YOUR HYPE GIRL

51 FEMALE FOUNDERS SHARE THEIR MOST
IMPACTFUL LEARNINGS, TACTICS &
STRATEGIES IN BUSINESS.

DOONE ROISIN

First Edition

Author: Doone Roisin

Editor: Marc Hoberman

❀ Created with Vellum

"One child, one teacher, one book, one pen can change the world."

— MALALA YOUSAFZAI

CONTENTS

*Dedicated to the leading women in my life
(you know who you are...)*

*But especially my beautiful mum -
A single mother who hustled hard to raise her only daughter in
the bush and teach her the lessons of life.*

UM... A LITTLE NOTE ABOUT SOMETHING...

When transcribing an interview, even the most eloquent of speakers resort to *ums*, and *so's* and *like's* and double *'ands'*. It's part of the natural rhythm of speaking. It differentiates us from robots. And Siri. So that's a good thing. While we've kept true to the content of our guests' answers, we've edited some sentences to help with clarity and make for easier reading. Just thought you should know!

INTRODUCTION

I am so grateful for you. Thank you for choosing to read this book.

At whatever stage of entrepreneurship you're in—whether you're in the dreaming phase, the "I'm gonna fuckin' quit this nine-to-five" phase, the plotting-and-planning phase, or the growing-your-business-to-the-next-level phase—by picking up this book, you're about to get direct insights and crazy tactical tips straight from fifty of the most exciting entrepreneurs in the world—that happen to be women.

More and more females are becoming entrepreneurs. Far more than any other time in history. Thank God! For centuries, business has been the exclusive realm of the male of the species, and women were relegated to the kitchen, running the household, and knitting sweaters. (Yes, I know, eye roll). Ironically, what many men seem to have missed is that running a household is full-time work and, in many cases, a bigger, more complex, and more demanding task than their husband's clock-in, clock-out nine-to-five. One can assume that if the roles were reversed, partners would be begging to get back to the office asap.

What this has always shown is that women have innate qualities that make them the humble superheroes of the sexes. We're multitaskers, tireless workers, and lateral-thinking problem-solvers who are emotionally intelligent, detail oriented, and intuitive. And it's about time that these skills and abilities are utilized in the world of business.

We've finally reached the golden age of the female entrepreneur. Welcome!

As I write this, 2021 statistics show that 252 million entrepreneurs out of approximately 582 million in the world are female. This is in addition to 153 million women who have already been running businesses.

Research also shows that women now account for 41 percent of the global workforce and control more than $20 trillion in annual spending. Predictions are that this number will go up to $28 trillion in the next few years.

So if you're female and thinking of joining the revolution, there's never been a better time.

The internet changed everything. We're living in a renaissance of information, where we can learn just about anything for free. We're globally connected, and rapidly evolving technology gives us the opportunity to make it all happen ourselves. We can set up shop online within hours, play out our own marketing campaigns on social media, connect with manufacturers on the other side of the world, and raise capital from online crowdfunding platforms.

The world is filled with examples of bedroom entrepreneurs. It's the new American dream.

And with so many of our modern-day heroes being

startup entrepreneurs, a fresh generation is growing up with a new set of idols—from Sara Blakely to Emily Weiss and every member of Klan Kardashian. Even athletes, pop stars, and Hollywood celebrities are becoming equally famous for their entrepreneurial side hustles. Entrepreneur is the new cool.

"All the women who independent, throw your hands up at me.

All the mamas who rock the dollars, throw your hands up at me."

Thanks, Beyoncé of the early 2000s. Years later, she gave us an updated anthem based on our progress:

"Who runs the world? Girls!"

It's more than a catchy pop tune. It's damn true.

But whether you're an Ivy League graduate, a seasoned hustler, or a green go-getter with a dream, starting a business is difficult. No one, however tactful, strategic, or lucky, can escape the many challenges that come thick and fast in the startup game.

Although women are becoming increasingly active in the business world, old habits die hard, and there are still extra challenges for females. Females are still often viewed in a different light to their male counterparts. No doubt it will continue to improve in the years to come; we're already seeing the right movements as the workplace evolves.

As an entrepreneur myself, and having spoken to so many others, it's clear that the startup journey can be a lonely one, and many find that one of the greatest challenges. Of all the successful female startup entrepreneurs that I've spoken to, all have the same piece of advice—it's vital to build a support network of like-minded female founders. Ongoing support and practical advice are invaluable. It's within this book and *Female Startup Club* that you're about to become part of a community of sisterly support.

A network isn't always easy to find, and that's why I started the *Female Startup Club* podcast and wrote this book. My concept for *Female Startup Club* was to connect female founders from all over the world and to compile advice from those that have found success. But it was important to me that the advice is strictly no BS and no fluff. I wanted to speak to successful (read: badass) entrepreneurs and get their real-world, practical, and actionable advice. I wanted to record their stories. Stories that give us human insight that we can relate to.

If there's one thing in common with all women, it's that unlike many men whose interactions are often emotionally restricted and limited in sharing, females are natural-born *talkers*. From a young age, and continuing throughout life, we share our life experiences and feelings and give each other advice. We don't hold back or filter—whether it's discussing our personal problems or providing every last minute of cringeworthy (or sexy) detail of our last Bumble date. So I wanted to do this through conversational-style chats. The kind of conversations that you have with your girlfriends.

I've done close to three hundred interviews since starting the podcast, and I've shortlisted fifty of my favorite episodes in this book. Although, truth be told, so far everyone has been a "favorite." So my goal is that this book will be the first in a continuing series.

There are many wonderful best-selling biographies of business titans. But what I've found is that, while these inspire us to dream big, they are often not genuinely relatable to our own lives, circumstances, and journeys ahead. The Oprah Winfreys of this world are rare outliers. The women I've spoken to are all examples of real "everyday" women that made their dreams happen. They're a mix of personalities, and no doubt you'll find chapters that you truly connect to. Although each guest is, of course, talented and driven, most started with relatively humble beginnings. Most started, just like you or me, with an idea. And a dream. A dream to say goodbye to their nine-to-five and risk it all on chasing their passion. A dream to change the world. Impact many. Enjoy life. And become financially independent. Many started their path without experience, many without financial backing or specific skill sets or support or a network of contacts. Many juggle the responsibilities of young children.

The interviews in this book ultimately show that whatever you truly put your mind to is possible. Your dreams *are* achievable with the right attitude, perseverance, self-belief, and hustle. These are women that largely began their journeys without any more advantage than you. These are examples of what can be done in today's world. And this can be you too.

MY STORY

I had a rather unusual and magical childhood. Raised by a hard-working single mom, I grew up in a middle-of-nowhere Australian town that was not remotely big enough to be called a "town." I'm talking ninety people, folks. We didn't have any money, and we lived in a humbly humble shed on the side of a mountain creek that my mum improved over the years. She's great like that. Without elec-

tricity or running water in the early days, we ate our home-
grown veggies from the orchard, our own chickens too, and
lived off the land. It was tough, but it was beautiful in its
own way. Like, really beautiful.

My school was made up of around twenty kids. For two
grades, I was the only student in my class. The bright side
was that I was consistently the very best in my class at every
subject (lol). My mom soon realized it wasn't a sustainable
life for me, and we moved to a small town near the
Sunshine Coast called Imbil, where I attended school until
grade 10.

It was then that my paternal grandparents gave me a
life-changing gift, by sending me to an all-girls private
boarding school in Brisbane. Or "Brisvegas" if you had the
joy of living there in the 2000s. The experience opened my
eyes to an entirely different world. I developed a great pride
in the power of sisterhood, and I met the most amazing
friends, many of them still a big part of my life today. A
special mention to Rebecca Tomlinson—my forever BFF
and soul sister from school. She deserves more than a quick
mention in my story. I'm so lucky to have her cheerleading
for me daily.

After school, I was faced with stepping out into the big
wide world and making decisions for my future. It was at
that age I realized I had the hustle gene. It came from
watching my mom hustle to put food on the table, and it
came from my grandparents who were both entrepreneurs.
They had bought a commercial cleaning business through
an ad in the paper and had made a fair success of it. A good
clean business. How cool is that?

My hustle gene made me dream big, and I was eager to
make my ambitions a reality and land my dream job. One
thing I've always been good with is setting goals and taking

the action needed to achieve them. You'll know this if you listen to the show!

At the time, my dream job was clear to me. There were no boy band posters on my dorm room wall. Instead, I had stuck carefully torn-out pages from *Harper's Bazaar* magazine on my wall, and that was my dream. I wanted to work for my favorite glossy mag. F-A-S-H-I-O-N.

So as a hustler does, I began to plot my path to make it happen.

I needed experience, I needed to land an internship, and the most realistic place was a local Brisbane magazine that was handed out for free with the *Courier Mail* newspaper. But they had no vacancies.

And even if they did, I knew I would be one of many young bright-eyed hopefuls in a winding queue around the block.

In my first act of entrepreneurship, I put a plan into action. I went to the local nursery and bought a thyme plant. I put it in a pretty pot, and inside, I placed my business card with a link to my website and a handwritten card that said, "Can I have a moment of your time?"

I dressed up in clothes that I thought looked like that of a delivery driver (yes, really) and arrived unannounced at the magazine's offices, proclaiming that I had a special delivery for the editor. My crazy (and possibly illegal) boldness paid off, and the very same day, I received a call. The editor was charmed and impressed, and although she didn't have an opening for an intern, she created a twelve-week position just for me.

Turns out thyme really is our most valuable asset.

Following my internship, I continued with my entrepreneurial spirit in the pursuit of furthering my career. I wanted to get an internship at a downtown design studio that was advertised asking people to send their applications to: yocheckthisshitout@laundrycreative.com. I knew their offices well from my morning runs along the Brisbane River, and I knew that, again, I had to apply in a nonconventional way that would make me stand out and shine bright. I texted my friend: "Hey, do you want to come and deface a building with me at 3:00 a.m.?"

You bet.

At 3:00 a.m., we went to the office building, and I stuck up a huge sign I'd manufactured from a magazine spread I'd worked on that was decorated with a generous amount of sparkly sequins. It said, "Yo, check this shit out at Doone-Roisin.com." I politely wrote a note to security that it was in fact a job application and asked them to look the other way and not take it down. (This one was definitely illegal.)

The strategy worked, and later that morning, I had a phone call from the founder.

These were two of many examples of my early entrepreneurial spirit slash hustle gene. Though I only realize this now in hindsight.

What I considered my dream job had evolved (as these things usually do), but I still set my sights on working in the fashion world. I got word about an opportunity to intern at a new company that was launching in Sydney. This company was called the Iconic—an e-commerce startup in the early days of online shopping in Australia. And it turned out to be a wildly successful company, earning its name.

Of course, I jumped at the opportunity, swiftly packed my bags, and moved to the big-city bright lights of Sydney. The experience turned out to be life changing because this wasn't just another established corporate gig. *This was a startup.*

To me, the startup world was wild. As the intern girl, I did everything to go that extra mile and get noticed. My hard work paid off, and I was offered the job of building their community and their social media.

Get paid to make friends on Facebook? Hell yes! My business card title read: "Professional Facebooker."

The startup environment provided a constant flow of excitement and buzz. I had landed my dream job, and I absolutely freaking loved it. I was obsessed, in fact. A startup means one challenge following the next, and I felt like I was where I was meant to be in the world and doing something I truly loved. Everything was exciting. Everything was new.

I learned all of the things in this crazy whirlwind (and look back on it with much love). Like the pure scrappiness of a startup. We had to constantly be creative in making things happen from the ground up. Scrappy on the inside, glamorous on the outside. Ah, the fashion world. Classic.

Today, The Iconic is a super wow business, employing hundreds of staff and turning over hundreds of millions of dollars. But back then, circa 2012, it was like a large crazy family of people who wanted to build this cool thing together. In the name of scrappiness, we furiously typed away at picnic tables, and even though we were an internet-based business, we had no Wi-Fi, and each of us had to manually connect with dongles. Ha!

To me, this is the romance of a startup. There's a romance in scrappiness. There's a romance in the adventure of forging a new path toward an impossible-seeming ambition. Just like the environment of my childhood, there was a romance in making the best of the little you had. We were funded btw—there was a lot of cash in the business—but we were lean AF.

Working in the startup world piqued my appetite to one day be a startup entrepreneur myself. I wasn't seeing myself in the roles around me or directly above. I saw myself in the guys at the top! I wanted to be a founder.

Although I had the seed planted, I continued to work for several big-brand companies like Finder.com (shoutout to Jeremy Cabral for being an absolute boss, mentor, and great friend in my life ever since), IMG, and Snapchat.

Looking back, there have been a few pivotal moments in my life, and perhaps the biggest, sparkliest one of those was meeting a certain dreamboat guy through a mutual friend. This is when Pierre-Antoine enters the picture.

I was working for an old-school corporate company at the time, and I wasn't enjoying the restrictive environment. This curious soul named Pierre-Antoine (also important to note he was hot and charming) asked me two questions that forever changed my life.

The first question was "Why don't you come join what I'm doing?" He was building a SaaS platform at the time—a marketplace—and they needed to build a creative content agency to fund the build of the software. I immediately said yes, and we became business partners.

Fast forward a couple of years, Pierre-Antoine (or P-A, as I call him with love) asked his second big question:

"Will you marry me?" (omg yes!!)

I continued the tradition of saying yes to P-A's questions. Obvs.

Pierre-Antoine is not only the absolute love of my life, but he also turned out to be my number one cheerleader.

When I decided to take the entrepreneurial leap for myself, he provided endless support and showed a belief in me that made me believe in myself. He is the best human I know.

They used to say, "behind every successful man is a strong woman." It turns out that the inverse is just as true.

Every startup journey begins with an idea, and I set out to work out what mine was. I thought a lot about my strengths: I had an e-commerce background. I had a social media marketing background. I loved the packaging and good design. I loved stuff that's tangible.

I settled on the idea of starting a small sparkly jewelry brand. I named it Kincs, and we launched in 2017. It turned out to be the adventure I had dreamed of. It took us all around the world. We went to China. Indonesia. (We actually moved to Bali for six months!) We went to Thailand. It took us to Paris Fashion Week. It was worn by influencers all over the world and featured in publications like *Vogue* and *Who What Wear*. You'd think everything was rosy. But not so much.

With all the many hats that a startup entrepreneur needs to wear, I realized that I had little time to focus on actually building the business side of things. It was more about newness, new collections, creating. Despite the many successes of Kincs, I started to feel like I had chosen the wrong product for me. I didn't want to build a company in the fashion world. What I really wanted to do was solve problems. And have an impact. Sometimes you need to try things to figure out what you don't like, to get you closer to what you *do* like.

Hungry for advice, I began talking to my girlfriends about what they were doing, how they were building their own businesses, what guidance they could give. The conversations were eye opening, and I got so much value

out of hearing other women's stories, experiences, and
lessons.

Around the same time, I was reading a book called *Tools
of Titans* by Tim Ferriss. I'm sure you know it. It's an
amazing book that is often mentioned as a source of inspiration by entrepreneurs (especially on *Female Startup Club*!). It
features high-performers, from billionaire entrepreneurs to
athletes and all sorts in between, and it has a no-fluff
approach. It's direct, no-bullshit, practical, real-world
advice.

I love Tim's direct approach, but I noticed something
missing. Where were all the women? Only about 10 percent
of the (huge) book featured stories from women.

I wanted to hear that same direct, no-BS advice from
successful women. But not the airy-fairy "believe in yourself" kind of thing. I wanted the nitty-gritty conversations
about actual steps to take. Practical, no-nonsense paths to
get to X. Although I did get a lot of value (and still do) from
the male voices in the book, I felt that the path of the female
startup entrepreneur was different, with specific challenges
that women face. Those from Venus and those from Mars
are, in many ways, different. We have different traits,
different strengths, different weaknesses, and different
obstacles. And the way we share stories with each other is
inherently different. Female entrepreneurs need female role
models. Fact.

I started asking my girlfriends if I could publish the
conversations we were having. I began to put them up on
Instagram. But, hard truths, no one wanted to sit through a
twenty-minute thing when casually swiping through their
feed. So a podcast enters the chat.

Podcast? Moi? You should probably know something

about me: I'm terrified of public speaking. Well, I was two years ago.

But the idea floated around in my head for some time. A few years before, I had actually bought a bunch of domains on a whim—Brisbane Startup Club, LA Startup Club, Paris Startup Club, San Fran Startup Club—so on. On the list was also Female Startup Club (.com). That one kind of stuck with me. It sounded cool. It made sense. It summed up what it's all about.

So I jumped in and started recording my first few episodes. I pushed through my public speaking shyness (I do like a challenge, after all). My guests were so super interesting and engaging that I started to forget I was being recorded—it just felt like the conversations I had with my girlfriends.

At the time, my approach to the podcast was rather casual. I did an episode here and there, but I was mainly focused on thinking up my next startup idea. At the time, I was doing a fair amount of traveling between Australia, the UK, and the US, so my (inefficient) strategy was to do face-to-face interviews bit by bit when I had the opportunity.

And then, March 2020. You know what happens next. The pandemic hits.

The pandemic changed the lives of pretty much every human on the planet. For me, it was a pivotal point in my career direction, and I decided to start taking *Female Startup Club* more seriously.

Among the gems of advice I have learned when it comes to entrepreneurship is that it's vital to set goals as early as possible. I decided that I would record one hundred interviews by the end of 2020. It was a scary, far-fetched goal. One hundred interviews is a lot of work when you break it down. But the best goals are ambitious ones, and I was up for a personal challenge that would call for hard work and hustle. After all, *Female Startup Club* was a female startup venture itself.

Now, the journey of an entrepreneur is, at times, lonely, but it's rarely the work of just one person. Along the journey, there are angels that join in on our vision and help us toward our goals. In my case, a humble and mighty thank you to my faithful behind-the-scenes team: Josephine, Jane, Francisse, and Bryan. And also to the folks that drive *Female Startup Club* forward in other ways: like our first and favorite sponsor, Klaviyo. (Love you guys!)

I tackled the obstacles that were in my way—from how to convince crazy impressive guests to appear on my show to how to finance the venture. And I got my hero sponsor on board—Klaviyo, the top email & SMS marketing software platform. They were my dream sponsor and the number one partner I had written down on my list. Not only have they been an invaluable cheerleader, but they truly care about supporting women- and minority-owned businesses of all sizes. They're a brand with heart, and I'm a genuine fan. I've used and loved their products, which is exactly why I approached them in the first place. If you've listened to the podcast, you'll no doubt have heard me wax lyrical about Klaviyo. Having a partner that I could genuinely enthuse about is important to me. I've always placed great value on being authentic with my listeners. And I genuinely believe they're a great resource for every startup entrepreneur out there—especially ones that happen to be women. If you don't know of Klaviyo, I'd suggest you check them out. Because they're a solid ten out of ten.

The impact of *Female Startup Club* has been, quite simply, mind-blowing. From the listeners that I meet on Instagram DMs every day to the people that have contacted me and shared how the show has influenced their own ventures and their lives. The power of a podcast in influencing so many people's lives from all over the planet is pretty damn crazy and extremely rewarding for me. *Female Startup Club* is needed in the world, and together, we're going to change the stats we're sick of reading about. My endless gratitude is to my community (you); thank you for putting a big cheeky smile on my face daily.

And then there's my guests—the incredible entrepreneurs that have appeared on the show. I've been blessed with the opportunity to speak with so many women that are true modern-day superheroes. Women that have had awe-inspiring successes against all odds. They are pioneers, inventors, problem-solvers, industry disruptors, and thought leaders. Each has shared their stories—failures, victories, lessons learned, business obstacles, personal challenges. They've all shared candid and frank advice, insights, and practical step-by-step guidance. They've inspired me, along with thousands of regular listeners around the world. I've heard from teenage girls with big future ambitions, I've heard from mega-successful entrepreneurs already in the thick of things, I've heard from women in the later years of life—all inspired to take a chance on their dreams. And I've heard from many men too (offline), who appreciate the different take that female voices give.

Females need female heroes, and if you're looking for one, you'll find fifty of them in this book.

Your Hype Girl is the first of many books by *Female Startup Club*. It's a collection of highlights from fifty selected podcast interviews, together with my own thoughts and insights. Wherever you are in your own entrepreneurial journey, I hope this anthology will inspire you to follow your dreams, your own exciting path, and make sh*t happen.

You got this, girl.

Oh, and by the way, maybe you'll be a guest on the show one day? I can only hope. You are my inspiration and the inspiration to future women and girls all around the world.

Your Hype Girl,
Doone Roisin

1

OUTSAUCING

ALISON CAYNE: HOW AN ENTREPRENEUR TURNED A COOKING SCHOOL INTO A SAUCY PRODUCT

Alison Cayne is the founder of New York–based Haven's Kitchen. Originally a cooking school that opened in 2012, Haven's Kitchen now helps all kinds of cooks in the kitchen with a celebrated range of ridiculously yummy-looking, vibrant squeezy sauces. I say "looking" because I haven't managed to get my hands on them, and I'm praying that one day they'll appear at my local Whole Foods in London! We covered Ali's eight-plus-year journey and so many of the lessons she learned along the way, including the moment she realized she would have to close down the best-performing side of the business due to the pandemic.

Ali got married at twenty-three and had five children in eight years. She describes having her own community at home, and enjoying cooking for her "community" led her to teach her kitchen skills to friends and friends of friends. "You know, they didn't know how to make a soup," she says. When Ali's youngest son went to day care, she decided to enroll in a program at New York University about food history and sustainability.

As part of a compulsory internship, she led school tours and introduced kids to ideas around farm labor practices, environmental sustainability, the impact of food choices on personal and community health, and the greater good. Grown-ups on the tours started asking for recipes and showing interest in shopping at local markets. They didn't know what to do with a yam, and Ali thought, *Hmmm . . . there's something here.*

Takeaway #1: Bring an International Concept to the Local Market

Like many startup entrepreneurs, Ali spotted something that was successful elsewhere but not locally available.

"Like in many places around the world, there are super cooking schools that aren't culinary professional schools. You visit, you go to the market. You learn how to make the regional cuisine. You have a fun day of it. You drink a bottle of wine. And that really didn't exist in New York. So I opened Haven's Kitchen in 2012, and it was just this idea to connect people with the joy of eating well and cooking and taking the fear and loathing out of it."

Takeaway #2: Create a Product in Response to Feedback

Ali's cooking school was housed in a beautiful, old carriage house that lent itself to having a café in front and two stories of private event space. Soon, she was doing three hundred private events a year, which quickly made the business profitable. But the heart of Haven's Kitchen remained the community built around cooking classes.

"In 2018, we launched the line of sauces really as a response to our students saying that they need a good, fresh, healthy sauce and everything in the supermarket is in jars and bottles, with lots of preservatives, lots of salt and added sugar. They just wanted the things they were learning how to make in class. Why doesn't that exist? So we made it exist!"

TAKEAWAY #3: Things Break and That's OK

The pandemic meant there would be no more corporate events for some time, and Ali realized she had to close the kitchen. Luckily, she was able to exit her lease, but the closing of the business and the letting go of around seventy-five staff made Ali tearful. It's in these moments that you learn and grow.

"That's the thing about the pandemic. It's just a pressure test for you personally. Relationships, businesses, ideas. People are either finding things that are getting them super locked and loaded or they're having some real crises in their personal well-being. I think of it as a house when it's built on a really firm foundation and moves when the winds come. But if it's not, then it breaks. And that's OK when things break. Because sometimes things are artificially held up. And so the breaking is the first step in the rebuilding, which is exciting if you can look at it that way."

TAKEAWAY #4: Make People Feel Good about Themselves

It's often important for a startup entrepreneur to have a clear mission statement—even if it's a simple sentence in their mind. It can help keep an entrepreneur on track with their original aim while being buffeted about in the world out there.

"The mission from day one has always been: there's a

cook inside of you, and you can feel creative and empow-
ered. People are flooded with images of the most beautiful
food and these incredible chefs. And so nothing you make is
going to compare, and it's just going to make you feel bad
about yourself. Our job has always been to get someone to
do something more because it's good for you, good for your
community, and good for the environment. It should be
really fun, really creative. The idea of squeezing a sauce is
very fun. It's like kindergarten. You feel like you're painting;
you feel like, 'I'm going to be creative.' It's not about
measuring out a teaspoon of this or whatever; it's just
squeeze here and maybe a little more. Squeeze there."

Takeaway #5: Invest in Unique Packaging

The Haven's Kitchen sauces are packaged in a nifty, slim,
see-through pouch instead of your typical bulky glass jar.
Getting your packaging just right can be the difference
between getting lost on the shelf and standing out as a must-
buy product. We're told to not judge a book by its cover, but
the reason we're told that is because we do. Beyond the eye-
catching packaging, Ali's packaging is environmentally and
business smart too.

"You know, the truth is that less than 25 percent of what
you put in that bin actually gets recycled. Most of it ends up
in landfills. So even if a pouch ends up in the garbage, the
amount of space that it's taking up in a landfill is significantly less. Not only that, but the production and the shipping. It takes twenty-four trucks to ship the jar equivalent of
one truck of pouches. The fuel use, the emissions, the water
consumption, the food waste—it's so much better with a
pouch."

·   ·   ·

Takeaway #6: Be Customer-Centric

Many businesses focus on their brand and can sometimes lose focus on the customers themselves—who are, of course, the core of any business. Ali explained her view on where she places her attention.

"We were fortunate because we had such a beautiful, loyal community already. One of the main things that I would say when you're trying to get consumers to try your product . . . The person on the other side has a problem. They might not know it, but they have a need. And if we're building something to fill that need, then our job is to make it less about our product and us and more about 'this is for you.' In business, the last several years have been very founder- and brand-centric, and for me, I feel like it should be very consumer- and customer-centric."

Takeaway #7: The Consumer Doesn't Always Know Their Needs

Ali explained how she placed great value in personally receiving people's feedback as part of the process of developing a product. She learned that interesting lesson, which is that consumers often don't know the answer to what they want.

"I learned that you can't really ask someone, 'What is it that you're missing?' Because they don't really know. I think a lot of what you're doing is trying to tease out and get an intuition about what your consumer needs. There's that old famous quote, I think attributed to Henry Ford: 'If you ask someone what kind of car they want, they'd say a faster horse.' Right? No one knew that they wanted a car."

· · ·

TAKEAWAY #8: Venus Is Not the Same as Mars

Every startup entrepreneur has to go through a journey of research, and so often this brings up surprising results. It's something I come across a lot in my interviews, and it always fascinates me how things aren't always what they seem! Ali explained one of her research surprises.

"I was surprised at how many men love our product. And then I did some further research into men and cooking, and it's really fascinating. People who identify as men are much more comfortable saying, 'I took pizza, and I put packaged lettuce on it, and then I put dressing on it, and I cooked dinner' than women and traditional cooking, who would say, 'I didn't really make dinner; I just took pizza and put some lettuce on it.' Men are much more comfortable with hacks. And we're really leaning into the men here because men are shopping more than ever. And now I think it's actually flipped in the US, where more men are doing the grocery shopping for their families than women."

THREE QUICK QUESTIONS

WHAT'S the number one marketing moment that made your business pop?

"We started doing Instacart ads in August, and we saw some of our stores triple in volume almost immediately. It was just, like, a flip of a switch, and boom!

(I humbly asked what Instacart was, and no, it doesn't count as one of my three questions . . . I make the rules!)

Instacart is a grocery store delivery platform. It operates a grocery delivery and pickup service in the US and Canada.

So you can shop for groceries online. Anyone in America who has a food or bev product and isn't doing Instacart ads, get on that ASAP."

WHERE DO you hang out to get smarter?

"Right now, I'm reading a book called *Caste: The Origins of Our Discontents* by Isabel Wilkerson. It's one of the best books I've read in my life. It's about the caste system in America and how race has been used to designate human beings as lesser human beings. It compares the American caste system with the Indian caste system, which is much more familiar to people. It's definitely opening my eyes to a lot of things that I (as a privileged white woman) didn't necessarily know or see.

On the business side, I'm reading *Who: Solve Your #1 Problem* by Geoff Smart. It's about finding the right people for your team. We are going to be growing our team. I am very nervous to hire because I love my team so much and we're so close, but it gives a really good framework for really vetting people well."

HOW DO you deal with failure?

"At first, I have the same reaction we all do, but then I start to look at the facts. It's what I've been taught to do by very smart mental health professionals. The facts are: I've raised this amount of money. I've grown my business ten times since the last round of funding. I have a team that works really hard, that respects me. You're going to get yourself out of the mental reel by looking at the hardcore facts. And I have them written now in the notes section of my computer so that when I don't remember them, I can read them to myself."

LISTEN to Ali's episode to find out how her products sold out in the first week of being launched, how empathy plays an important role in business, and what we can learn from a thirty-dollar cookie.

2

FASTER THAN A SPEEDING BULLETIN

ALI KRIEGSMAN: HOW AN ENTREPRENEUR TURNED A NEWSLETTER INTO A THRIVING TECH PLATFORM

Ali Kriegsman is the cofounder and COO of Bulletin. Bulletin is a premium B2B wholesale marketplace where retailers and buyers go to discover, shop, and support the best brands on the planet. The new retail concept gives small, women-run merchants access to shelf space in the company's physical stores. In addition to all the good that Bulletin represents for women, the company donates 10 percent of its profits to Planned Parenthood of NYC. Ali spoke about the humble origins of Bulletin, which started out as an e-commerce newsletter. And about how that grew into pop-ups and retail stores and went on to be accepted into Y Combinator—which led to a major pivot into a thriving tech platform. If you want to read more about Ali's journey, I can highly recommend her book, *How to Build a Goddamn Empire*. She aptly describes it as a "no-BS book on entrepreneurship."

Ali grew up with entrepreneur parents and describes her homelife as "feast or famine." The unpredictable financial situation of her parents' ventures made her averse to the idea of being an entrepreneur herself, and she gravitated toward the stability of a nine-to-five career.

In her early twenties, she kicked off her career with a job at Condé Nast, the famous publishing house and legacy brand. Shortly after, she left to join a tech startup and worked in sales—something she was very successful at, regularly being the number one salesperson in the company. However, she found the task unfulfilling. As she explained, "I was giving the same drab, dry sales pitch every single day, you know, making the same joke planted at the exact same moment of the pitch days on end."

Her entrepreneurial journey started when her cofounder, Alana Branston, suggested they create a newsletter showcasing independent talent on Etsy. Their side hustle ended up getting a $20,000 grant, and that allowed the pair to dive in full-time.

Takeaway #1: Start by Marketing to Your Network

Startup entrepreneurs are often low on cash and can't always afford advertising. But Ali showed that being creative and "shameless" in connecting to her personal and professional network was an effective starting point. In the first few weeks, they had amassed around five hundred subscribers.

"We emailed everyone we knew and their mother. Also, every list I was on in college. We emailed it to absolutely everyone we knew or kind of knew."

Takeaway #2: Do Your Own PR

In the questions I ask at the end of every interview, I

always ask what the number one marketing moment was that made the business pop. So often, the answers have to do with early exposure in the media, and many startup entrepreneurs have shown that with persistence, it is possible to achieve success without a PR firm.

"I've been our press person from the beginning and helped get us placed in places like BuzzFeed and Refinery29. I would say press was really instrumental for us at that point.

I want to say that by the time we started doing our pop-up markets, which was the next evolution of the business, we had maybe ten thousand subscribers. And a lot of that was driven by press at the time."

Soon the business was proving profitable, although not quite as lucrative as their ambitions. The pair were making around $6,000 in monthly revenue; however, their costs were low. They had a Squarespace site with drop-shipping, so they weren't holding inventory and were taking a 40 percent commission on sales.

Takeaway #3: Take Your Online Business into the Physical World

Startup entrepreneurs shouldn't be averse to pivoting their businesses. Sometimes it can be vital to growth, as was Ali's case.

Wanting to increase their revenue, Ali and Alana pivoted their business by taking their online business into the real world. They started "Bulletin Market," a series of pop-up markets all over Brooklyn and Manhattan, charging brands anywhere from $100 to $400 a weekend depending on what part of the market they showcased in.

Ali realized that it was hard work for brands to set up a

pop-up store, so her USP (Unique Selling Proposition) was
to do the hard work herself.

"We bought all the tents and tables and set the whole
environment up for brands, so all they had to do was come
and merchandise their table, which made us competitive
with other pop-up market series like Smorgasbord or Long
Island Flea, where you have to schlep everything yourself."

Takeaway #4: Female Entrepreneurs Need to Prove Revenue to Investors

Ali found herself working seven days a week, but it was
paying off, and they were bringing in around $15,000 a
weekend.

It's no secret that seeking investment is a different game
for female startup entrepreneurs. Sadly, gender biases are
still commonplace in the venture capital space.

"As women in business, we knew that in order to get on
an investor's radar, we needed revenue. Women can't really
get by with just having a massive user base or a massive
customer base or certain press hits or a waitlist. In my experience, women get measured by their proven track record,
whereas men get measured by their potential. So early on in
the business, the goal was to make more money, versus
make this more scalable."

Wanting more capital for their business, Ali and Alana
applied to "every grant program known to man" and finally
got accepted into a Y Combinator program. For those unfamiliar with Y Combinator, they're a famous seed money
startup accelerator in the tech space that helped launch
companies such as Airbnb, Dropbox, Twitch, and Reddit.

.   .   .

TAKEAWAY #5: **Pivot Your Investment Pitch (& Piggyback)**

Applying for grants can be a slog of a journey, and many rejections usually come with the territory. Sometimes it can be a good idea to pivot your pitch—to reframe it in a way that catches attention.

Ali's applications to Y Combinator had been rejected several times, but she finally caught their interest by positioning her vision as an "Airbnb of retail space." This reframing did the trick, as it piggybacked onto a recent success and helped explain the vision neatly in a few choice words.

"We believed at the time that it should be just as easy to take over physical space and physical retail space and showcase your wares as a brand as it is to launch a Facebook ad. So our whole thesis was that taking over physical space is going to become programmatic, the same way that running ads on Instagram or Facebook is programmatic. And so we built a technology platform."

THREE QUICK QUESTIONS

WHAT'S **the number one marketing moment that made your business pop?**

"Rebranding the store, refocusing it to just be women-owned businesses, and really specifically deciding that this metropolitan, progressive, liberal female customer is our customer. And orienting our Instagram around the store experience, the branding, and the brand voice. Everything changed after that."

.   .   .

WHERE DO you hang out to get smarter?

"As I'm approaching thirty, I'm really trying to become more emotionally intelligent, not as it pertains to other people but as it pertains to myself. I just finished a book called *The Big Leap* that I loved. It's about facing what the author calls your "Upper Limit Problem," where it's like, why do we self-sabotage? Why do we feel like nothing's ever enough? Why don't we reach our potential? What gets in our way? I'm also reading a book called *Designing Your Life*, and it talks about how you can structure your day in a way that gives you energy."

HOW DO you win the day?

"I journal in the morning. I bought a beautiful fancy journal and a beautiful fancy pen because I've always told myself to journal, and I always do it when something's wrong or something great. Now I journal every morning for thirty minutes. I also like to read in the morning, and I also work out before work. In the evenings, I smoke a joint. I'm a very anxious person, and my brain will whiz out of control at all hours if I let it."

LISTEN to Ali's episode to find out how a pivot to tech helped scale her business, how important it is to rearrange your vision board, and why being an entrepreneur is like being a pop star.

3

FIFTY SHADES

ALICIA SCOTT: HOW AN ENTREPRENEUR BROUGHT BEAUTY TO AN OVERLOOKED MARKET

Alicia Scott is the founder of Range Beauty. The cosmetics brand was created out of a need for diverse shades that catered to the needs of so many consumers that were under-represented in the market. They also utilize botanicals in their makeup line specially formulated for eczema and acne. We spoke about how she went about making a new foundation formulation from scratch, her advice for women starting out, and plenty of fascinating things that are pen and notepad worthy. First fascinating thing worth mentioning? She counts Bobbi Brown and Beyoncé as mentors!

Alicia's previous career was in the fashion industry. From a young age, she was fashion obsessed. Designing her own clothes as a child led to studying fashion at Virginia Tech, which in turn led to moving to New York and working in the industry. Much of her work was behind the scenes, and at fashion shows, she was exposed to many makeup artist and model interactions.

. . .

TAKEAWAY #1: Keep Your Eyes Open for Gaps in the Market

While observing these interactions, Alicia came across a problem that she felt needed a solution. It's a common character trait amongst many entrepreneurs—having your eyes and ears open for opportunities, problems that need solutions.

"I noticed the pattern of a lot of the Black models coming to set with their own makeup kits. I asked a model why, and she told me this story of how a designer once said to her, 'I can't do the look because I don't have anything in my kit for your skin tone.' I was shocked because, especially living in New York, you just kind of think that we have everything at our fingertips. It was upsetting to me that she felt that she was 'a problem.'"

TAKEAWAY #2: Say Your Idea Out Loud

Sometimes we keep our great business ideas to ourselves, but as with so many things in both business and personal life, there is great power in saying things out loud. Alicia found that voicing her idea was really the start of her journey.

"I always say my first step was speaking about it out loud. One of my good friends, Alisa, was the only person I knew in the entrepreneurial world. We were sitting in the living room, and I was thumbing through a magazine. There was an article about the best lipsticks for Black women, and it prompted me to tell her my idea. She was quick to say, 'Do it!' And she asked me tons of questions. I feel like when you say it out loud to someone, you actually start thinking out loud. It really starts to make it more tangible than when it's just in your head."

·   ·   ·

Takeaway #3: Become Best Friends with Google

I hear this so often from entrepreneurs. The internet is very much a free university, and it has a huge number of answers for how to get started with pretty much any venture or industry you're looking to get involved in. There's never been a time in the history of the world with as many opportunities for information-sharing as the era we're in now.

"I became best friends with Google, and I started searching. Even though YouTube wasn't as big back in 2014, there were still plenty videos on there: how to make your own lipstick at home or how to make your own lip balm. The internet provided many answers to things like how you start your own makeup line or what do you need to have a startup business."

Takeaway #4: Use Social Media for Market Research

Alicia tracked down manufacturers (again with the help of Google) and eventually made her first order, which was just the start of her three-year-long product development phase. Far before she launched the brand, she began using social media as a way to understand her target market. Social media can be a great tool for entrepreneurs to get a handle on what their market is talking and thinking about in real time. And it can be far more honest and candid than traditional market surveys.

"I used social media at the time as a research component. I wanted to have our social media before the product was launched. I would see these brands put out lines, and there were a lot of women of color who would comment, and I would comment under there like, 'Oh my gosh, you should check out that address.' I would also take those comments that I would see and use it to apply to the line. So it was kind of like my market research tool."

Takeaway #5: Be Resourceful to Keep Your Costs Low

Alicia had little capital to get her startup off the ground, but that didn't stop her from making things happen. Cash-strapped entrepreneurs need to become masters of thriftiness, and Alicia was creative in finding ways to save money on things that are usually expensive.

"I am someone who is just like if I don't have to spend a lot in the beginning, I'm not going to. So I did my own website through Squarespace. I got their nine-dollar plan that came with two or three months of free trial. For packaging, I found a graphic designer on Instagram. She was an intern at a cosmetics company who wanted new work for her portfolio. So she charged me fifty dollars for three different packaging iterations."

Takeaway #5: Start with Professional Not Perfect

Startup entrepreneurs often strive for perfection from the get-go. After all, it's their vision, their baby, and it's only natural to want to have everything just perfect. But what Alicia found, as have many successful entrepreneurs, is that perfection can and should take time. Entrepreneurs should strive for professional in the beginning, and the process of perfecting should be allowed to happen organically over time.

"There's a difference between something being professional and something being perfect. Perfect is just unattainable [at this stage]. Make sure that it's professional, make sure it's sellable. And I tell people I went through four different brands since. So if I would have put up all this money in the beginning, it would have been such a waste and such a loss."

TAKEAWAY #6: Raise Capital through Pitch Competitions

Early on after launching, Alicia was contacted by a buyer from Target. She was shocked at the opportunity after she realized it wasn't spam mail! The buyer was friendly and supportive, but it became clear that Alicia needed considerable capital for inventory, marketing, and logistics in order to supply such a big retailer. Alicia considered her options and chose to take advantage of the opportunity of pitch competitions.

"I start looking into grants and pitch competitions. And that's really what lit the fire. All of 2018 was basically going crazy with more and more pitch competitions. I won a lot of grants. I got a lot of exposure. And in December, I left my nine-to-five, and it was just the best thing ever!"

THREE QUICK QUESTIONS

How DO you win the day?

"In the morning, I have to start with prayer and meditation. If I'm rushing, if I oversleep and don't start with that, my day is significantly different. I do mantras that set my day up. Like "I am worthy of my success;" "I am worthy of everything that's coming to me;" and "I am worthy of being the creator of all these things."

. . .

WHERE DO **you hang out to get smarter?**

"I listen to Michelle Obama's podcast and Bobbi Brown's podcast. I read a lot of blogs by company founders, so I kind of steered away from books lately. I hang out in the shower —I see it as my "think tank." That's where I get my best ideas and my best thinking happens."

How DO **you deal with failure?**

"My reaction to failure has definitely changed as I've gotten older and as I've progressed as an entrepreneur. It used to completely wear me out; I would dwell on it. Now my mindset is that whatever is meant for me will be, and it will come to me when it's intended to."

LISTEN **to Alicia's episode to find out how she "dated" manufacturers, how she met Beatrice Dixon, owner of The Honey Pot Co (who's in chapter 6), and who became her famous mentor.**

4

SODA THING IS

ALLISON ELLSWORTH: HOW AN
ENTREPRENEUR MADE SODA HEALTHY

Allison Ellsworth is the cofounder and Chief Brand Officer of Poppi—the fastest growing nonalcoholic beverage in the nation. They dubbed their product "prebiotic soda," and the industry-disrupting drink, which incorporates apple cider vinegar, is the market's answer to a desire for healthy soda that's actually good for you. Hooray to that!

Allison secured funding for her venture (originally branded as "Mother Beverage") on *Shark Tank* in 2018, and despite the untimely economical gloominess of COVID, she forged ahead and launched nationwide in retail, quickly becoming an Amazon best seller as well.

As is the story with most startup entrepreneurs, there's an "aha" moment where, through a personal problem or need, a gap in the market becomes apparent. Before braving the startup world, Allison worked in oil and gas research. Stressed, run-down, and spending a lot of time on the road, Allison was feeling increasingly unwell. She felt tired and bloated, and her skin was breaking out. She went to see doctors and was prescribed "this pill and that pill," but nothing seemed to be working. So as one does, she began to

Google search solutions and went down the rabbit hole of how to heal your body through diet.

One thing that kept coming up over and over again was drinking apple cider vinegar to detox and reset your body. She decided to try it, and within two weeks of drinking it daily, she was shocked at how much better she felt.

"One thing that kept hitting me in the back of my mind was that I can't drink this every single day. Like this is not sustainable. Anyone that's had straight vinegar . . . that's not exactly enjoyable."

TAKEAWAY #1: Experiment with What You Have at Home

So many startup entrepreneurs that I've spoken to began creating the formula for their product at home without any budget. It shows that with some effort and creativity, developing the first iterations of a product doesn't always need big capital investment. Allison spent about three months in her kitchen playing around with formulas for an apple cider vinegar drink that both tasted good and didn't have the crazily high sugar content of typical sodas. She describes her first version as "rocket fuel." It was heavy on the vinegar and had a strong taste, but it was a good start. She began sharing her concoctions in mason jars with friends and neighbors, and soon she was getting very positive feedback and requests to buy more. Having a full-time job, she continued her little venture purely as a side hobby, simply happy to be helping people out.

TAKEAWAY #2: Test Your Product at a Local Market

Local farmers markets are great places to test out your product. It's inexpensive and low commitment, and it provides direct feedback from customers. Pregnant and having just bought a house with her husband in Dallas, Allison didn't fancy the idea of going back to work, so she took a chance and set up a stand at a local market to see what response she would get from her side hobby.

The product sold out within the first week, and sales doubled in the second week. By the third week, Allison had an astonishing break. She was approached by a Whole Foods buyer who was at the market with her mom and happened to come across Allison's booth. She explained that it was not something she would normally do, but she loved the product and gave Allison her business card.

TAKEAWAY #3: Becoming an Entrepreneur Is about Going with Your Gut (the irony isn't lost on me!)

Successful startups often have surprisingly humble beginnings, and the decision to turn a scrappy hobby into a business takes bravery and confidence in one's intuition. It's that intuition that is the secret sauce for entrepreneurial spirit.

"I was bottling this myself at home in my kitchen—straight-up grassroots style. But there was just something that I think you get as an entrepreneur or when you're doing something, like this gut feeling that you just know you're on the right path."

Allison was adamant about forging ahead with her venture, and at first, her husband (and future CEO) was nervous about it—"You're pregnant. We just bought a house. You can't quit your job!"

TAKEAWAY #4: You Can Be a Mom AND an Entrepreneur

Critics have been proven wrong time and time again about women needing to choose between being a mother and a businesswoman. Allison took the leap of faith and convinced her husband she could handle both.

"It's something I think can be really scary for women—like I'm starting a family, I have to choose. And I think that's so 1950s, right? You can do both. I started the company pregnant. I think women are superhuman when it comes down to it."

With her powers of persuasion, Allison, now six months pregnant, convinced her husband to quit his job and join her in the business. They took out their life savings, maxed out their credit cards, and opened their own brewery-like production facility.

A friend from the farmers market gave the pair advice on what equipment they needed to source, and spending around $30,000, they set up a small production warehouse ("around fifteen hundred square feet and no air-conditioning") and got to work.

The early days were a true grind.

"It took us about ten months from the time of the farmers market to the time we got into Whole Foods. So by that time, I had the baby. I remember being on the bottling line, going into labor, strapping the baby to me, and being back on the bottling line like two weeks later. It was a whirlwind! My husband got a second job to pay our mortgage at night; it was just a full-on grind of startup life."

Takeaway #5: It's Your Job to Believe in Yourself

Putting all your chips into a new venture is filled with uncertainty and often very little hard evidence to go on. Those around you can see it as a madness. But the main fuel that every entrepreneur needs is an unwavering belief in their gut feeling and intuition.

"It just doesn't faze you when you have that gut feeling. You know you're doing something right. Just take it a day at a time. Don't give up and don't let people around you bring you down either. Just go, just hustle. So I always try to tell people that because it's hard."

TAKEAWAY #6: Investment Should Be More than Just Money

As the business rapidly grew, Allison realized that they needed to seek investment to scale. What she also realized was that she didn't just want money alone but a partner that could help strategically. Investment offers can be tempting for startup entrepreneurs, but it's important to realize that investors are people you are "stuck with," and they need to be the right fit.

"We almost took on what people say is 'stupid money,' where we had people interested but they weren't going to bring any strategics to the table with it. And I think that people can get a little bit blindsided by that. When you start taking on investment from people that just have money and they don't bring any other value other than that, it's not a great partnership. Maybe later on, once you're an established brand and all you need is capital because you've figured everything out. But at the beginning, it's almost like a marriage. And you want to be really careful with that."

Allison and her husband applied to appear on *Shark Tank*—a process that proved to be a lot more grueling than they expected. Their pitch was a success, and they received an offer from Rohan Oza. He was the investor they had their sights on, describing him as "the shark of all sharks in the beverage industry." Oza explained to them that he had been searching for a product just like theirs. The partnership with Oza proved to be a great strategic alliance, particularly with his help in rebranding the product. The rest, as they say, is history!

THREE QUICK QUESTIONS

WHAT'S the number one marketing moment that made the business pop?

"It was definitely our viral TikTok moment. I think that video has over fifteen million views and over four hundred thousand comments, which means people are actually engaging with it. It changed our whole strategy and the company, and it was a major moment in the company history."

WHERE DO you hang out to get smarter?

"I am obsessed with the news. Every morning I listen to two podcasts from both sides of the left and the right. I love to know both sides. I don't want to be blindsided by just what one person is saying. I want to know all views. And I think that's really important to make my decisions in life."

HOW DO you win the day?

"I get blindsided by it a lot because I do have kids, and I want to focus on them and the company too. So for me, it's probably like getting my nails done or something simple to take in that me time in the morning. It's my coffee. And at night I'm all about balance. And I love to have a little dessert every night. So live your life. Love your life. Have some balance."

LISTEN to Allison's episode to find out how she redeveloped her branding, why you don't need an MBA from Harvard, and how she got a big marketing boost from a dancing J.Lo.

5

IN THE BLINK OF AN EYE

ANN MCFERRAN: HOW AN ENTREPRENEUR
TURNED BEING TEASED INTO A
MULTIMILLION-DOLLAR-A-MONTH BUSINESS

Ann McFerran is the LA-based founder behind the beauty brand Glamnetic. Glamnetic is famous for its innovative magnetic lashes, and through their creative, top-quality products, they strive to make people's beauty routines a whole lot easier. Ann's story is quite simply amazing (I also considered saying "crazy" or even "colossal"). Ann shared her story with me of how she went from being a BCEO (Bedroom CEO . . . a new term for you!) to speedily making seven figures a month in sales.

Ann is originally from Bangkok and moved to the US at the age of seven when her mother remarried. Finding herself in an all-white neighborhood, she was teased for being Asian, and that led to low self-confidence. As a teenager, she discovered the power of make-up—particularly false eye lashes—which gave her an instant, much-needed confidence boost.

After many years of different careers, including being a successful artist and a stock trader, Ann wanted to start her own business, and her instincts took her back to her passion for lashes.

TAKEAWAY #1: Improve on an Existing Product

It's the typical startup entrepreneur story—Ann's idea for her business came from a personal desire for a product that didn't exist. It's come up many times in my interviews with entrepreneurs—that it's all about keeping your eyes open for opportunity, wherever it may be. Often, popular products that already exist can be improved on, and if you're wanting a specific improvement, chances are there are many people out there like you.

"I had seen magnetic lashes come out, just the normal ones, and they were very thin and plasticky. They had two magnets on them. This is an interesting idea, but I like glam beautiful, thick lashes. I want to add more magnets. I want to have five. And I even came out with six magnets."

TAKEAWAY #2: Enroll at YTU

YTU? YouTube University! (I made that up, but it's cute, right?) I've heard this from so many female entrepreneurs who are YTU alumni—that almost everything you need to know can be learned from the internet. Gone are the days where the only way to educate yourself is through college. There really is no excuse to not learn!

"I began learning through YouTube, literally just from YouTube. Teaching myself everything in product development, just understanding every part of development. I taught myself all that. And that's where my journey started."

· · ·

TAKEAWAY #3: **Enrol Again at YTU**

Without any marketing capital, Ann decided to photograph friends wearing her product. How did she learn photography? YTU! Her photographer friend was shocked at the quality of her images (her professional artistic critique was "Holy Crap!"). Ann discovered that the first photo that she took was later painted as a mural in Spain. She had no idea how it reached Spain, but it was a pretty cool validation nonetheless.

"I love YouTube school!" Ann beamed.

TAKEAWAY #4: **Surround Yourself with Good People**

Ann was running her startup out of her small bedroom in a little backhouse in Korea Town. With no money for employees, a one-desk bedroom office, and a hectic schedule, she found it challenging to find people to join her. However, she knew that she needed to surround herself with good people. Eventually, she met Kevin.

"He came in a month into the business, and he believed in me enough to want to be a business partner. He helped me build infrastructure around the brand in terms of the finance and operations. I was thinking more about the creative and the marketing. As you get larger, that's something that's very important to deal with."

TAKEAWAY #4: **Don't Underestimate a Bedroom Office**

The life of a startup entrepreneur is, more often than not, not glamorous. Getting a business off the ground requires one to do whatever they need to, often without much capital. Ann, like so many, started her business from her bedroom. While a fancy office sounds like a nice idea, in reality, do we really need much more than a chair and a desk?

While there may not be much glamour in bedroom officing, Ann explained something that truly is, something that happened while she toiled away in her small bedroom.

"We actually hit our first, like, million dollars a month at month six."

TAKEAWAY #5: **Communicate with Your Customers Directly**

Ann's main marketing drive was through social media, particularly by marketing through influencers. She also made videos and ran online ads where she would appear as the founder and speak candidly about her product. Ann put a lot of value on communicating with her customers and found that being involved "on the ground" can be invaluable.

"I was talking to the customers every day because I used to do the customer service myself. So I understood the customer really well. And I would even text some of them and say, 'Here's my phone number, text me.' It allowed us to really understand the customer and really home in on the messaging in a big way. That's allowed our marketing channels to thrive."

THREE QUICK QUESTIONS

WHAT'S **the number one marketing moment that's made your business pop?**

"I think when I learned to become absolutely obsessed

with optimizing every aspect of the business in the same way that I became obsessed with optimizing beauty. There are so many channels, and there are so many possible ways to advertise and get your product out there. I think once somebody becomes obsessed with it, then they're going to figure it out."

How do you win the day?

"I have to have my eight hours of sleep, despite working from 9:00 a.m. to midnight, sometimes 2:00 a.m. When I get out of bed, I start working immediately because I enjoy it! I don't drink any caffeine. My employees are like "you're a robot.""

How do you deal with failure?

"That word doesn't exist in my mind, like *failure* or *I failed*. I never ever say that in my life. Life presents you with random things you have to deal with, and if they don't work out, then it's fine. You move on to the next thing. It's just how you define it in your head."

Listen to Ann's episode to find out how she was inspired by psychobiology, how she got free clothes, and how she found herself in an area densely populated with cows.

6

HONEY TALKS

BEATRICE DIXON: HOW AN ENTREPRENEUR
FOLLOWED HER DREAM AND MADE VAGINA
POTION

Beatrice Dixon is the cofounder of The Honey Pot Co—a plant-based feminine care brand. A brand that cares for our vaginas. In six years, The Honey Pot has grown from a kitchen-based operation with a client base made up of friends and family to a massive operation with products flying off the shelves of every Target and Walmart around America. We spoke about the event that really led to Beatrice and her brother getting started with the brand, when you should and shouldn't fundraise, and why their brand resonates with so many women. Sometimes companies can get long winded about explaining themselves. Beatrice keeps it to the point, an elevator pitch for when the elevator is just going up one floor: "We're a vagina company." Love that.

TAKEAWAY #1: Follow Your Dreams (and Listen to Your Grandma)

It's quite a magical thing, and I've never heard this one

from a startup entrepreneur, but there's a first time for everything, right? We always hear about female entrepreneurs following their dreams, but in Beatrice's case, it was quite literal!

"I was dealing with bacterial vaginosis for almost a year. I had a dream one night, and in it, my grandmother told me that she had been walking with me and seeing me struggle. She told me that what she was giving me was going to solve my problem. She had a piece of paper with a list of ingredients. She kept telling me to memorize it. That's what I did. And I made it, used it, and it worked!"

With such an intriguing story, I was eager to know just what grandma suggested!

"Coconut oil, water, apple cider vinegar, lavender, rose, garlic. Very simple ingredients, but the point of it was for me to make a formula. Because everything is blended together cold, I didn't have to do anything crazy or heat things up and things like that. It was really like a vagina potion. You know, I love that it sounds magical, and I feel like it is magical."

TAKEAWAY #2: Test Your Product at a Trade Show

Amazed at how well her dream potion worked for her, Beatrice started making it for her friends for free. But soon, those friends and friends of friends were insisting that they pay. So Beatrice had a small email customer business but no website or plans to grow. She kept an eye out for opportunities and came across a trade show that seemed like a good fit. Trade shows are often excellent places to show your product as they're a mix of the general public and industry professionals—a perfect audience to get initial feedback.

"An opportunity came to go to a trade show. My brother (Simon Gray), who became my cofounder, put together some money with the help of a friend. We bought bottles, caps, labels, and ingredients, and we set up a little assembly line for us to make the product. And we just got started. We sold six hundred bottles in a weekend."

TAKEAWAY #3: Grow with White-Label Products

Beatrice realized she was on to a good thing and was eager to get started developing her concept and brand. However, she had limited financial resources to get started. She turned to white labeling products—a sometimes efficient and inexpensive way to grow your range.

"You need people to consume your shit. If they're not consuming it fast enough, then you're not making money fast enough. What we realized is that we needed to bring in other brands because it wasn't like we could brand everything ourselves at that point. We connected with a brand that did 'mommy' products—a white-label brand. We just kind of created this marketplace—a little vagina story in a way. And what we saw was huge growth. Huge meaning we went from like $30,000 to maybe $240,000."

TAKEAWAY #4: A Great Product Leads to Word-of-Mouth Marketing

Beatrice soon made the leap to supplying The Honey Pot Co products to Target—a dream retailer for many startup entrepreneurs. The connection happened thanks to word of mouth, and Beatrice puts it down to having a good product. If there's one thing I know for sure after interviewing so many founders, it is that for any brand to succeed, it all starts with a product worth shouting about.

"Our brand's marketing was really through word of

mouth because our products are good, you know. And so the
way we got into Target is that the buyer went to get her hair
done, and her hairdresser was talking about feminine care
(because that's the buying she was involved with). Her hairdresser asked if she knew about The Honey Pot Co, and she
said no. She came and looked at stuff, and then she
contacted us."

TAKEAWAY #5: Use a Retail Broker

Beatrice continued with some advice about dealing with
a major retailer, explaining that she hired a retail broker to
help with negotiations. Many startup entrepreneurs aren't
aware of this option, but it can really increase your chances
of success, especially if you are new to the world of retail
and buyers.

"You have to get a broker once you start getting into the
process because brands speak their brand language, not
buyer language. So we had to get a broker, and we had to do
mountains of paperwork."

TAKEAWAY #6: Struggle First before Asking for Money

When it came to fundraising, Beatrice decided to first go
through the startup struggle alone. Going this route often
leads to an entrepreneur really getting to understand their
business, and this can be an advantage before seeking
investment. It also means you raise money at a higher valuation because you have proof of concept and have built up
customer loyalty.

"Don't raise money until you're kind of desperate to raise
money, especially if you do what I do, because every investor
is going to want to know what kind of handle you have and

what you have done. There are people that raise capital before their businesses launch. Those people typically have connections. Those people typically have relationships. But in the consumer-packaged goods space, it's really important that you understand your business first and that you know what it's like to struggle before you go and ask somebody else for their money."

THREE QUICK QUESTIONS

WHERE DO **you hang out to get smarter?**

"In books and with smart people. Currently, I'm reading *The Mountain Is You* by Brianna Wiest. It's about responsibility and accountability, and it is really powerful."

How DO **you win the day?**

"It's easy to get lost in thinking about the past. Always be thinking forward. I focus on the right now, this minute. Who are we talking to? What are we doing right? What's the task?"

How DO **you deal with failure?**

"It's inevitable. And there's no way to control it, so bring that shit on!"

Listen to Beatrice's episode to find out how she avoided running two businesses, what she learned about bar codes, and why she told a marketing agency to kiss her ass.

7

SURE CAN DO

BECCA MILLSTEIN: HOW AN ENTREPRENEUR MADE TINNED FISH SEXY

Becca Millstein is the cofounder of Fishwife. Fishwife is a new female-founded and female-led food company aiming to make ethically sourced premium and delicious tinned seafood a staple in every cupboard. In fact, more than a staple, Becca and fellow cofounder Caroline Goldfarb aim to make tinned fish *sexy*. It may not sound possible, but they've hit the nail on the head with their surprisingly stylish branding, female-centric storytelling, and good-for-the-planet ethos. Fishwife works with small-boat fisher folk, sustainable aquaculture farms, and micro canneries to bring the vibrancy of European conserva culture to the North American table. Becca explained what makes a distinguishable brand, what that actually costs, how to find the right folks to do it, what it actually means to create a sustainable tinned fish company, how to start small and build within your means, and how to build a brand that's truly authentic and unique.

Before getting into Becca's entrepreneurial story, she explained the inspiration behind the Fishwife name, which, as it turns out, is a shout-out to the early female entrepreneur.

"Googling, I found the term *fishwife*, which was just so perfect for what we were trying to achieve with the project. It was a term that was used for the wives of fishermen who would sell their husband's wares at the market. They gained a reputation for being really bossy and swearing, as they needed to move this perishable product fast. It came to take on this gendered insult for a loud, bossy woman. And then it has this dual meaning as these fishwives gained professional rights earlier than maybe some of their contemporaries because they had this power to control these businesses. So it has this dual-toned entrepreneurial approach as well."

The pair's idea for the business came from a discussion during a hike. Becca and Caroline were throwing around ideas for a business they could do together, and they got onto the subject of fish. Both had been really enjoying eating fish during quarantine, trout in particular. Having both spent time in Spain, they had been exposed to an altogether different way of looking at tinned fish.

"In those European exploits, we'd both been exposed to the elegance and sexiness and casual allure of going to a Spanish wine bar and getting a tin of beautifully decorated sardines. And then you go to an American grocery store, and looking at the shelves, it's just totally clinical, absolutely devoid of any sexiness. And we were like, why?"

Becca was fortunate enough to have friends in the food world, including entrepreneurs and journalists, and she discussed the idea with them. They all quickly jumped to validate the idea, and the pair got started the very next day.

· · ·

TAKEAWAY #1: Get Branding Inspiration from Instagram

From the get-go, Becca put her focus on branding—one of the key aspects that she realized would separate her brand from the rest. Having previously worked in the music industry, helping artists with creative direction and marketing, she knew that Instagram is a wonderful resource for inspiration, both in terms of getting ideas for branding direction and as a platform for finding talent.

"Instagram was very helpful; it's an amazing database of information. You can find different artists, illustrators, and graphic designers and pass through who would best be able to communicate the conceptual design concept on a project."

TAKEAWAY #2: Hire Independent Artists

Becca shortlisted about twenty illustrators and asked friends who they liked best. There was one clear winner, and the entrepreneurs got in touch through a DM and began working together on their visual concepts.

"I think it's the best of all worlds if you can find independent artists because they need support, and it's helpful for them to get their work out there in this capacity so then they can grow with you."

Becca also found that hiring an independent freelancer was much more budget friendly than going the traditional branding agency route.

"His fees were that of an indie illustrator designer, and that was really affordable for us in this bootstrap phase. For our illustrations plus another independent photographer, we probably spent about $5,000. And I have people telling me that the visuals that we put out were equivalent to a quarter-million-to-half-a-million-dollar job!"

. . .

TAKEAWAY #3: Source Suppliers by Talking to as Many People as Possible

Becca's next step was to source a partner for canning the product. Her mission was to find a suitable microcannery that would agree to low minimum orders. Not having personal experience in this world, Becca turned to everyone she knew.

"I hear this from entrepreneurs all the time. When you start a company, you just have to talk to so many people, like you talk to everyone."

Becca's research paid off, and she found a suitable cannery that offered a low minimum initial order that she was comfortable with. It took a lot of time to get there, but the challenge of workable minimum orders is something many startup entrepreneurs have to deal with. Her story goes to show that it is possible to find what you are looking for, and it's worth the effort of thorough research.

TAKEAWAY #4: Be Scrappy with Your PR

Fishwife's marketing started off with a bang from the get-go. In part, this was thanks to Caroline's existing social media following (Caroline was working as a successful comedy writer and is the creator of the @officialseanpenn Instagram account). In addition to their social media campaign, they also had early success with mentions in the traditional press—from Condé Nast Traveler to Vogue. Many startups are cash strapped and unable to afford the high cost of hiring a PR agency. Becca got it right without the help of a traditional PR agency and found it was in her favor to be scrappy.

"I had some familiarity with putting together press releases and all that stuff from working in the music industry, and then I had amazing journalist friends that were willing to look over my press release and make sure it was all good. I'd say just try to do everything yourself for as long as you can because you'll learn how to do it. So when you do eventually hire someone, you'll have a really strong understanding of it."

Takeaway #5: Test Your Customers as Quickly as Possible

Becca started her business with the philosophy of moving quickly. It's a common piece of advice for startup entrepreneurs to "move fast" and "break things" by getting your MVP (Minimum Viable Product) out there as soon as possible. Becca found the most useful part of this strategy was getting the opportunity to get feedback from customers as early on as possible.

"My advice is to get customer feedback as soon as you can by launching the brand, and you hear this all the time. Like Nik Sharma, who's a very hot brand guru, would create fake websites to just test a brand and get feedback on it. You've just got to think of those hacks and a way to get your brand in front of people to see if they would want to buy it."

THREE QUICK QUESTIONS

How do you win the day?

"I am a runner; running is where I come up with a lot of ideas. I try to leave my phone outside my bedroom because it's terrible. I'm not good at it, but I am working toward that goal. I did it for a week, and it made me feel like a complete person again."

WHERE DO you hang out to get smarter?

"For the first four months of the business, I just listened to all of *How I Built This* (hosted by Guy Raz) and learned so much. So if you're starting your business, definitely listen to that podcast because it will teach you so many things."

HOW DO you deal with failure?

"I think you've just got to say, OK, what did we do wrong here? Try to lay the groundwork for failure by always being honest. If you were acting genuinely, and you were trying to do the right thing, then that's all you can do. That's all you can say, and you'll learn from it."

LISTEN to Becca's episode to find out how she learned about sustainability, what challenges she faced with early success, and what question you should ask your waiter.

8

ROYAL FLUSH

BETHANY EDWARDS: HOW AN ENTREPRENEUR MODERNIZED PREGNANCY TESTING

Bethany Edwards is an inventor and the founder of Lia— an earth-friendly health care company on a mission to revolutionize reproductive health through the development of innovative products. The company recently launched its first product, which is set to be a total game changer. The FDA-cleared Lia Pregnancy Test is the world's first flushable pregnancy test, and it's changing the historically wasteful product into a plastic-free, flushable, biodegradable form. It's as brilliant as Bethany is. She gave fascinating insights into what it takes to develop an idea like this that doesn't yet exist in the world.

Bethany's vision has opened a truly important dialogue for an antiquated industry, which has had the same stiff plastic products for over thirty years. Its effect on the planet is shockingly astounding as Bethany explained:

"If you're born in the 1980s, your mom's positive pregnancy test is still in a landfill somewhere. Just in the US, from pregnancy tests, there's two million pounds of plastic waste, which is enough to stretch from here to the International Space Station and back about seven times!"

Bethany's entrepreneurial journey was inspired by a talk she heard by Richard Fry, who was speaking on behalf of the Industrial Design Societies for America. In it, he expressed his views that we should no longer be designing products to be recycled. Instead, we should be designing them in a way that they can be completely disposable.

This got Bethany thinking, and she identified pregnancy tests as a product that needed to move with the times.

Takeaway #1: Start with Market Research

Time and time again, startup entrepreneurs have found that after having the initial seed of an idea, thorough market research can be invaluable. Bethany spoke to hundreds of women, both through one-on-one interviews and through surveys.

Her research revealed that there had been no notable innovation in the industry for decades, and beyond the clear need for a planet-friendly option, the aspect of privacy was a problem for many women. Over 92 percent of the women she surveyed valued privacy when taking the pregnancy test, regardless of what result they were hoping for.

"That really got us into this idea of designing with paper, not plastic. If we can be really smart about the materials that we're choosing, that will allow us to design a test that is also flushable, which provides the additional level of privacy because nobody is seeing these tests in the trash."

Bethany considered the idea of packaging as well when it came to the issue of privacy. Wanting to move away from the old-fashioned, overused, and indiscreet branding in the space, she developed branding with a name that was "human" and personal, with green colors (instead of the usual pink, purple and blue) and no smiling, happy baby pictures. In addition, she kept the words *pregnancy test* discreet, only placing it on the little tear tab.

TAKEAWAY #2: Learning from Scratch Is Possible—There's No Excuse in Today's World

In getting started with developing her idea, Bethany had no knowledge or experience in the industry. But she proved, as so many startup entrepreneurs have shared on this show, that you can find out all you need to know from available material and speaking to professionals in the space.

"I think the entrepreneurship journey is a little like this video game that I used to play as a kid called *Quest.* You had to go around and talk to a person, and they would give you advice, or they would give you little trinkets that you would then use to solve another problem. It was a lot of that, especially in the early days."

TAKEAWAY #3: Raise Money through Pitch Competitions

We've heard it plenty of times before: pitch competitions are a great route to get early-stage funding. Not only is it a viable option for getting investment, but it's also a chance to plug into a network and gain expert business advice.

Bethany had success after entering "every pitch competition we could find," and she did so with a conceptual idea, a "terrible looking prototype," and an early proven concept. Essentially, it was "a kind of sketch on a piece of paper."

TAKEAWAY #4: KISS (Keep It Simple, Stupid)

Bethany put down her pitching success to two things. The first was "just having the strong, strong desire to make this a reality." Passion can go a long way.

Second, Bethany found great strength in being able to explain her concept in a neat, succinct way with simple language. Entrepreneurs can often make the mistake of pitching with a complicated explanation, and this can send investors running. The most effective pitches are ones that investors can get their heads around quickly. So it's worth reworking your pitch until it's as simple as possible.

"Having had some marketing background, I was able to find a way to talk about it in a very simplistic way. So to be able to be like, 'they are flushable, biodegradable pregnancy tests.' Just like snappy and quick. We would explain some of the privacy stuff by pointing out that it has been the plot of so many sitcoms and movies—like people finding pregnancy tests in the trash. We were able to quickly be like, look, it's flushable. It's biodegradable. It's 0% plastic. Easy language."

THREE QUICK QUESTIONS

WHAT'S the number one marketing moment that made your business pop?

"It was really being strategic in lining up some awards with the announcement of our FDA clearance. I looked for events and awards that we could enter around that time frame (of the FDA clearance) because I wanted to try to line up that announcement really well. So we were fortunately able to get on stage at TechCrunch in Berlin. And I announced that FDA clearance live on the international stage. We ended up winning, and that drove like 320 million press impressions in four weeks. It absolutely helped lead us to be able to secure funding."

How DO you win your day?

"Coffee, coffee, coffee. I have to have coffee. Also, a little time in the morning is something I really value. Recently, I'm starting to try turn my phone on "do not disturb" just to be able to unwind a little bit later into the evenings."

IF YOU ONLY HAD $1,000 left in your business bank account, where would you spend it?

I automatically think of something that would bring in more money, which would either be promotion of the product or a networking event where there's potential funding. So those are the two I think of first. But then I would also say the third one would potentially be to splurge on a team outing.

LISTEN to Bethany's episode to find out how she launched with scalability in mind, how she built her future retail strategy, and how she found inspiration in coffee filters.

9

FERTILE GROUNDS

CARLY LEAHY: HOW AN ENTREPRENEUR DEMYSTIFIED WOMEN'S HEALTH AND FERTILITY

Carly Leahy is the cofounder of Modern Fertility—a forward-thinking women's health care company that set out to launch the world's first at-home fertility hormone test in 2017. Since launching and at the time of writing this book, they've successfully raised $22 million, been named Fast Company's number one company for innovation in health care, and expanded their product range to a pregnancy test and ovulation test, as well as an app for women to track their cycle.

Their mission is to empower women during this important but often overwhelming life milestone by helping them understand their bodies in an easy-to-digest way and taking the fear out of the journey.

Carly's career background has included lead creative roles for companies such as Uber and Google, which she ascribes as a major factor in the success of her business. It's clear that with Modern Fertility, her skill in brand creation and marketing really shines through, and I've admired Carly from afar for quite some time. In this chapter, you'll find so many tactical pieces of advice and information that you can take directly into your own venture.

Through a "you guys have to meet," Carly had coffee with Afton Vechery (her future cofounding partner), who passionately introduced her to the world of fertility and the problems that she spotted in the industry.

Carly's initial reaction was that "baby stuff" was not her thing:

"It was a complete blind spot. I thought that being a feminist meant pushing away all the motherhood stuff. I always thought I wanted to be a mom, but I was focused on my career and not ready for it. I don't love not knowing what I don't know. I consider myself an intelligent woman, and I really don't know the fundamentals about my reproductive health."

However, Carly was inspired by the chat and started reading clinical papers and books on the subject.

"Fertility declines over time. And that that doesn't have to be scary. It is what it is. And women need to be able to have tools to help them understand where they are in that trajectory, especially as we're waiting longer."

TAKEAWAY #1: Blind Spots Can Be a Great Start

From speaking to so many entrepreneurs, I've found it interesting how often startup entrepreneurs successfully make their impact in an industry previously unknown to them. The standard textbook advice is to stick to something you know, but it seems that in some cases, a lack of experience and naivety can actually become your strength.

"I really do think that sometimes your blind spots are the places where you're most well equipped to come to the world with a brand. Because you can help break down things but not dumb things down."

Takeaway #2: Get Help from Experts

If you're approaching an industry that you're inexperienced in, a resourceful entrepreneur will find that there is plenty of information out there that's readily available. Carly and Afton filled in the gaps by speaking to experts who could fast-track their learning. (I also recommend becoming acquainted with the school of YouTube.)

"If you are a learner, and you're not afraid to talk to people and ask for advice, you can really do it no matter what your background is. We built the company on lists. We would look at each other's list and add things and trade things. If we don't know about this? Let's find an expert here and an expert here. We spoke to the people who are really smart, who knew the things that we were trying to figure out."

Takeaway #3: Consider Your Brand from the Beginning

Common advice for early-stage startups is to not think about the brand—some suggest that brand building should come at a later stage. But Carly considered herself a "brand person" and felt quite differently.

"For us, it wasn't just about making sure women had access to lab testing. It was about making sure you feel comfortable understanding what's going on in your body. There are sometimes weird undertones that are associated with understanding fertility. So very early on, we really cared about how we felt, what we said, what we meant, why we matter."

An example of one of the ways they developed the brand was with a unique, customized dashboard showing various indicators around hormone levels:

"We did a color study because we didn't want her to think there was a 'good' or a 'bad.' There's no green or red."

Takeaway #4: Create a Sticky Community by Being Relatable

While still in the early stages of developing their digital experience, Carly began creating a community through a blog. Carly explained that the ROI (which she said with air quotes) was not something easily quantified; however, it was undoubtedly a vital move in launching the business.

"There wasn't a great resource for women to be able to proactively understand what was going on in their bodies. We could be the thought leaders; we could really talk to women in 'human speak' about what was going on—and not just about our product but about anything related to fertility and reproductive health."

Takeaway #5: Don't Advertise, Educate

In today's world, consumers are sophisticated and can pick up even the most subtle advertising tricks. Today, the consumer wants transparency. Carly made sure that the blog's focus was on education and not direct "buy our product" advertising. This created a safer space for women to discuss an intimate subject and ultimately built trust around the brand.

"It's about finding out what people care about. It's about creating the best possible content. And we just kept at it until we started gaining traction, and we started seeing that women were really finding us through our blog. We would never do an advertisement. The more that we're able to just provide the education, the stronger our whole ecosystem becomes."

Takeaway #6: Hire Freelance Marketing Experts

Startup entrepreneurs that start lean need to make a judgment call on what kind of initial team to build to have the biggest impact. Carly found that what made the biggest difference was an amazing marketing team: "It's a game changer in terms of guiding the ship."

Carly came across a company called Marketer Hire where you can hire marketing contractors. Many of the marketers have strong experience working for large brands such as Airbnb or Uber. With my own businesses, I've found these kinds of resources can be extremely useful. Many super talented marketers are moonlighting with a side hustle. Without the commitment of employment, you can get access to the person who's done that exact thing you need and has the proven results.

"They've worked in one of these companies you've heard of that has done really well. So don't stress about hiring, getting your full marketing team in the door, day one. It's just not going to happen. It took us years to do that."

Takeaway #7: Make a List and Take Baby Steps; It's All about the Compound Effect

I asked Carly what advice she would give to a female entrepreneur with a big dream, and she explained the importance of list-making. By showing up every day and taking small actions toward your goals, the compound effect over time will lead to your success.

"Start a list of all of the things that you need to do to accomplish what you want to accomplish and then chunk it up; break it up and chip away at that list every day. There's no way you're going to be able to accomplish everything in a day. It can be completely overwhelming to get started because there's so much to do. But make yourself an outline from today to the launch of your company. What would that look like? What would you do tomorrow to chip away at that outline? Stay diligent, diligently attacking that list every single day. It really does take every single day."

It's a secret of many successful entrepreneurs. Instead of grand gestures and energetic leaps, constant baby steps, one foot in front of the other, are exponentially powerful.

"The compound effect of all of those small steps that you might not think are big ideas, but on the day that you don't feel like doing anything, just do the least hard task and just get one little thing done, and it will all compound."

THREE QUICK QUESTIONS

WHAT'S YOUR "WHY"?

"I want to help people gather more mindfully. I want to create experiences that will be memorable. Someone told me once, "How you live your days is how you live your life," and for me, it's all about these really small moments and making them count."

WHERE DO you hang out to get smarter?

"I highly recommend a book called *You Never Forget Your First*, which is a biography of George Washington (by a woman). Like 99 percent of the biographies written on George Washington have been written by white men. And she totally annihilates the way history has been written before. I love nonfiction. I think especially in times of crisis because it helps me remember that there has been so much suffering in history that it actually helps ground me."

How do you win the day?

"In the morning, it doesn't really matter what the sweat is, sometimes it's a bike ride, sometimes it's a run, sometimes it's a walk, sometimes a few push-ups. There's something about your body having persevered in and of itself. It feels really powerful to me—even before the day starts, you've already accomplished something. I went through a phase of having freezing cold showers for the last four months. So it's that same feeling where I was like, I can do anything I want because I just overcame this freezing cold shower."

Side note: I too have done a four-month stint of cold showers over the Swiss winter, and I can confirm it's pretty life changing.

Listen to Carly's episode to find out what she learned about building a brand from her time at Apple and Google, how she got her business started with Y Combinator, and why she treats her brand as a best friend.

10

BEE THE BEST

CARLY STEIN: HOW AN ENTREPRENEUR DISCOVERED THE HEALING POWER OF BEES

Carly Stein is the founder of Beekeeper's Naturals. Beekeeper's Naturals launched in 2017 and is an inspiring company on a mission to reinvent the medicine cabinet. How? By using unique remedies from the beehive! The beekeeper-led team is committed to providing the cleanest, most powerful solutions to modern health issues like brain fog, chronic stress, poor sleep, and scratchy throats. I spoke to Carly about her really special story, and she gave great pieces of advice while explaining her journey.

Having done some research on Carly's brand and its ethos, I was feeling inspired, and I checked what was in my medicine cabinet. My findings were that I didn't have anything natural in there, which is surprising because our fridges are full of natural products and so is our skincare. Carly had spotted a gap in an increasingly ingredient-conscious market.

"When you're sick, your body's in a vulnerable state. The last thing you want to do is be introducing chemicals, refined sugars, flavors, preservatives, and dyes. There are some wonderful aspects of modern medicine, of course, but in a lot of cases, the medicine that we buy at the drugstore is meant to mask the symptoms and get us through our day. But it's not really helping us in the way that it should."

Takeaway #1: If You Want Something Done Right, Do It Yourself

Carly had been a lifelong sufferer of chronic tonsillitis, as well as having an autoimmune condition that meant she wasn't able to take antibiotics. She couldn't find help through western medicine, and the natural remedies available on the market weren't helping either. On a trip to Europe, she discovered propolis (a resinous mixture that honey bees produce by mixing saliva and beeswax), and it was the first thing she ever found that helped her ailments.

Like all good entrepreneurs, she searched for it back home to see if it was available. Back in Canada, she struggled to find it, and when she did, she found it had a clear flaw. To get around that flaw, she realized that universal wisdom—if you want to get it right, do it yourself.

"I finally found some propolis at this farmers market in British Columbia, and it was forty dollars for the tiniest tincture, and it was organic and artisanal and all the things. And I went back and used it, and I had a really severe allergic reaction. I actually ran a toxicity test on the product, and I found out that there was pesticide exposure. How are there pesticides? Isn't that the whole point of organic? It made me realize that if you want something done right, you have to do it yourself. So I need to start beekeeping and run quality control. Next step: How the hell do I do that?"

· · ·

Takeaway #2: Passion Comes before Profit

It's probably the most common piece of advice in this book—that a startup entrepreneur can learn anything with all the readily available information of our times. Carly did all she could to start learning about beekeeping. From Google University to buying Beekeeping for Dummies and taking science courses. But her breakthrough came from attending a beekeeping association meeting. There she met John, a third-generation beekeeper and retired biochemist.

"I convinced him to let me be an apprentice. I started working for him for free. It was an incredible learning experience. I didn't know it at the time, but looking back, I was creating this product line and just perfecting it for myself. And, you know, it was actually a really beautiful, accidental way to start a company because I think a lot of the time when people start companies, they're thinking about the longer term. They're thinking about profitability and how you can scale."

I loved this concept—the freedom of developing your business with a focus on personal passion rather than having your sights on profits. Truly learning about a subject requires focus, and it's a phase that should be driven by passion, not future profits.

"A lot of people cut corners in the pursuit of profit. I was just making what works for me and doing it as best I could. At the start, I never thought it could be a company. I studied sciences. I never took a business course in my life. I never thought I could start a company. But I started sharing these products with my roommates. And next thing you know, people on campus were Facebook messaging me."

The other piece of advice I picked up here was the idea of working as an apprentice. It may not be lucrative financially, but it's one of the best ways to learn, get real-world experience, and be guided by a mentor. And it's a whole lot cheaper than school fees.

TAKEAWAY #3: Be Aggressive in Your Pursuit of Information

Carly had previously worked as a trader at Goldman Sachs—a lucrative and sought-after career. But it made her unhappy. She told me that she actually made a "happiness spreadsheet," and it prompted her to consider ditching her nine-to-five (or more like 8:00 a.m. to 11:00 p.m.) and taking a chance on the bee idea.

Personal happiness and a feeling of fulfillment are common drivers for startup entrepreneurs to take a brave leap. In Carly's case, this really was a brave leap because she had no experience in her new venture and had a lot to learn. But she's an example of how you can make it all happen if you want it badly enough.

"I knew nothing about business and how to start a business. I knew a hell of a lot about the products and the science behind them, and my biggest asset was that I knew a lot about how to research effectively. I knew what constitutes good science, what kind of trials to look at, and what kind of science was being manipulated for a certain result versus what to understand. But on the business side, I had no idea. And you don't need to have an idea. You just need to be aggressive in your pursuit of information and understanding."

TAKEAWAY #4: Meet Your Customers Where They Are

Carly experienced great success early on with rapid customer growth and customer acquisition. Carly felt that this was down to two things: good product and relatability.

"I think, for one, we're obsessive about product. I'm a great guinea pig for all of our products. I won't bring something to market that I don't use. You can only get so far with a company built on promise."

With regards to her marketing, she attributed her success to having relatable content for her audience. This is where Carly having once been new to this subject herself became a strength.

"We focused on marketing messaging that people understand, trying to bring this down to everyone's level, because the average person doesn't know what propolis is, so how can we make this understandable in a quick snap? Even if something is the best miracle product ever, and it is a cure-all, it's really important to be specific and meet your customer where they are and speak to the problem that they are going through."

THREE QUICK QUESTIONS

WHAT'S the number one marketing moment that made your business pop?

"I don't think that I could point to one silver bullet. We've had a ton of celebrity endorsements, but I don't think it was one thing. I think it was slowly grinding away, creating our Instagram following, and interacting with our customers. We've created a lot of micro-moments by focusing on connection. You build connections by solving people's problems."

. . .

WHERE DO you hang out to get smarter?

"I have a lot of entrepreneur friends, and I spend a lot of time trading stories with them, learning about what's working for them, sharing what's working for us. I have a really incredible network of female entrepreneurs. I cannot tell you how many times my brilliant girlfriends who run brilliant companies have given me advice that's fundamentally shifted my path. So, trying to find people who care about the things you care about and can provide a different perspective is really important."

If you're looking for a community of like-minded folks going through the same challenges as you, tune in to the end of this book where we introduce you to Hype Club.

HOW DO you deal with failure?

"Failure is so important. I fail at things all the time. I'm teaching myself and constantly reteaching myself to see failure as an opportunity to build that resilience muscle. That is the most important thing you can do as an entrepreneur."

LISTEN to Carly's episode to find out how she raised capital, what she found in Copenhagen, and what caused her embarrassing fangirl moment.

FIVE OTHER TITLE IDEAS

Oh, come on, you know that the word *bee* is *so* good for word play. Here were my other ideas for chapter names that didn't make it:

To Bee or Not to Bee

Staying in Buzzyness
Be All You Can Bee
The Bee's Knees
A/BEE Testing

11

VICE PRESIDENT

CATHARINE DOCKERY: HOW AN ENTREPRENEUR MADE NICE IN THE INDUSTRY OF VICE

Catharine Dockery is the founder of Vice Ventures—a fund that invests in businesses. Sounds like pretty standard stuff, right? The twist is that the startups she invests in are rather nontraditional. The mix includes cannabis, alcohol, CBD, addiction recovery, and sex tech.

While investigating work with an alcohol brand, Catharine found that there was common feedback. She discovered that many investors have a "vice clause," which precludes them from investing in certain "taboo" industries, even if the opportunities were huge. This is how Vice Ventures was born, and this is Catharine's story.

TAKEAWAY #1: Be Open Minded about Opportunities

While many startup funds shy away from nontraditional products and services, Catharine decided to keep an open mind, and this led her to many lucrative opportunities— simply by being open to all ideas. Regarding her current portfolio, she explained:

"We invest in 'vice,' which we define as cannabis, alcohol, nicotine, sex tech, sexual wellness, porn, ketamine, and psilocybin. We look at the whole gamut."

For those not familiar with psilocybin, it's the active ingredient in magic mushrooms.

TAKEAWAY #2: Don't Be Scared of Cold Contacting

Catharine had worked in many jobs, including working on the floor of the New York Stock Exchange, writing a popular blog called *Dockery's Daily Docket* (with over five thousand followers), and working as a Chief of Staff for Bonobos. Wanting to start her own thing, she had an "aha" moment and found a wide-open opportunity in investing in the vice industry.

But Catharine didn't have her own financial backing. Her father was a bartender, and she was still paying off a student loan. But like many successful entrepreneurs, this didn't stop her from moving forward.

Catharine's first move gives two important lessons—the first is that despite a lot of contrary advice, cold calling can really be effective. Second, start by approaching the very best in the industry—as they say, "(s)he who dares wins"!

"So the first person that I emailed, I was like, who's the richest and most powerful and brilliant person I can think of? And I was like, Marc Andreessen. So I sent a cold email, and he responded in no time."

Days later, she had a commitment from Marc, and she described it as "one of the best moments of my life, without question." Following that deal, she focused on raising money, and within five months, she had raised $25 million.

Not too shabby.

.   .   .

TAKEAWAY #3: Get People's Names Right

After Catharine's initial success, things went all-out crazy. In her first year, she saw two thousand companies that were seeking investment (we like to be totally accurate on *Female Startup Club*, so we confirmed that it was exactly 2004). Out of those, she invested in just eight. I wondered what the first thing was that she looked for in a company seeking investment. And it all started with the finer details.

"I know it sounds stupid, but if they can't get the name right of the person they're trying to get funding from them, what do their financials look like? Where are the other typos?"

TAKEAWAY #4: Ask All the Questions

Catharine advised that for women wanting to become angel investors, it's all about asking the right questions.

"You have to ask a ton of questions. You need to ask what they believe. Are they only going to be online? Are they going to be in stores? Who's doing the branding? Have you done testing of the product on fifty random people?"

TAKEAWAY #5: Start with Investment Funds

Although Catharine has had huge success in investing in private companies, she still recommends that early investors start with traditional investment funds as a safer way to grow capital.

"You're rolling the dice with more than one hundred companies. So you're kind of guaranteed a return. I wish that I had invested in a fund instead of investing in private companies to begin with. I think the returns would have been a lot better for me."

. . .

THREE QUICK QUESTIONS

WHAT'S BEEN the number one marketing moment that's made your business pop?

Interviewing on CNBC was a big deal. We got something like 250 emails after that from people who were looking to invest.

WHERE DO you hang out to get smarter?

With my husband. I hang out with him all day. He literally is the smartest person I've ever met in my life; like literally, I have gotten so much smarter dating and marrying him.

IF YOU ONLY HAD $1,000 left in your bank account, where would you spend it?

I would probably give it to my employees; I think I would split it between both of them, like a small bonus. Please stick with me; don't leave me please!

LISTEN to Catharine's episode to find out how she deals with regulations, what she sees as unique opportunities for female investors, and why she woke up her husband at 1:42 a.m.

12

IT'S WHAT'S UNDERNEATH THAT COUNTS

CAYLA O'CONNELL DAVIS: HOW AN ENTREPRENEUR USED A RECYCLING PROGRAM AND A BOOTY CALL SERVICE TO DRIVE GROWTH

Cayla O'Connell Davis is the whip-smart CEO and cofounder of Knickey—a pioneering women's underwear brand offering consumers high-quality basic briefs made from certified organic cotton. What makes them different? The philosophy behind the brand is to champion fashion that is sustainable and eco-friendly. And why underwear? What's a better place to start shifting the industry than with clothing that every human on the planet uses every day?

Although only in its second year of trading at the time we recorded our interview, Knickey has already proven to be a success. Through creative marketing, Cayla has managed to attract the attention of her market, convert an audience to her way of thinking, and in turn, convert them into happy and loyal customers. I spoke to Cayla to hear her story, which, we might add, includes undie recycling and booty calls. Buckle up, this one's a goodie.

The seed of Cayla's idea started while she was a student:

"While studying a master's degree in fashion at Parsons, I had pulled back the veil on all the detriments and atrocities that fashion has on the environment and also the people. I thought, *Oh my gosh, I'm participating in the system, and I need to figure out how I can really try to change it from the inside out.*"

TAKEAWAY #1: Simply Start with a Direction

Many entrepreneurs that I've spoken to began their journey with a concept of a direction, as opposed to having a specific product in mind. Sometimes that's more powerful than starting with a product idea—products can develop, change, and pivot, but knowing your values and mission gives a solid foundation.

"It started from just a place of wanting to make an environmentally friendly product and to move education and move the needle for customers more broadly to change their thinking about eco-minded products. It was not being done successfully. I thought, *If we're going to change this industry, we have to change the way it operates fundamentally and start from the inside and enact change internally. So we started with that concept first.*"

TAKEAWAY #2: Create a Product That Everyone Needs

Cayla's "aha" moment did indeed come. With so many different directions she could go in the fashion industry, she settled on underwear and its universal power. Sometimes an entrepreneur will spot a niche, and some advice that the more specific the niche the better. But there's the opposite argument too, which is to tackle something that absolutely everyone needs.

"I thought, *OK, we need to focus on basics because these are high-frequency items that people are going to buy regularly and put on every day throughout their lives.* It's a great point of education."

Takeaway #3: Start with Making Better Products

In today's global marketplace, competing on price alone is a losing battle in most cases. One of the first pieces of business advice I received was "If you compete on price, you'll always lose. There's always someone who can do it cheaper." Cayla agreed with a succinct pearl of wisdom:

"It begins with just making better products from the start."

Takeaway #4: Market Research Can Reveal a Different Reality

It's a surprise that many startup entrepreneurs experience—an idea makes perfect sense in your head, but sometimes market research shows that the reality is quite different. In Cayla's case, she discovered her USP actually needed to be a value-add instead of the driving force. Even if a market appears to be sensitive and caring about a cause, when it comes down to it, consumers don't always put their money where their mouth is.

"People constantly tell you, 'Oh my gosh, I would totally buy an eco-friendly product if it were available to me because I want to do right by the earth.' But what we found in practice was that when it came down to it, people were much more motivated by cost and convenience."

· · ·

TAKEAWAY #5: Bootstrap and Focus on Your Business

Cayla decided to not seek outside investment but rather bootstrap and self-fund her venture. This can mean a tougher and slower route for a startup, but she explained the thought behind her decision, choosing the route that would allow her to focus her attention on growing her venture:

"I feel like self-funding has allowed us to really focus on running the business and growing the business rather than fundraising and answering to external parties."

TAKEAWAY #6: Be Creative and Bold with Your Marketing

Cayla's first marketing strategy was to give free gift samples to media—a move that proved successful with a feature in Vogue that gave her that all-important early-stage boost.

She realized that she needed to keep evolving her marketing strategies, and she came up with two bold and creative ideas. Her first was to offer "undie recycling," where people could send in their used undies to be recycled into insulation. Yes, it's true (and they received more than you think)! Her second marketing initiative was the "Booty Call," inviting customers to call their hotline and discuss anything and everything about intimate subjects in a fun and light-hearted way. In fact, Cayla often answered the calls herself.

Both marketing strategies proved to be great successes that resulted in increased sales and customer loyalty to the brand. Wondering what the undie recycling program was all about?

"It's such a unique thing. It's the first of its kind. And we're really addressing a real problem, which is that there is no responsible way to get rid of your old underwear. You can't donate it, can't give it to a homeless shelter. It will just get sent to a landfill by a third-party recycler. And we've been able to collect that, palletize several tons of undies, and make that into insulation and industrial rags for commercial rugs. So that has been an awesome component of our business that we're so thrilled to see people resonating with."

WHAT'S the number one marketing moment that made your business pop?

"Launching the recycling program. It has brought us so many wonderful customers and so much brand loyalty that I think it contributes longer term to our lifetime value overall."

(LTV = very important)

WHERE DO you hang out to get smarter?

"I'm a big podcast person. I can recommend *Matters of Scale* by Reid Hoffman; it's really quirky, great guys, incredible business founders. *Planet Money* is my all-time favorite; I recommend that for any founder."

IF YOU ONLY HAD $1,000 left in your business bank account, where would you spend it?

"I would spend it on product and inventory. One hundred percent. We have found that when we have product, people buy it."

. . .

LISTEN to Cayla's episode to find out how she crafted her marketing narrative, what she learned working for a startup, and how she increased her company's general cheekiness.

And finally, here is my list of selected underwear puns that you were (almost) spared from:

Undie-niable Truths
Under Wears & Whys
Panti-Capitalism
A Brief Introduction

13

SAALT OF THE EARTH

CHERIE HOEGER: HOW AN ENTREPRENEUR MODERNIZED REUSABLE PERIOD CARE

Cherie Hoeger is the cofounder and CEO of Saalt—a company that's on a mission to modernize reusable period care. In 2018, Saalt launched its flagship product, the Saalt Period Cup, with the vision of making cleaner, more sustainable period care accessible to everyone. Cherie began networking with impact partners to provide period cups to underprivileged girls and women so they could confidently manage their periods, stay in school, and lift themselves out of poverty. Now, in their third year, Saalt has donated over twelve thousand cups in over twenty-two countries to create a wave of informed cup users who then act as mentors for other donation recipients. In this conversation, you'll hear how Cherie and her husband got their impactful start by launching the brand to their focus group of one thousand people and how they're driving growth through impact and education.

TAKEAWAY #1: **Improve on Existing Products**
Cherie's idea for creating her period cup was sparked by

a phone call she had with her aunt who lived in Venezuela. Her aunt explained that she'd gone without pads and tampons for years, and the political instability there had caused huge shortages of basic consumer staples like food and hygiene supplies. Grocery stores were literally empty.

"That dependence on disposables really kept me up at night. I immediately thought of my five daughters and what I would do in that situation. So that led to a lot of research into what reusable options were out there. And that's when I was first introduced to the period cup."

Cherie discovered that period cups are cleaner and nontoxic, and they can be worn for twelve hours at a time. These elements really sparked her interest in a product she was previously unaware of.

"I bought several cups to try out but couldn't find one that really worked well with my anatomy. And I also found that there weren't many cups that were made out of high-quality, medical-grade silicone that were also FDA compliant. And so I got help to create a custom model on 3D CAD and got to work creating this cup that I hoped would be best for beginners and also the mainstream consumer. It took about fourteen iterations to get it right."

TAKEAWAY #2: You Need to Have Complete Confidence in Your Own Product

Ultimately, it's vital that a startup entrepreneur has confidence in their own product—total confidence is what drives momentum and inspires others. Cherie found that the initial capital needed to get started was high, and her confidence led to her risking her own retirement funds.

"When you're creating a silicone menstrual cup, you need to find a supplier who makes medical devices. The mold itself cost $25,000 of an investment just to have it created because you're literally etching that mold in steel that is then liquid injected with silicone. So we had to make sure that it was right, which is why it took fourteen iterations. We had to be super confident in our product. And because we're going to have a small and a regular size, then that's another $25,000. $50,000 of our own retirement funds were invested into this product. So you can imagine how nerve-racking it was to be able to get this right. And when we finally pulled the trigger, it was a big step. That's what you need to do as an entrepreneur; you need to have confidence in your product and decide to move forward."

Takeaway #3: Consider People, Planet, and Profit (the Three P's!)

Cherie explained her company's vision as creating products that are clean, sustainably sourced, and good for the planet. Your vision as a startup entrepreneur affects the way you operate from the very beginning and has to be kept in the forefront of your mind when designing and manufacturing your products.

"Yeah, absolutely. Because there's a deep core if you want to make sure that you're providing products that are both good for everyone's bodies and the environment and all your stakeholders. So you actually have language written into your bylaws, into your operating agreement, saying that you measure the impact of your decision on all stakeholders, not shareholders. So it's not just about profit. Bottom line, it's about people, planet, and profit. It's a triple bottom line approach."

. . .

TAKEAWAY #4: **Validate Your Idea by Creating Loyal Focus Groups**

At some point, every startup needs to go through a proof-of-concept stage—an exploration of opinion and feedback from potential customers in the target market.

"We started a focus group early on Facebook with the goal of getting a thousand members to join. And the idea was if we could get at least a thousand people who resonated with our new brand and mission and also our product, then we would have something that we could sell."

To gain her target of a thousand members, Cherie had to be creative.

"We started hosting these lunches in different states to recruit people to join our group, and we bribed them with free food and asked them to bring their laptops and invite their friends to join."

Once she reached her thousand-member target, she began to ask many questions in order to get feedback and understand her market better. While startup entrepreneurs hope to have smooth-sailing, positive feedback, that's not always the case, and it can sometimes be a real eye-opener.

"It was a roller coaster of emotions to hear this real and raw feedback from our customers. But it was so important because it prepared us for the problems that we needed to address as a customer service team and also really helped us gain confidence in our product, that it really worked for people."

TAKEAWAY #5: **Build a Community of Microinfluencers**

Cherie's list of a thousand members proved to be more than simply a group of people to give feedback. Cherie found that the power of gathering so many potential customers was that she had effectively built a community around the product, and when it was time to launch, she had the help of a thousand microinfluencers. Microinfluencers can prove to be powerful marketing allies and create an effectual and noticeable impact on getting the word out there. Although many focus on the big influencers, sometimes it's the microinfluencers that engender more trust among their followers. And the cumulative effect of numbers can make that crucial difference.

"When we launched, we gifted them our packages. On social media, they were able to show us their unboxing experience and share it with the world. It really helped us launch, so when we put our website out there, it wasn't just crickets. We had a team of a thousand people who were helping launch at the same time."

TAKEAWAY #6: Invest in Educating Your Market

One of Cherie's early battles was around educating her potential customers. To do this, she aimed to make the information understandable, unlike many products in this space that she felt had "ambiguous information." As part of that education, she realized that she also had to tackle the stigma that existed around period care.

"Actually, that stigma really represented both our biggest challenge and opportunity. Challenging the fact that we had to overcome the stigma meant we could retell the story in a different way, and we could show that instead of something that was gross and reusable, we would show something that was clean and sustainable, would actually be better for you and the planet, and would actually be a cleaner period experience. And so we really took that stigma head-on, especially in our branding and our messaging and our voice and our imagery, and we showcased the cup as this beautiful high-end product that opened like a beautiful lipstick."

Takeaway #7: Split Test Your Brand's Voice

It's vital for a startup brand to get its marketing tone of voice just right. In developing her voice and identity, Cheri sought feedback from her focus group, doing split testing and seeing what her target market resonated with. She tried different languages, from approachable to authoritative, and it was clear that the approachable style was what customers gravitated to.

"We actually have a name for it. We like to call it "Your best friend's older sister." And the reason why is because when you're learning about period care as a teen, you don't always want to go talk to your mom about it. And then your best friend, well, she's going through her period at the same time you are. But your best friend's older sister—now she's cool. She knows the deal. She's been through a lot of cycles before. So you could turn to her to know how you should cover your period care."

THREE QUICK QUESTIONS

What's the number one marketing moment that made your business pop?

"Putting those production dollars behind a really great brand campaign. We were able to film our last one during COVID. Everything had shut down, and we had this decision to make—should we postpone it? And so we pivoted. And what we were able to do was to put on a callout to female directors to help us with this. We used four different female directors that all filmed in their separate locations around the world."

WHERE DO you hang out to get smarter?

"I find a lot of value from interacting with different entrepreneurs and then having regular coaching. I'm part of a national coaching program called Strategic Coach, and I really look forward to every quarter because I get new tools and ideas. I'm also part of a local forum, Entrepreneurs Organization, and they're worldwide. You can talk about your problems, the ups and downs. Because as entrepreneurs, it's hard to be able to really share those really high moments and the lower moments because people who aren't entrepreneurs don't always understand."

How DO you win the day?

"I have a very strong morning routine, and I feel like that really grounds me every day. There's a book called *Essentialism* that I love, and it helped to identify my "vital few." Part of that for me is my family and my health. It's my contribution to the world in my relationship. And as long as I'm hitting those five vital few in the morning, then I feel fulfilled during the day."

LISTEN to Cherie's episode to find out what she thinks of email marketing, what she did to quadruple her revenue, and what event happened in the business that became known as Smelly Gate.

14

SERIOUS FLOWER POWER

CHRISTINA STEMBEL: HOW A GIRL WITH A DREAM BUT NO EDUCATION OR INVESTMENT BUILT AN E-COMMERCE EMPIRE

Christina Stembel is the founder and CEO of Farmgirl Flowers. Farmgirl Flowers is a pretty darn clever business, which totally disrupted the e-commerce flower industry. Inspired to find a solution to her (and others') frustrations with online flower ordering (#goodgriefthatdoesntlooklikethepicture), Stembel offered customers fewer and better options plus enthusiastic customer service.

Christina started the business in 2010, and petal by petal, she bootstrapped the brand to over $60 million a year in revenue. That's why we added "serious" before "flower power" in this chapter's title.

Speaking to Christina felt like a business masterclass. She explained to me how she started with dreams just like every future entrepreneur, stumbled across a gap in the market, built her business with no marketing budget, and forged forward with total belief in herself.

TAKEAWAY #1: Disrupt an Industry

Disrupting has become a trendy buzzword. But it's for a reason. Many successful entrepreneurs find their gap by looking at an already existing industry and spotting a flaw—something that's not being offered or, often, something that can simply be done better. Big industries already have a proven market with available and quantified statistics and an audience that no longer needs to be educated about the product or service. Existing industries also often have many customers that are frustrated about something, and spotting what that is can lead to super success.

"I was interested in entrepreneurship for at least a decade before I actually got started. Flowers was an industry I found that was huge. The most recent innovation was in the mid-nineties, and it wasn't a great innovation. It actually made it a more generic industry. Living in Silicon Valley, I was seeing everybody around me disrupting everything, from toothbrushes to potato chips and everything in between."

TAKEAWAY #2: Identify a Real-World Problem

While Christina worked as an events planner at Stanford University, budget cuts made her realize just how much flowers cost. This got her thinking about the industry and her own experience with sending flowers to her mom through online stores. She was always shocked at the prices, and when her mom sent her a photo of what she received, they never looked like they did in the picture. That's not even close to "all white"! She found that others felt the same, with endless #fail posts of flower delivery disappointment.

.   .   .

Takeaway #3: Go to Google University

The internet is the most incredible resource for learning absolutely anything and everything, and it means that entrepreneurs have no excuse for not knowing how to do something. If you're looking for answers, it's all out there.

"There's no excuse not to learn anything because you don't have to go to the library. You don't have to go look at books written twenty years ago. You just go to Google, and it's the best research tool out there. I spent hours and hours and hours on Google and then just practiced [how to create flower bouquets]."

Takeaway #4: Spend on Legal Early

Christina's initial startup capital was all from her own savings, built by working at coffee shops and restaurants and living frugally. Christina had an initial capital of $49,000, which goes to show that if you are frugal and consistent with saving, you can make it happen. I asked Christina what she spent her initial capital on and if she would have done anything different in hindsight.

"I used it for practicing the flowers, building a website, doing all of those things, and living, paying my rent every month as well. We had the burlap wrap that I created, and now you see that worldwide. It gives a lot of brand equity, and that's worth a lot of money."

However, Christina explained the importance of investing in legal protection early:

"If I could go back, I would spend $25,000 on legal fees."

That reminded me of a little acronym to keep a mental note of (that is quite aptly named after a woman): "ELAINE" (Early Legal Advice Is Never Expensive).

· · ·

Takeaway #5: Marketing Doesn't Need to Be Expensive

As a marketer myself, I know this advice too well. Big marketing spending can definitely lead to success, but if you don't have the budget, it's not an excuse to "poor me" yourself. There are endless ways to be creative about marketing without spending much at all.

"In the first two years, I didn't have a single dime for marketing. I literally took my product, and I put it out at coffee shops all across the city in different neighborhoods. And I made little marketing cards myself. I did that in ten to twelve coffee shops around the city, and 100 percent of our growth was due to that. I did nothing else."

Takeaway #6: Always Do the Numbers, Even If You Don't Like It

"I don't really like numbers. I hate numbers. It's the worst part about my job. I'm usually doing them at two in the morning. I'm doing all the accounting and finance then because I hate it and I procrastinate and work on the fun stuff like product development during the day when I should have been doing accounting. But it's that important."

It's interesting to hear that the CEO of a company with over $60 million in annual revenue doesn't like numbers, right? Entrepreneurs are often visionaries and concept people, and that's super important, but all successful businesswomen will tell you that you've got to keep your eyes on the numbers. At the end of the day, numbers are everything.

THREE QUICK QUESTIONS

. . .

WHAT'S **the number one marketing moment that made your business pop?**

"If I have to choose just one, it was an article in the New York Times when we were just starting out. I used to think PR was so fluffy, but to this day, it's still one of the best investments we made. Don't underestimate the power of PR and budget for it."

WHERE DO **you hang out to get smarter?**

"I read a lot, and I will say that as someone who never went to college, I read every business book I could get my hands on. I found *The Lean Startup* to be amazing, and it shows you how to figure out how to do it in a scrappy way and not be afraid to get out there. I listen to all of Brené Brown's books every year."

IF YOU ONLY HAD **$1,000 left in your bank account, where would you spend it?**

"That has happened to me many times, where I've had less than $1,000 in my bank account, and my answer would be: I wouldn't spend it. The first thing I did when COVID-19 hit was to turn off all the credit cards. I turned off all auto-payments on our bank account. I did everything I could to protect every dollar. You do everything you possibly can to not spend that $1,000."

LISTEN **to Christina's episode to find out how she treats her employees, how a cup of tea can grow your company, and how *The Fresh Prince of Bel-Air* inspired her.**

15

SHIPPING UP

CONNIE LO: HOW AN ENTREPRENEUR MADE VEGAN SKINCARE ETHICAL AND AFFORDABLE

Connie Lo is the cofounder of Three Ships. Three Ships is an all-natural vegan skincare brand on a mission to make clean beauty accessible for all women. The products are 100 percent plant-derived, certified cruelty-free, and best of all, forever under forty dollars. Founded in 2017, Three Ships was founded by chemical engineer Laura and business grad Connie after the two wondered why clean, vegan skincare costs so much. With only $3,300 in their bank accounts, these female founders started making their own formulations in Connie's apartment kitchen with the goal of creating effective and affordable natural skincare products. We talked about pro tips for retail expansion and how to make a partnership successful. Connie gave insights about key moments of growth and how to be scrappy in the beginning, as well as some of the key trade shows you might want to invest in.

TAKEAWAY #1: Don't Follow the Herd

Connie's father was an entrepreneur, and as a child, she would often join him on business trips. This inspired her to start her own business one day. For many women that dream of becoming an entrepreneur, it can be a daunting prospect as it requires treading a path of your own.

"When I was at university, I started to compare myself a lot to what my peers were doing. So I remember comparing myself and being like, Oh, wait, marketing and sales and entrepreneurship, that's not where all the smart kids are going. So for anyone a little younger, maybe even in school still, what I recommend is just really listen to your gut and trust your intuition because that is what I did not do and I regretted it."

Connie studied accounting despite not enjoying it, and after working full-time as an accountant for eight months, she realized that she had taken the wrong path. Thinking back to her classes at university, she recalled the extracurricular classes she took that really got her excited—marketing, sales, entrepreneurship, and negotiation. Shortly before taking her exams to become a Chartered Accountant, Connie bravely switched careers to marketing and sales.

Connie loved her new job, and during that time, she met her future cofounder, Laura (Berget). Laura had been talking to a mutual friend about her ideas to start a natural makeup removal company, and Connie's name came up as the friend remembered her making her own natural skincare products in high school.

TAKEAWAY #2: Choose a Partner Who's Different from You

When it comes to choosing a cofounder, one sometimes tries to connect to someone that has the same personality type and skill set, but often, the most successful partnerships are those that are made up of polar opposite traits. After all, there's no advantage to duplicating yourself. What one really needs is a partner to balance out strengths and weaknesses.

"We realized we were complete opposites in terms of personality types and skill sets but completely aligned in terms of values. And at the end of our first meeting, Laura just asked me, like, Hey, you want to be my cofounder on this? We were both just twenty-three. We got started on the product literally the next day."

Connie and Laura had *big* dreams but a very small working capital of just $3,300. Most startup entrepreneurs have the obstacle of limited capital in the early stages of getting their company off the ground, and it can be a great challenge to know where to invest the money for maximum impact.

Takeaway #3: Start with Trademarks and Incorporating

Connie's first two moves were to incorporate the company and to apply for a trademark. Without any budget for lawyers, she took the time to fill out the incorporating forms herself.

"By incorporating, you're making your company a separate entity. So that way, say someone sues your company, they're not able to go after your personal assets. Although let's be real, at the time, Laura and I had very little personal assets, but still, we just wanted to set ourselves up for success."

The trademark process can take a very long time, sometimes several years, so it's a good idea to get that started as early as possible. One of the important reasons for applying for a trademark is that it uncovers whether your brand name is available. This can help avoid a lot of time and expenses when you're further down the road and discover your name isn't available.

TAKEAWAY #4: Create an MVP as Cheaply as Possible

Connie set out to create a minimum viable product (MVP) as quickly and cheaply as possible. The pair set about developing their products at home in the kitchen. Although they ultimately wanted to use water-based ingredients, they made do with what was practical without a manufacturer and started with oil-based products that were more accessible to create at home.

TAKEAWAY #5: Print Your Own Packaging

Out of Connie's small startup capital, she decided to spend around $600 on a laser printer. Although it was an expensive purchase relative to her funds, it enabled her to create her own packaging without having to invest in high minimum orders from printers.

Connie found this to be a good investment as she could continue to develop her branding based on customer feedback.

"We were able to iterate on our product packaging really quickly. I recommend that you don't spend on things like labels and custom packaging at the beginning unless you're absolutely sure that that's going to be your final product for at least six months to a year."

TAKEAWAY #6: Put Sweat Equity into Marketing

In order to save on the heavy costs of a marketing

agency, Connie decided to focus most of her time on doing the brand's marketing herself. Much of her early marketing was split between Instagram marketing and attending flea shows.

Connie started her Instagram page well before she had her first product ready, with the aim of starting to build an online presence as early as possible. She researched competitors to get a strong understanding of what was happening in the skincare space, and she proactively commented on posts. Many people posting in the beauty space described their skin types, so Connie noted these, and when she launched a relevant product, she'd DM people to introduce herself and the product and offer a discount.

Although Connie and Laura were both in nine-to-fives, they took every opportunity they could to attend flea markets—at least one per weekend. Flea markets can be invaluable places to get direct customer feedback and also great places to find early customers.

"The customer feedback loop was so important, and we learned so much about our products and our customers and product market fit just by going to these markets."

THREE QUICK QUESTIONS

WHAT'S YOUR "WHY"?

"I do what I do really for the customer reviews. Whenever we read customer reviews, that really is what funds our team. We have a channel specifically dedicated to positive reviews."

. . .

WHERE DO you hang out to get smarter?

"Podcasts like this one are amazing for having a wealth of knowledge. Other podcasts I enjoy are *How I Built This* and Joe Rogan. I just love hearing different perspectives. Another thing that our team does is have a monthly book club where we all share an audible account and read the same book."

HOW DO you win the day?

"I always want to be able to check off things within three buckets, so one is work, one is self, and one is life. Getting some sort of big project done covers work. For self, I usually work out and also meditate. Then life would be something that's like friends and family. So having a call with my mom or going on a walk and talking with a friend. My best days are the ones where I have something within each bucket."

LISTEN to Connie's episode to find out how she marketed through subscription boxes, what made her leave her nine-to-five, and when to stop talking on the phone.

16

JUST CHILL

CYNDI RAMIREZ-FULTON: HOW AN ENTREPRENEUR MODERNIZED SELF-CARE

Cyndi Ramirez-Fulton is the founder and CEO of Chillhouse. Chillhouse is a "destination for modern self-care" in New York's Lower East Side, and it's redefined what it means to slow down and pamper yourself in New York City. The boutique-style cafe and day spa is an experiential space with innovative services, such as a CBD manicure and the popular "Hangover Cure" massage, and it also offers a line of products ranging from press-on chill tips to candles. We spoke about how she brought the vision into reality, how a cult product can be used as a major discovery tool, and how the ultimate girl boss of entrepreneurs got involved with Chillhouse in the beginning, getting Cyndi to think bigger and dream bigger.

If you haven't come across the queen of Chill's ultra-millennial space on Instagram yet, I highly recommend a browse so you can truly understand why her brand is so special.

Takeaway #1: Identify a Gap in the Market

Cyndi's mother was an aesthetician, and she explained that "subconsciously, I always kind of knew I was ingrained in the space." A few years prior, Cyndi and her husband were looking to get a massage in Manhattan and were underwhelmed with the options that were available. It's these little moments that can spark a thought for a natural entrepreneur. Someone with an entrepreneurial spirit will always have an eye out for a gap in the market.

"Your options were either you spend an obscene amount of money for a sixty-minute massage or you ended up somewhere kind of weird and sketchy in like a basement. So we kind of just realized that there was something missing somewhere in the middle."

The couple began talking it through and developing a concept where several services could be offered under one roof—but specifically with an experience that's hospitality-like and fun, something the pair felt was lacking in the space.

TAKEAWAY #2: Start with a Core Offering and Then Evolve

Cyndi opened her first location, starting with an offering of her favorite things—beverages, manicures, and massages. Her plan was to start with this simple core offering and then expand from there. Startup entrepreneurs are often tempted to launch with their full range of services or products, but as Cyndi showed, it can be a smart move to start simple and grow organically from there. Cyndi's idea turned out to be on point, and the first Chillhouse quickly attracted an appreciative audience.

"There were people that were really gravitating to the brand just because of what we represented. We are fun. We don't take ourselves too seriously. We talk about self-care from a very holistic standpoint, where it's not just about how do you spend all your money? It's more about just how do you make sure you're thinking about yourself regularly. And here are all the ways that we can help you achieve that goal."

Chillhouse developed an impressive online presence, with "Chill Times" and visually powerful Instagram content. I'm totally hooked; it's worth a snoop.

Takeaway #3: You Know Your Brand Better than Anyone Else

I spoke to Cyndi about her journey and process to develop such effective branding. She explained that on the whole, her branding has stayed pretty consistent but also that it definitely evolved as she expanded from her first location. Cyndi began conceptualizing her brand by doing lots of mood boarding and looking at different types of brands, such as food, fashion, and beauty.

When it came to the design, she worked with an architect who was also an interior designer, a process she described as being great fun.

"I was telling him, 'Hey, this is what we have going on from a branding perspective. How do we align this with the store?' But I will say that I was much more hands-on in the design of the second one. The first time it was all 'go ahead,' and I just didn't want to step on his toes. I kind of wanted to let the expert lead the way. But this time around, I was like, 'No, I know my brand more than anybody else. I need to make sure that I have final say over every single element that happens in the space.'"

Takeaway #4: Pitching Is All about Research

Cyndi explained how she prepared for her investment pitching by doing plenty of research—both within her direct industry and associated ones.

"The process is pretty much getting to work from a research standpoint, putting together a business plan simultaneously. We were doing a lot of real estate scouting at the same time. We were also doing a lot of research into competitors, even though we don't have direct competitors, but understanding the nail industry, understanding the massage and spa industry, and even the cafe industry. So getting a better sense for what our margins are going to be. And, of course, putting together your financials based on that and coming up with pricing. And then based on where you end up with all that, you put your deck together and get to work."

Cyndi had great success in raising capital from friends, family, and angel investors, and she proudly managed to get to this point without the constraints of institutional investment.

"We've raised about a million total. But that's really just to power the stores. The rest of the business has been pretty much bootstrapped. So that's something I'm pretty proud of because we haven't raised institutional capital yet. I think there are different expectations with your business when you do that. And I'm not saying we're not going to do it, but it's kind of cool to have gotten this far without it."

TAKEAWAY #5: Seek Mentorship from Another Badass Entrepreneur

Sophia Amoruso was an early mentor of Cyndi's. Mentorship is such a critical part of the entrepreneurship journey, and so many startup entrepreneurs I've spoken to have cited a good mentor as a vital element of their success.

"My God, that's such a crazy story. I feel like she probably thinks I'm such a psycho any time I share this story because I was always a huge fan of hers. In my early twenties, she was an entrepreneur I could actually relate to. She didn't have a fancy pedigree, college education, or anything like that. It was more so that she just kind of went with her gut, with her intuition, and she just worked her ass off. And she was unapologetic about her personality. She was unapologetic about her leadership style. I just love that she was super raw."

Prior to launching Chillhouse, a good friend of Cyndi's was scheduled to interview Sophia on a promotional trip for her Netflix show. She was unable to make it, so last minute, she put Cyndi's name down in place of hers. Cyndi jumped at the opportunity and got her chance to meet her business hero, albeit briefly as she was "among like fifty girls."

Some time later, after launching Chillhouse and setting up her social media accounts, Cyndi experienced an influx of followers that included celebrities and entrepreneurs she really admired. Among those, she saw that Sophia was a follower too, which she excitedly explained as "whoa, big stuff!"

"At one point, it was just a random day. We had a party that canceled at the last minute, and it was a lot of money that we had lost as canceling had no repercussions. And I just took to Instagram and started complaining about the situation. I was like, 'Please, like, if you ever find yourself wanting to cancel, please consider the business.' Blah, blah, blah. Sophia DM'd me as I'm complaining. She's like, 'I love what you're doing, let's talk!'"

Every entrepreneur's dream, right? Cyndi explained her fangirl moment:

"I'm like, of course you DM me when I'm complaining about customers. That is such a Sophia thing to do!"

I asked Cyndi how the relationship developed from there.

"She came on board, ended up flying to LA, and I went to her house and chatted with her. She became an advisor and an investor shortly after that. And then, just having her to bounce ideas off of has been incredible. She's one of the few really badass entrepreneurs that we have. She's very supportive of female businesses; she's made a whole career out of it. We were blessed to be her first adviser role and her first investment."

THREE QUICK QUESTIONS

What's your "why"?

"I do what I do because I create experiences that I want for myself. Truly, there is nothing that I've done that I wasn't like, "I need this." So my "why" is to create a better lifestyle for myself, as selfish as that sounds, because I know that if I'm creating a better lifestyle for myself, I'm creating a better lifestyle for other people in our community."

How do you win the day?

"My best days are really the days that I go to sleep early and wake up early and hang out with my baby. I have a solid hour with him. Prior to having a child and prior to the pandemic, we were running to the office; it was always a rush. And it's so nice to actually go to sleep early and wake up and have a normal night's sleep. And it's not always like that because we still have a baby that's six and a half months old. So it's not perfect every day. But the days that it is, it feels so good. And those are always the days that I'm the most productive."

If you only had $1,000 left in your business bank account, where would you spend it?

"I'd probably spend it on gifting. If I'm trying to survive and get our sales back up, it would be going toward making sure I'm working with the people that we already have in our network, our community, gifting people that I know can amplify our products and our services."

Listen to Cyndi's episode to find out how she got her products into retail, why she values digital ads, and how her brand is like a hug from a big sister.

HAIR TO THE THRONE

DIANNA COHEN: HOW AN ENTREPRENEUR MADE A BUSINESS OUT OF HER FAVORITE DAILY RITUAL

Dianna Cohen is the founder of Crown Affair, a company that's reimagining hair rituals and taking a considered approach for the top of your noggin. The story begins with the innocent sharing of a Google Doc with friends that went viral—a true, modern-day fairy tale! Dianna shared the lessons she's learned along the way, the approach she used for her pitch, and the importance of community and story-telling.

Before I had hit record, Dianna and I discussed our shared love of hair brushing. It was always clear to Dianna. But it was the first time I really thought about it and realized how much I enjoy the daily ritual too. Business ideas truly can come from any part of your life.

Dianna grew up in a small town in South Florida called Lighthouse Point. At school, she was a sports-playing tomboy and also totally in love with art history. Passionate about beauty and design, she followed her dream and moved to New York to do *The Devil Wears Prada* thing. Dianna started working a variety of jobs in fashion and beauty before launching her own brand strategy consulting agency called Levitate.

TAKEAWAY #1: Share Your Knowledge

I asked Dianna how she went from owning her own agency to creating hair care products. I had read that it started with a humble Google Doc, so was intrigued to know more.

"I'm a full hair care nerd. I invest in quality tools and products. My fiancé laughs at the way I position my hair on the pillow. I'm so delicate with it, and I'm mindful of it and respect it. And not everyone was doing that. I was traveling a lot, and I would tell friends, and they'd be like, 'Wait. What are you doing with your hair routine?' So I finally put it into a Google Doc. Like, the sixteen things that I do. It was a Sunday, and by Friday night, I had dozens of people on it. I had no idea who they were. It was like people requesting access, and there were tons of comments. And I thought, *This is so crazy.* You can YouTube how to get Chrissy Teigen's Coachella ponytail but nothing about how to actually care for your hair in a way that felt really accessible and relatable."

Sometimes we don't realize how valuable our personal knowledge is until we share it with others. I asked Dianna how that resulted in her developing products while still running an agency.

"My fiancé's best friend was a big part of this journey. He's a bioengineer, and I sent him and his wife the Google Doc, and they were amazed at the results from my advice. We just started working on stuff. We were like, 'OK, can we take our favorite $200 hairbrush and reverse engineer it? And can we make it better? How do we find vendors that are sustainable and can do this at a more accessible price point?'"

Dianna continued to explain what became clear to her.

"The category is really dated. It's very wholesale driven. There hasn't been a ton of innovation on the ingredient side (in the way that skincare and color cosmetics have been democratized over the last ten years). The same thing is just not really happening with hair care. So that was really the spark of the journey."

TAKEAWAY #2: Get Physical Samples

The first early steps in any business are to invest in physical samples as a starting point so you can put them to the test and see what kind of reaction you get from potential customers.

"So the first two things that I did were: we actually had samples that people could try and did small focus groups to get feedback. If you look at these samples, you would laugh. But you know? It's just great to actually have a physical product that people could give real-time feedback to."

TAKEAWAY #3: Design Your Universe

Building a brand is very much about creating a universe. Developing the visuals of your brand can really help shape that universe, as we're ultimately visual creatures. So it can be a smart early investment to work with a good graphic designer—one that is on the same page as you.

"The other thing that I had was our (still current) creative director. He is one of the most talented graphic designers that I've ever worked with. I had told him about my vision for Crown Affair. And we had the really early stages of what this brand felt like and what the universe that we're currently building felt like. And that felt so different for a hair care brand. I think so often it's such an afterthought."

TAKEAWAY #4: LISTEN TO INVESTORS' **Advice**

Dianna reached a point where she realized that if she was to continue, she would need to raise capital. This resulted in a grueling marathon of investor pitches. For some entrepreneurs, the experience can be crushing, while for others, it's a chance to grow and perfect their pitch. I asked Dianna what she took away from the experience.

"Raising money for our first seed round was one of the most valuable experiences of my life. I had over two hundred investor meetings, and you just eventually know how to do it. You learn so much about how to take a meeting. Like, listening and understanding what they're looking for and then really positioning and building this narrative around what the brand could be and what the opportunity is. Also, a lot of these people are so brilliant and so interesting. So whether they end up going forward with the deal or just to be able to have these conversations . . . I think that measuring the journey and not the end result is such an important part of being an entrepreneur."

I'm always astounded at how many investor meetings startup entrepreneurs go through. It reminds me of an interview of a vocal artist who compared being on tour to being an athlete. One of the great things about having so many meetings is that you always get something back for your efforts—and that's free advice.

.   .   .

TAKEAWAY #5: SKU Count Isn't Everything

How many products you have in your range can be a big and important decision for an entrepreneur. There are different views on this. Some advocate for keeping the product line small and focused, while for others, having a generous range can attract attention and reach more customers. Dianna explained what worked for her.

"My entire vision was that every single product we're making is a hero product. We are working outside contract manufacturers to truly innovate on these products. In this category, people just go to contract manufacturers, and they're like, 'Here's twelve shampoos.' But, for us, part of my ethos is that I never want to launch anything to the world unless it's truly unique and makes me feel different. SKU count is not the issue in this category."

TAKEAWAY #6: Investors Invest in People

While investment pitches usually focus on the business itself, for many investors, what they're really looking at is the person behind it. It's really the entrepreneur that they're investing in at the end of the day.

"Many investors are like, 'Are you going to be the next Warby Parker for this?' And I reply, 'That was ten years ago. This is what we're doing. Either you're in or not.' I think that the best investors invest in founders. There might just be a global pandemic. You might need to pivot your entire business. And that's why it's important to bet on people, not the product, at the end of the day."

TAKEAWAY #7: Your Customers Are Just People; Keep Them Front of Mind and Let Them Be Your Cheerleaders

In the same way that investing is really about people, so is marketing. It can be overwhelming to think of your customers as an endless, faceless group of numbers. Dianna's advice is to remember that each customer is just a person.

"The most important thing with marketing is people. Customers, your community, everyone is literally just a person. You have to treat them like people and build up your army of people who believe in you and are excited about what you're building. If you're listening and thinking about launching a business, it is so important to remember that people want to support what they are part of creating. And I think so often (especially as women) we don't want to share things with the world until they're perfect. And people really do want to be a part of that process. So when you do go live, they're so excited to be like, 'This is awesome!' Even if it's just a quick email or coffee or selling products early, people get really excited, and they root for you long term."

THREE QUICK QUESTIONS
What's your "why"?

"My "why" is making people feel different about themselves. I love putting things into the world (whether it's Crown Affair or just in my personal life) that change the way people identify, about how they view the world. That is my mission for everything I've ever done."

WHERE DO **you hang out to get smarter?**

"I listen to a lot of podcasts. My favorite podcast is called *Poetry Unbound*, and it's led by theologian Pádraig Ó Tuama. I also love Adam Grant, Seth Godin, and a lot of marketing writers. I read their daily letters. It always sparks something —even if it's not in the moment, maybe a few months later."

How do you win the day?

"It's definitely doing my morning papers that I have in a journal. I feel really complete when I put my *Five-Minute Journal* away at night. And a big, big win is if I get a bath and dinner is made by my fiancé. There's something really powerful about having the phone in the other room and getting into a warm bath. It resets you in a really nice way. My best ideas come to me in the bath—that's where the magic happens."

Listen to Dianna's episode to find out what she learned as an intern, what her plans are for the future, and how she connected with a seventy-year-old winemaker in Napa.

CEREAL ENTREPRENEUR

EMILY ELYSE MILLER: HOW AN
ENTREPRENEUR REIMAGINED BREAKFAST

Emily Elyse Miller is the founder and CEO of OffLimits. Emily created OffLimits out of her love for breakfast food and her desire to put human beings before profit. OffLimits is a groundbreaking cereal brand that besides being 100 percent organic and super delicious, tackles important topics like humanity, inclusivity, and mental health. She's created two cereal products—"Zombie" and "Dash!" The "cereal character" of Dash! will no doubt go down in history as the first-ever female cereal brand character! Emily explained how she turned her love of art and design into a cereal brand, how collaborations are a driving force behind the brand, and how to pitch ideas and partnerships.

TAKEAWAY #1: Start by Looking at What You Love

When considering your startup idea, a good place to start is to consider what you love, what inspires you.

Emily grew up in the hospitality world and is a self-confessed breakfast addict. Although she's always in some way stayed close to food, she ended up studying fashion design. This led to a brief career in the trend-forecasting and editorial space, but she found that there was a demand for more people who could write about food, especially as food culture was on the up. Emily took advantage of the opportunity, and it led her on quite an adventure!

"I started traveling all over the world writing for different outlets and started a series called *Breakfast Club*, where I would invite about thirty or so creatives in each city to work with chefs. They were incredible chefs, and their restaurants were typically closed in the morning, so it was perfect for them to open up early and prepare a family meal but for breakfast. And all these creative people got to be in a space that wasn't typically open in the morning, and there was no pressure to post on social media. It was really just, "Let's all connect!"

The series gained popularity and soon led to a cookbook deal—an exciting and challenging project that turned out to be one of the stepping-stones to creating OffLimits.

"I spent the next three years researching, developing, and writing a 380-page recipe cookbook about breakfast. We featured over eighty countries. That was a really rewarding project. And after that, I wanted to escape the freelance grind and work on something that combined both art and food. And that's kind of how I started thinking about OffLimits."

TAKEAWAY #2: **Build a Creative Team**

When, as a startup entrepreneur, you reach the stage of having to build a team around you, it can be important to consider exactly what kind of focus you want your team to have. Sometimes that could be "numbers" people, out-the-box marketing minds, young and on-trend, or older and more experienced. In Emily's case, she went about building her team by focusing on creative minds.

"I am really pushing to champion a lot more creative founders, having been in art classes, design, school, etc. my whole career. In college, they teach you how to work for other people. But if you're in business school, you're taught how to be financially independent. I really want to empower more creative entrepreneurs to not work for other people and start their own thing."

TAKEAWAY #3: Create a Brand That Connects to New Audiences

Something that I noticed when I was going through the brand and looking through the website was that it really felt like a cereal brand for adults versus a typical cereal brand that's designed for young kids. And that came through in the flavors too. However, Emily explained that the adult placement was unintentional. But what was intentional was to build a brand that connected to new audiences—niche audiences that were typically left out of competitors' targeted marketing.

"I really hope that OffLimits and the characters can be role models for kids. New flavors with new characters are coming out where everything is kid friendly. I would just say coffee, which is kind of like the early-bird work-hustle character, also deals with social anxiety or just anxiety in general because of the pressure to succeed. She needs a cereal that can keep her up and going and inspired and working. So I would say maybe that's the only character that isn't kid friendly, but moving forward, all of them will be."

Emily explained further how she found inspiration for

the characters in her branding by considering the lifestyle of creative professionals:

"The inspiration for the characters is the kind of extreme personalities that creative people have, sometimes individually, sometimes like, in a day, you can go through all of these different emotional cycles. But also, each of the characters inspire the flavor. And that's how we came up with that."

TAKEAWAY #4: Start a Conversation

When considering her branding, Emily noticed that the famous age-old brands like Kellog's had fun and bright characters, colors, and stories, while the healthier options tended to have quite bland branding—not the kind that would lead to nostalgia. Growing up, Emily's mom didn't approve of sugary cereals, so Emily never got to enjoy the fun characters. In fact, the name OffLimits is inspired by sugary cereals being off limits in her household.

Besides wanting to introduce relatable branding, Emily felt that there was a responsibility in creating a meaningful mascot character. Unintentionally, OffLimits ended up creating the very first female character for a cereal! I had never even noticed that before. Cap'n Crunch, Tony the Tiger, Coco the Monkey, that Lucky Charms leprechaun— hey, where are the girls at?!

"When you have something character-driven that relates to young people, you have this insane opportunity and, honestly, a responsibility to be championing important conversations. And it's been decades. None of these brands are doing that. So I was like, 'OK, cool, we're going to have the first female cereal mascot, which is Dash.' We didn't even realize Dash was the only female mascot until halfway through!"

Takeaway #5: Commit Long-Term

Emily explained how starting a cereal brand is a challenging journey—the reason why one doesn't see as many startups in the cereal business as one does in, say, the beauty or beverage space. For startup entrepreneurs wanting to build a valuable business, one needs to keep focus on long-term growth over short-term gains.

"Cereal is really difficult, and the minimum order quantities for even starting are really capital intensive. So it's a commitment, and it definitely requires being fully invested in the space and long-term growth because this is not like a short-term gains kind of product to create. You only really start seeing profitability down the line when it comes to bulk ingredients and things like that."

The quality of ingredients is an important element to Emily's philosophy, as is choosing to use a lot of organic and plant-based ingredients.

"We work with Intelligentsia coffee on Dash cereal. So we source really good quality beans and work with smaller suppliers whenever possible. I'm looking into upcycling ingredients and all of these different other sustainability efforts that we can be challenging not only ourselves to implement, but the cereal industry at scale too."

THREE QUICK QUESTIONS

.   .   .

WHAT'S the number one marketing moment that made your business pop?

"When NYU students were coming back to school, there was this issue because they all had to quarantine in the dorms for two weeks. And NYU completely messed up their food schedule. These kids were posting TikToks of their vegan meal that had steak in it. And they would get their entire meals for the day at 6:00 p.m.—it was just so dysfunctional. And it became this thing on TikTok. So literally within twenty-four hours, we made these snack packs of cereal and toys and everything. Our social media manager somehow got on the group chat for all of the NYU students, and she really did some stealth investigating. We're just three people, and we spent three hours in Washington Square Park packing up bags and then going to each of the dorms, delivering them individually to all the kids. So then all the kids started posting about OffLimits, and it was a great outcome."

WHERE DO you hang out to get smarter?

"Other founders are my number one resource. I think if you're starting out, it definitely is worth reaching out to some of your favorites. And even if you can't get a hold of the founder, just like people on the team to pick their brain or listening to podcasts like yours. And then I think my favorite book is *The War of Art* by Steven Pressfield, which is kind of like motivate yourself, stop blaming it on you being a tortured artist. It's kind of just a reminder when you get in these little depressive phases to get it together and be consistent."

As a side note, Female Startup Club *has a private online network for founders. Check out our website for more details!*

. . .

HOW DO **you win the day?**

"Coffee! I look forward to it, and that's the only thing that gets me out of bed. It would be a lie if I said I get up early every morning and I do my morning routine and all of that kind of stuff. I feel really good when I do those things. But to be realistic about it, it wavers all the time. So being really normal and kind to myself I think has been more what I try and do daily than the actual physical things that make me feel better."

LISTEN **to Emily's episode to find out how she raised capital, how she collaborated with a streetwear brand, and why zombies don't always say the right things.**

LET'S TALK ABOUT SEX, BABY

ÉVA GOICOCHEA: HOW AN ENTREPRENEUR TOOK THE TABOO OUT OF THE TABOO

Éva Goicochea founded maude, a company that champions a path to modern intimacy, sexual health, and education. Through maude, Éva has pioneered changes in how we view (and speak about) intimacy, mental health, and sexual well-being. In our conversation, we spoke about the challenges of building a brand in an industry that's often regarded as taboo, which it totally shouldn't be. We're in the 2020s for Pete's sake!

TAKEAWAY #1: Analyze What's Happening (before Making a Website)

Éva studied marketing. In her early twenties, she found herself working as a legislative aide in healthcare before a few more career changes. After moving from Sacramento to New York, back to Sacramento, and then to Los Angeles, she became excited at the idea of joining a healthcare startup. But the choice left her wanting more. Considering her own path, Éva had a long-standing interest in sexual well-being. She noticed the space hadn't really advanced that much in one hundred years. I wondered how she got started with maude. What were her first steps?

"The idea came about in 2015, and in typical fashion, I built a website first, which was not the way to do it. I don't recommend that because we started getting inquiries about product and press, which was funny. I think when you first start, you need to really think about the industry that you're going into and what the landscape looks like. My first recommendation is to really analyze what's happening in the space that you're going into. And then start doing some customer research. We did a big survey early on. We purchased some formal research. You really have to build a foundation, and for us, that took a year."

Takeaway #2: Know Your Economics

There are so many things to consider after research and when you take the next step. There's the challenge of raising capital and finding a manufacturer. Some entrepreneurs focus on one at a time, but often, both need to be tackled simultaneously, as was the case with Éva.

"It was both. I think one [focus] was to work on the product to make sure that you had the business model and what the unit economics were so that you could raise capital. You definitely need to know what your economics will look like—what the cost will be—and then you can build out a model. After that, I raised half a million dollars, which was really hard. It wasn't easy. It was definitely a friends and family round. We had some institutional capital in 2017, and then we launched the business in 2018."

Takeaway #3: Seek the Help of Professionals

Éva launched her business with two lubricants, a vibrator, and condoms. In general, these kinds of products are standard for many manufacturers. Sometimes an entrepreneur's product has to be built entirely from scratch, but before going that route, which is generally very expensive, it's often a good idea to do your research by speaking to experienced professionals in the space and find out if there is something similar that can be expanded on.

"There are some really best-in-their-class manufacturers in our space that we went to. I think when you're starting to go into formulating products from scratch (as opposed to, for instance, condoms—you can't really build a condom from scratch), it would take a lot of money and time. I think it's about the FDA. It's a medical device. In our space, it's one thing because you're trying to find FDA [approved] manufacturers, and you're trying to work with formulations that are really body safe, and you work with chemists. If you're going into something completely new, there's much more research to be done. And I would recommend as much as possible to get in touch with factories that have chemists, where you can start learning about it more than just saying, 'I'm going to go build something off the shelf.'"

TAKEAWAY #4: Be Clear on Your Values

Marketing products deemed to be in the "sin" space can present a real challenge. Just think about two of the biggest social media platforms: Facebook and Instagram. Both have conservative policies around marketing anything related to sexual content.

"It was a learning curve. One of the things I really recommend is that we built a brand book essentially outlining that we're not an explicit brand. That's actually just not our DNA. And the reason is: we believe sex is human, and it's an everyday thing, and there's a real need in this space for people to treat it that way. We navigated those platforms by making sure our messaging was true to those values. And it ended up allowing for us to advertise more, as we're not trying to push the envelope of being explicit around sex. We're actually trying to do the opposite, which is to destigmatize it by *not* being explicit. Now we're able to advertise. We definitely cannot advertise the vibe, and of course, it frustrates us to no end. But the opportunity is also to make a vibrator a basic, and that's what we're trying to lead the way on."

Takeaway #5: Create a New Language

Online platforms' restrictive policies about marketing sexual products present obstacles for those with positive and healthy attitudes, but you can understand the general need for them. I empathize with platforms in having to deal with this complicated space—and at the same time, I empathize with someone like Éva, who is normalizing sexual health and well-being. I was interested in whether Éva agreed with these social media policies, especially considering her background in making policy.

"I agree with some of the policies, and the reason why I agree with them is because they're blanket policies to, essentially, prevent the stuff that shouldn't be on Facebook. Instead of fighting that particular language, I think what we're working toward is building a new language. So separating, say, adult products and services (which, in their case, might be like porn, strip clubs, etc.) and saying, 'Look, there's an actual category that's really sexual wellness and health, and that's a separate category.'"

. . .

THREE QUICK QUESTIONS

WHAT'S **the number one marketing moment that made your business pop?**

"It was having a social and press presence well before launch because it allowed for us to create a community and really start to get the feedback loop. You need to make really great decisions when you launch."

WHERE DO **you hang out to get smarter?**

"I wish I could go to libraries right now, but I think it's usually just reading. It doesn't matter where I am. Reading a physical book or a paper is where I feel like I'm getting the most information because there's no distraction. They can't open a new tab! A book that I recommend right now is *The Subtle Art of Not Giving a F*ck* by Mark Manson. It's been helpful because I think that with what we've been going through with COVID, we're reevaluating what matters to us."

HOW DO **you deal with failure?**

"I'm not one to think of failure as failure. I don't think that you're ever going to know why you went through it. I don't necessarily think that life works that way. I always say, "Life is not a VCR." You can't just put the tape in and hit rewind and fast forward. Acknowledging that you're going to learn a lot from whatever happens is really important.

And then it reframes failure entirely. I have screwed up so many times, too many to count."

LISTEN to Éva's episode to find out why she thinks language is so important, what she makes of today's sex education, and what exactly a "squat thrust in a cucumber patch" is.

20

SERIAL NUMBER

GRETTA ROSE VAN RIEL: HOW AN ENTREPRENEUR FOUND SUCCESS AGAIN AND AGAIN AND AGAIN AND AGAIN (AND AGAIN)

Gretta Rose van Riel is one of Australia's top young serial entrepreneurs. Sometimes "serial entrepreneur" can be bandied about without much to back it up, but Gretta is the real deal, with five multimillion-dollar startups to her name.

At the tender age of twenty-two, Gretta founded her first startup, SkinnyMe Tea. With a startup capital of twenty-four dollars (not a typo), she achieved mega global success and, within five years, sold over eleven million cups of tea worldwide. That's a *lot* of tea.

Some of her other ventures include The 5TH, a global watch brand with a unique twist on selling (she has since exited); Drop Bottle, a pioneering drink bottle that combines function with trend-setting form; Hey Influencers, a killer platform for brands and influencers; and Skintox (among a bunch of other super cool projects she has in the works). I know, she's a real badass.

Gretta is, of course, a woman many talents, but perhaps above all, she's a true master of social media and an algorithm guru. Her Instagram accounts are followed by over 16 million subscribers, and her Pinterest account averages over 5.8 million impressions a month. Just one of her impressive feats was growing a new Instagram account from zero to almost fifty thousand followers in just one day!

Gretta started her career working for an agency in digital marketing after getting her degree in media and communications. It seemed like a dream job at first—well paid and room for growth. But she quickly realized that she didn't enjoy the corporate structure and that her job was "basically making my boss look good." So she began to search for a side hobby to keep her inspired and busy after hours.

After considering several ideas, she opened an Instagram account with the aim of selling clothes. It was a casual side hustle, but she came across a marketing tactic that would set her up for major future success.

TAKEAWAY #1: **Fake It Till You Make It**

Social media presents all sorts of incredible opportunities for startup entrepreneurs to gain traction. But it's a competitive space, and it's important to have a clear marketing strategy to promote engagement.

In Gretta's own words, her strategy was "a little dodgy" and "sneaky," but it certainly paid off, and she discovered how to work Instagram's algorithms in her favor. While she only had a few not particularly coveted-after items to actually sell, she would list highly sought-after items that she didn't really own. She'd focus on hashtags and tagging different accounts, and people would "go crazy" about the items and engage with reposts and comments. She'd then break the bad news: "Sorry, that's been sold."

Her strategy built hype around her account, so when she

did post the fairly random items she actually had to sell, people jumped at the opportunity because of the perceived scarcity and exclusivity.

What she had discovered was that Instagram favors engagement for organic reach.

"Basically, the way that the Instagram algorithm works is that it shows your post to 3 percent of your followers, and then how that 3 percent responds determines how much of the next 3 percent it will show, and so on and so forth. So it's a closed loop, but once it gets up to maybe the 10 percent or 20 percent saturation point, if it's performing exceptionally well still, then it will push it through to a more viral reach. So organic reaches when your followers see your post, and viral reaches when people who are not following your post see it."

Always one to keep herself busy, at the age of twenty-two, Gretta was experimenting at home with making tea blends, and they proved popular with friends and people around the office. Gretta found herself getting busier and busier making her tea concoctions to keep up with the demand, but she wasn't charging anything for it. At the time, she felt awkward about asking for money.

Takeaway #2: You Don't Always Need Big Capital to Get Started

Of course, it depends on the nature of your product or service, but many successful startup entrepreneurs have proven that you don't need much capital to get started. Gretta decided to take a chance at turning her tea-making hobby into a side hustle, and she famously did it while living at home with her parents and with no more than twenty-four dollars in the bank.

Needing a platform to set up an online store, Gretta turned to Google and came across Shopify—the number one e-commerce platform that requires no coding skills to get started. Setting up her store without any prior experience took her around eight hours on a Sunday. Most of that time was spent carefully writing the copy for the info page —explaining in detail the ingredients and benefits of each tea blend.

TAKEAWAY #3: Library Research Is Free

With her hobby now becoming a side-hustle venture, Gretta spent more time developing her products further. She wanted to expand her offerings to include a wide range of benefits for different health needs. Of course, twenty-four dollars was not going to cut it for hiring a research and development department, so she made use of the local Melbourne University library and did her own research.

"I took a reverse approach. I know that I want the tea to perform these certain actions. I would look up the most next-level medical case studies and trials of different herbs. For example, if I wanted a weight-loss tea, I looked up herbs that assist in obesity management. Or for an appetite suppressant, there's a couple of ingredients that when combined, delay gastric emptying by 50 percent. It delays how frequently your stomach empties itself into your intestines, and the food is kept in your stomach for longer, so you feel fuller for longer."

TAKEAWAY #4: Stick to What You Know

When launching a new product, it can seem over-whelming for an entrepreneur to juggle all the different marketing channels that are available. But in Gretta's case, she found that it was enough to stick to the one thing she knew worked and simply repeat and repeat.

What Gretta knew was how to grow an Instagram account, thanks to her successful experience with her previous clothes business. To build her initial following, she focused on following everyone in the country that she knew. She built up around one thousand followers—which was an impressive amount back in 2012 when most people considered around fifty followers a decent following (boy, oh boy, how times have changed!). Once she hit that critical mass, an organic following started to build as people became intrigued with why the account had so many followers. In this game, success begets success.

"We launched, and we sold a few packs of tea, and there's that profound moment where the thrill is addictive. I wanted that thrill again and again."

Takeaway #5: If It Works Once, Then Repeat and Repeat

Sometimes it can take a few times to find something that works with your marketing. Gretta was lucky in that her first strategy was paying off. She found that the more she focused on building her Instagram following, the more sales she was making. Sometimes it's tempting to overcomplicate things early on with new avenues of customer acquisition, but if something works, it can be a good idea to simply stick to it. In sports, there's a common piece of wisdom that it's best to spend more time improving your strengths than your weaknesses.

"I didn't really have a background in business at all. I've never read a business book. I literally was just throwing things against the wall, and if it stuck, I'd just keep doing that. It was just so obvious to me because that's all I knew. It wasn't like, 'Oh, I should hire a CEO. I should try email marketing. I should try YouTube influencers . . .' It was so much more simple because I was just like, 'Okay, I'm onto something. I'm just gonna keep repeating that.' I think that there is this overcomplication of business as a whole, and you do really need to lean in and find the things that are working for your business and just keep doing this until they don't work anymore."

Gretta's business exploded, and within the first six months, she was selling an average of twenty thousand units a month. She casually entered a competition for the best Shopify store and won first place—an accolade that introduced her to a host of business mentors.

Takeaway #6: Failure Doesn't Mean Going Back to Scratch

From the outside, it can seem that someone like Gretta was fearless and confident, but as she experienced more and more success, her fears continued to mount.

"I was worried about everything; it was just constantly problem-solving, constantly putting out fires. My biggest fear was that we would be over as quickly as we began. I was really worried that something would happen, and I'd have to go back to how everything was before."

One day, a friend, who was a successful businessman that helped ailing companies turn their fortunes around, gave a piece of advice that changed Gretta's anxious way of thinking.

"He said, 'Let's look at this realistically. It's Thursday night right now. If everything went under tomorrow, which is Friday, what would you be doing on Monday?' And I replied, 'starting again.' It was just the most obvious answer to me, but no one had ever asked me that question. So that's one of my favorite quotes—if you do need to start over, you won't be starting from scratch; you will be starting from a place of experience. That finally relaxed me because I was like, 'Even if the worst happens, I know what I'm going to be doing now, and I have learned so much, and what I'm doing is repeatable."

THREE QUICK QUESTIONS

What's your "why"?

"I always kind of wondered what motivated me, and I did this psychometric test when an investor was considering working with me. It basically covers a lot of the commonalities of successful founders. Everything came back really good, except one thing. They were like, "We're a little concerned that you don't seem to care about money." I think ultimately, I've realized over time that money comes and goes, and that's a great thing, and it's more than fine. But what really, really excites me every day is ideas and solving big problems. So I think my earlier startups have always been quite problem and solution focused. But I think as I progress as a founder now, I'm going to be able to get into solving bigger and bigger problems."

What's the number one marketing moment that made your business pop?

"I think collaboration has always been the central key with my business. You could say social media, but behind the social media, the way that we've always grown has been through collaboration. So leveraging someone's preexisting audience to build your own. So whether it's leveraging that to build your email list, or it could be via influences to build your following, or it could be collaborating with another brand that's not a competitive brand but more a collaborative brand because basically that is your growth lever in business."

HOW DO you win the day?

"My number one tip is breath work. We all have within us the capacity to instantly change the way that we feel through the power of breath, and if you are feeling stressed or anxious, or if you're in that fight-or-flight mode, which a lot of us are in day-to-day business, it's just about being more mindful, slowing down. One of my favorite exercises is called "box breathing," where basically it forms a box. So you breathe in for five, then you hold for five, then you breathe out for five, and then you hold for five. So that one I do a couple of times throughout the day, ideally."

LISTEN to Gretta's episode to find out how she raised capital, how she expanded her business empire with new ideas, and what unusual ways she spends birthdays and Valentine's Day.

21

PIMPLE AND TO THE POINT

JAMIKA MARTIN: HOW AN ENTREPRENEUR TACKLED AN OLD PROBLEM FOR A NEW GENERATION

Few (if any) humans escape the horror of acne and breakouts. The reality is that acne is super common well into adulthood. A quick Google search told me that it affects up to 54 percent of women older than twenty-five years old. Those "perfect-skinned" celebrities are no different. Recently, many of them have spoken up about their all-too-human skin problems.

You may have come across Mindy Kaling's zit cream selfies or TikTok star Bella Thorne's filter-free posts of visible acne scars. Chrissy Teigen posted a photo zooming in on her cystic acne. Riverdale star Lili Reinhart said on social media, "My breakouts don't define me. To anyone out there who feels embarrassed or ashamed by breakouts . . . I feel you."

Jamika Martin is the founder of ROSEN Skincare. ROSEN is a direct-to-consumer acne care brand with a difference, disrupting the old-school approach to treating breakouts that big brands have clung to for decades. It's made with the millennial and Gen Z demographic in mind and boasts out-of-the-box branding, language, and price points. Jamika and I spoke about her bootstrapping journey and how she's approached working capital. She shared how to price beauty products and explained the key to building a strong marketing foundation.

TAKEAWAY #1: Find a Space That Needs Innovation

For many female startup entrepreneurs, the idea behind their business comes from personal experience as a consumer. That was very much the case for Jamika.

"I have close ties to the acne space because of my own personal journey with breakouts. I've dealt with that most of my life—pretty much breaking out in fifth or sixth grade. I shopped for treatments in places like Target, where I could afford and where I knew . . . and since sixth grade, I've just seen pretty much the same brands, same packaging, same formulas. But at the time, there definitely was a lot going on within the beauty space. And that was something I was personally interested in. And so I just remember thinking, *Wow. There's literally so many cool brands out here, but there's nothing happening in this space.* I had that initial discovery in 2016. So I was second year in college. I was set on that idea and inspired to play around with it. I launched in 2017, which is when I ended up graduating college."

TAKEAWAY #2: You Don't Need Experience to Get Started

I read that Jamika started without any background in the skincare industry or experience formulating products. I find it fascinating how some female startup entrepreneurs tackle

a complex industry without insider knowledge. I've heard
enough stories to drive home the point: with the right mindset, you can overcome just about any barrier to entry. I asked
Jamika how she went about getting started.

"My major was business economics plus two accounting
classes. So it wasn't really like business—more in the area of
how the economy works. But I did an entrepreneurship
minor while I was there, and that definitely helped with just
the idea of starting a business. I had a little bit of a baseline
there, but I didn't have cosmetic experience . . . although,
obviously, I had a lot of experience on the consumer side of
what I wanted to see and what my experience was, but as far
as formulation and production, that was all stuff that I
learned on my own, whether it was independent course-
work or a lot of trial and error."

TAKEAWAY #3: Replicate What Works

Jamika reached out to people around her that she
respected for advice and feedback on how she was going
about things—for many startup entrepreneurs, having
support can be invaluable. She recalled a particular early
nugget of advice.

"I was sitting with a mentor right after I graduated, and
she asks, 'OK, so you have five customers. Where did they
come from?' We keep getting traffic from YouTube. I had
sent a friend a package, and she did a YouTube video on it a
few months ago. And then she's like, 'OK, so keep doing
that.' That was very crucial for me, to really focus in and
understand where you're coming from and replicate that."

·   ·   ·

Takeaway #4: Work Out Who You Are

As in life, it's vital for entrepreneurs to have a clear understanding of who they are and what they stand for, which they can then articulate to others. In the craziness of the world out there, there are endless opinions and voices. It can get confusing if you haven't set your story from early on.

"I spent a lot of time trying to figure out our brand and who we were. I ended up working with a consultant early on, which was very hard for me because I didn't have a lot of money. But it was such a reassuring experience. With who we were, what we stood for . . . I couldn't ever say it very succinctly, and I couldn't clearly articulate it to people. And so once I worked with that person, I felt like everything was very clear. Like, 'This is who we are, this is what we do, and this is who we serve.' And so I would say that's a core area that really impacted our growth. Our trajectory was just focusing on marketing and understanding who we were as a brand."

Takeaway #5: Gift Your Product to Influencers

Like many of the startup entrepreneurs who've shared their strategies with me, Jamika's marketing began with reaching out to influencers on social media. As with others, she found it was a very effective route to customers and driving brand awareness to broad audiences.

"For the first year, all I did was focus on Instagram and gifting influencers. I tried stuff with Facebook ads, but I didn't know what I was doing. It is very easy to dump money there, and when you're bootstrapped and you're not making a lot of money, even five bucks a day adds up. So it was super risky. I started with a handful of influencers, and then I remember having a list. Like, 'I'm going to send out ten packages this month.' And just slowly scaling that up because it was working for us. In the first month I made money, I think we made $1,700 online. And then in that first year, year and a half . . . we probably got to $8,000 or $10,000 a month in revenue—and that was all from gifted influencers and chugging along on Instagram."

Takeaway #6: Consistently Chug Away at Marketing

Today's marketing landscape can be a real challenge for entrepreneurs. Traditional marketing provided relatively clear strategies, but in today's online world, there are seemingly endless options and platforms. It can be overwhelming to know where to put your focus. I wondered how Jamika's marketing progressed as she gained experience and whether there were any specific steps she took that made a quantum leap.

"The key was really homing in on the influencers and getting to a place where I could understand who's going to perform for us. Understand what types of influencers, what types of posts work. But, really, our growth has been fairly incremental. It hasn't been like we turned this ad on, and it was crazy. It's always just been a consistent chug, month over month of growth—which is, of course, still exciting. But no one thing kinda shot everything out. And I think that's also really key because you've got to keep persevering. You've got to keep chipping away every single day. And it's those small actions that you continually do. And then over time, you look back, and you're like, 'Holy shit! How did we end up here? This is working. This is amazing!'"

This reminded me of what was probably my first business lesson ever. Remember the fable of the tortoise and the hare? If you didn't have it read to you as a kid, the takeaway is that in a race between a slow, consistent, and focused tortoise versus a speedy, energized, but distracted rabbit, put your money on the tortoise.

TAKEAWAY #7: Make Sure Your Margins Make Sense

Our listeners often reach out to me for advice, and I remembered a *Female Startup Club* listener asking about how to tackle pricing products in the beauty product industry. Like many other retail products, it can be a real challenge to balance the tight margins and the need to survive as a business. Jamika was just the person to ask!

"I try to aim for a 75 percent margin on my products, and that might give a little bit when you go into wholesale, but you can bring in other things, like the scale. It gets cheaper when you make more products, but if you want to do direct-to-customer (DTC), maybe you want to do this forever and never sell in retailers. If you're selling to retailers off the bat, they're taking half at least. So you want to have a good margin there. For DTC, you make 100 percent of the price, but then you have different fulfillment requirements. You're paying more per product to fulfill because it's being shipped out. For a package, you might have a cool mailer or stickers or all these other things versus retail. I would also say (depending on how small you are) you can look at what costs are going to look like down the road—to see if you're going to hit economies of scale. You might have a horrible margin right now because you make one product at a time. But you might say, 'OK, if I start ordering fifty pounds of clay or if I start ordering five hundred pounds at a time, then it goes from being twenty cents an ounce to two cents an ounce.' But don't go too far because you don't want to be not making any money for too long."

THREE QUICK QUESTIONS

WHAT'S YOUR "WHY"?

"I think my "why" is just folks like me, people who grew up hating their skin and looking in the mirror and literally crying. I think that's my way of just seeing the impact that I can have on individuals. Of course, it's easy for me to get caught up in "let's hit this many sales" and stuff like that. But then there are times where I really get to connect with individuals who are impacted by ROSEN. And just seeing those individual stories and seeing so many parallels in my early journey with skincare and acne, that's definitely what keeps you inspired and why I do all of this and why I want to continue to grow."

WHERE DO you hang out to get smarter?

"I get smarter as I talk to other founders and as I connect with other people within the space."

How DO you win the day?

"I like to get up early so that I can get started at a reasonable time. I just started going to a coworking space, and they close at 5:30 p.m., which is useful because I have a tendency to easily keep going and going. Once I stop, I go to the gym, and then I'll come home and simmer down from working.

Because I can get so focused, it feels very tense sometimes for no reason."

LISTEN to Jamika's episode to find out how she expanded her marketing to other channels, what she learned about cash flow, and what she thinks about the power of scrappiness.

22

NEXT OF SKIN

JENNA OWENS: HOW AN ENTREPRENEUR INTRODUCED CBD TO SKINCARE

There's been a rapidly growing shift in the world around the discovery (or more accurately the rediscovery) of medicinal uses of marijuana. Knowledge of the plant's healing properties dates back at least five thousand years. The Ancient Egyptians reportedly used marijuana to treat glaucoma, as well as general inflammation. Chinese Emperor Fu Hsi called cannabis a popular medicine in 2,900 BCE, and the Chinese had identified more than one hundred medicinal uses by 100 CE. In the year 1993, Cypress Hill noted, "Forward motion make you sway like the ocean. The herb is more than just a powerful potion."

With cannabis rapidly being legalized throughout the US and the world, there's a huge opportunity for entrepreneurs to enter the CBD space. But it's not an easy space, as weed still holds a sinful stigma, and many investors and suppliers remain dubious (I was so tempted to say 'doobie-ous,' but I won't).

Jenna Owens is the founder of Fitish. Fitish is a skincare company committed to embracing balance, using ingredients that do exactly that for the skin and body. Jenna founded the company in 2017, and she's been actively growing the line with beauty and wellness products geared toward active people. She believes that the anti-inflammatory benefits of CBD, along with botanical extracts, have an unmatched ability to cleanse and nourish the body. Her aim is to create common rituals of self-care within an active lifestyle naturally and effectively. I spoke to Jenna about her big life pivot, her key learnings about growing and scaling a skincare company, and things you can start doing today to increase your average order value (AOV).

TAKEAWAY #1: Do Something That Fulfills You

I've found that this is one of the most common motivators for the female entrepreneur: a desire to build a career around something that is meaningful. This can sometimes surprise others as often female startup entrepreneurs develop out of an already impressive career. Perhaps the right word is *aligned*. Jenna is a perfect example. For over a decade, she had been a much-loved figure in the public eye as the candid, shoot-from-the-hip cohost of *The Kidd Kraddick Morning Show* on 106.1 KISS FM.

"I think that my trajectory is similar to a lot of women, even if they didn't have a job on a radio morning show. You reach a point in your life that you just realize, 'I don't feel fulfilled.' I had this job that to the outsider, looked like a dream, and I loved a lot of elements of the job. However, I got up at 3:30 a.m. every single morning, and I felt very rundown all the time. I wasn't feeling as creatively stimulated, and I thought that with my platform there was maybe something more out there for me."

· · ·

TAKEAWAY #2: Be Honest with Your Audience

The name of Jenna's future company, Fitish, and the seed of the company's ethos trace their origins to her talk show days. Instead of following the damaging trend of our times of pretending our lives are glossy and perfect, Jenna encouraged her listeners to be candid and honest about their health and beauty routines. In doing so, she created an organic following that later served as an early customer base for her ventures.

"I would be quite honest with women because I felt that at the time, we were inundated (and still are) with women who want to be perfect on social media. Like, 'This is me. I do everything perfectly all the time. I work out for two hours a day. I use one hundred products before I go to bed every night . . .' And that is *so* not me. I find it much more attractive and likeable and comforting when I hear women who are just quite honest about who they are."

TAKEAWAY #3: Test the Market—You Can Always Pivot

So many of the entrepreneurs I've spoken to began with a business concept that was completely different from the one that they ended up pursuing. While it could be seen as an initial failure, there seems to be a pearl of wisdom there. The most impactful step an entrepreneur can take is to simply get *started*, wherever that may be. There's great power in momentum, taking that step from the bedroom to the real world. Once we physically begin something, a whole world of opportunities presents itself, offering things we could never have imagined. Jenna knew she wanted to be in the fitness space, so she started testing out an early business idea, one that was as inexpensive to launch as possible.

"When I went to start the business, I thought, *Well,*

maybe I can offer women twenty-minute workout programs. Because that wasn't really around at the time. They were all sixty minutes long. That was a way for me to charge an affordable price. They were $19.99 to access all these programs. So it was more affordable than other things on the market. It also only cost me about $9,000 to film all the videos. And so I knew that I would probably recoup the costs, but it was also a really good indicator of 'Do I even have customers?' Like, if I want to come out with a product, do I even know the business side of things?"

TAKEAWAY #4: Keep Your Eyes Open for Opportunity

I was intrigued to discover how Jenna made the leap from fitness to skincare. What this shows is that early testing doesn't need to be your final business. As is often the case—and was certainly the case with Jenna—just doing something in your target space, no matter what it is, gives you the opportunity to observe the market and spot a gap.

"I remember I was working out one day, and all the women are wearing these expensive workout outfits. And in Dallas, at least, they're wearing concealer and mascara to exercise. It was a very specific moment for me. I had been sitting on this idea of what kind of product is it that I want? I knew I wanted to create a beauty product because I was very passionate about that space, but I didn't know exactly what it was. Women—at least where I live—they're not showering after they workout at the gym. They're going home later to do that, but they're freshening up so they can go grab a margarita across the street or go on a date, putting on perfume and using dry shampoo and doing this whole thing. And I thought, *Well, why aren't there more products for women like that?*"

(Living and regularly working out in London, I recognized the same gym bathroom scene. So it's not just a Dallas thing; it's a woman thing!)

Takeaway #5: Keep Costs to a Minimum

I asked Jenna how she actually got started. What were the steps in those early days for her to be like: "OK, I've made a little bit of money. I can reinvest that back into phase two. What is the new evolution of the brand going to be?" Jenna had her eye on CBD as a possible ingredient because it is a good anti-inflammatory. She discovered that there wasn't anything topical in the market at the time. As with several interviews I've done with early adopters in the CBD market, finding suppliers willing to work with the ingredient can be a challenge and an obstacle.

"I started researching the CBD element, which is quite a bit harder. Beating doors down at labs who are saying, 'No.' They don't work with CBD. I was fortunate to find a lab that didn't have huge minimums, so I took a little bit of money that I had made from the videos. I believe my first order cost me about $20,000, and I actually chose a makeup setting spray that didn't have CBD and one that was a cooling spray. I ordered the same bottle for both of them in order to make my money go further. They have different boxes, but to keep it cheap, I ordered the same bottle with different art. There was a lot of confusion in the beginning because they have the same bottle. But that was a way to do it, to meet the minimum requirement of five thousand bottles. I started out pretty small and was just really excited when people actually started buying it."

. . .

TAKEAWAY #6: **Early Adopting Means Challenges and Rewards**

Many investors and suppliers have clauses that preclude investing or dealing in what is known as the "sin" space (think CBD, sex toys, alcohol, etc.). I wondered if Jenna experienced these obstacles. If so, how did she overcome them?

"Payment processing was one of the biggest hurdles we had to overcome. We had all these orders about to come in, and our credit card processor put together that we were in the CBD space or something like that and shut down the payment plan. Payment providers that, of course, instead of taking 3 or 4 percent off every order, they're taking, like, nine. Or they're routing that through a bank account in Ireland. And then your customers are going to see an international charge and wonder, 'What's going on?' It was really difficult."

Jenna sold her products on Shopify, which is the obvious go-to platform for any entrepreneur in the e-commerce space.

"We're sold on Shopify. I couldn't say enough good things about that platform, and they have been so supportive of us as a business. However, at that time, they used Square as their payment processor, and they were like, 'We don't mind CBD, but our payment processor does.' So they allowed us to find another payment processor to use. I can go on and on, but at some point, you say, 'You know what? These are the risks that you're going to take.' Being in a business that you hopefully will reap the rewards of, being a first mover in an industry, you've got to hold out and figure it out."

Gosh, there are so many little obstacles that one doesn't think about beforehand. But this is all part of being an early adopter, and if you get through all the hurdles, there's a big pot of gold at the end, or perhaps a gold pot of pot! I couldn't resist.

TAKEAWAY #6: More SKUs = More Sales

It can be a tough question for many startup entrepreneurs: how big should the product line be? Some theories suggest that less is more; others say more is more. Jenna gave an interesting insight into one of the main moves she made to boost her business.

"It was important to look at the space and do my market research and realize that a lot of these other CBD brands don't have nearly as many SKUs as we do. And so I realized that when we doubled our SKU count, our average order value (AOV) went up from fifty-four dollars to about seventy-four dollars. And now I know there's a tipping point there. You're not going to have an average order of more than one hundred dollars all the time, especially when your products are really moderately priced. But the fascinating thing is I can only attribute that to adding more SKUs."

THREE QUICK QUESTIONS

WHAT'S the number one marketing moment that made your business pop?

"We did a campaign where we brought some clients in for a video testimonial and got them all done up. Oh my gosh, even the men who were filming were crying! And it was amazing because I guess you just don't realize how powerful skin issues can be and how powerful overcoming them is, and we underestimate the confidence that is then associated with that transformation."

WHERE DO you hang out to get smarter?

"The golf course. And I know that that sounds really funny because I'm not that great of a golfer! Men are really relaxed, and then they're just shooting the breeze around with one another, and they'll just broker these deals."

How do you deal with failure?

"Drink some wine! Just kidding. It's about *transparency*. A lot of brands will only post really positive reviews. I post all the reviews. I mean, unless they're really defamatory and crummy or bullying. But if there is value in educational moments there, I think that people care very heavily about who's behind the brand, what's going into this, and whether you are honest. I think we should just be honest about the struggle, about creating a business."

LISTEN to Jenna's Episode to find out how she pivoted to pets, what she wished she learned in high school, and how she celebrated Halloween.

23

JING AND YANG

JING GAO: HOW AN ENTREPRENEUR BROUGHT PREMIUM CHINESE PANTRY STAPLES TO THE MODERN KITCHEN

Jing Gao is the founder of Fly By Jing—the first premium Chinese food company that brings thoughtfully crafted pantry staples to the modern kitchen. And they are famous for their hot sauces. Fly By Jing's hugely popular signature hot sauce "Sichuan Chili Crisp" quickly became a favorite with quarantine homebound cooks.

Jing's successful Kickstarter campaign led to over three thousand customers at launch. She explained the key moments of growth that led to an eight-figure-revenue business in just two years and gave key lessons that entrepreneurs in progress can keep in their back pocket.

Currently based in LA, Jing was born in Chengdu and raised abroad in Europe and Canada. Growing up in a family that was regularly relocating, Jing felt pressure to adapt culturally and lost touch with her Chinese heritage.

On a work trip to China in her twenties, Jing began to reconnect with her own cultural identity, and delving into Chinese culture, she realized something that would be the early seed to her entrepreneurial journey.

"I was learning more about Chinese food; I was realizing just how little of that five-thousand-year heritage really made its way to the West. There were all kinds of false narratives that existed—everything from the value of Chinese food to how it should taste, what ingredients should be in there, whether it's healthy or not, and the price point."

Back in the US, Jing attended the largest natural foods expo in the world and saw an opportunity in the limited Asian flavor options on display.

She realized that one of her personal sauce recipes, which she used for her own cooking, was shelf-stable and could be jarred and sold. So she began selling to friends and family and launched a humble online shop.

TAKEAWAY #1: Tell a Compelling (Read: Spicy) Brand Story

Jing started a crowdfunding campaign in the hope of raising funds for producing her first batch at scale. It was a great success—in fact, at the time, it was the highest-funded craft project on the platform, at $250,000.

Crowdfunding platforms can seem like an easy route to funding for startup entrepreneurs, but truth be told, it can be deceptive. Achieving success in a crowded marketplace takes damn hard work and careful strategies. A big part of getting a crowdfunding campaign right is crafting a captivating narrative around your product.

"I think the product itself should be able to tell a story. So for us, the message, and that was inherent in the product, was about that 'Made in China' or Chinese food products can be some of the highest quality in the world. A lot of the food products that made their way out of China had traditionally been lower priced and, as a result, had used much more basic ingredients. So just telling that story of the craftsmanship that goes into it, the sourcing, the ingredients —that was compelling as a story."

TAKEAWAY #2: **Drive Hot Traffic to Your Crowdfunding Page**

There are a kazillion techniques and tricks to growing a successful Kickstarter campaign. The potentially most important one also happens to be quite obvious (there's no secret sauce!). It's to focus on driving a ton of traffic to your page, as this gets the attention of the platform's algorithms and ranks your campaign higher.

"A lot of it is getting people to come on your page. So whether it's like every single person that you've ever met in your life, just emailing them, asking them to come and support or reaching out to bloggers and media. I emailed a few writers who I thought had written about similar things in the past and might be interested and ended up getting placements in New York magazine on the day of launch, which was really great because Kickstarter works on these algorithms that they'll show you to more people, the more traffic you're getting. And so you want to actually hit your goal on the first day for it to snowball." (Hot tip!)

Jing found her Kickstarter audience made a perfect initial customer base for free word-of-mouth PR.

"I think the great thing about Kickstarter is that it's a platform that attracts people who are trendsetters or innovators. They're willing to take a risk to support something brand new. And they usually tend to be the people in their communities that people trust for advice on things like food or travel or gadgets."

. . .

TAKEAWAY #3: **Add a Personal Touch to Your Marketing Campaign**

In today's world, with so many businesses being automated and dehumanized, adding a personal touch can be extremely effective for building rapport and creating an engaged community. Customers respond positively to personal communication, especially from a founder. Adding a personal touch, although hard work, is low on cost. And it can prove to be more effective than an expensive ad campaign.

"I think that my initial backers felt a connection to me because it was such a personal campaign. So when they receive the product, they feel a personal connection to the founder. It was really important for me in the beginning. I was trying to write as many personal notes as possible to my customers, and any customer service issues—shipping issues, delays, whatever—it all came directly to me, and I was answering every single one. And that began building our community, which now it's like extremely strong."

TAKEAWAY #4: **Trust Your Gut**

Trusting your instincts is vital for startup entrepreneurs. Startups are about vision and often need to navigate unchartered territories. It's very much part of the job description of a startup founder to have a strong instinct and listen to it closely when decisions need to be made.

"I think my strongest trait was just trusting my gut and saying that the US market is ready for really high-quality Chinese food. That insistence on the quality, on the techniques that inherently made the products unique in the market, because I knew how difficult it was to get there and that it was unlikely that anyone else would go to such lengths. And so it just made the product instantly unique."

Takeaway #5: Constraints Lead to Creativity

The financial constraints that many startups face in the early days can often prove to be a blessing in the long run. Having big early capital injections can lead to a degree of laziness, while conversely, having to deal with financial limitations can really lead to creative out-the-box thinking—the kind that can make all the difference.

"So we were bootstrapped. Kickstarter was the only funding we really received for the longest time until just last month. So without resources, without even employees, how do you make decisions? How do you just do more with less? And I think that's a startup entrepreneur superpower—sometimes restraints or constraints actually help you think more creatively."

THREE QUICK QUESTIONS

What's the number one marketing moment that made your business pop?

"A major moment was last November when we launched our rebrand. So if you Google the initial Kickstarter, it was a very different branding system. It was initially something that drew your attention, but eventually I felt like the brand outgrew it. With the new rebrand, our tagline is not traditional but personal, which really encapsulates our story and our mission. A lot of people have formed ideas about what

Chinese food is, but we wanted to express that there's so much more diversity that exists within Chinese food."

WHERE DO you hang out to get smarter?

"I listen to so many podcasts, podcasts exactly like this one. I've been very lucky to have a great support group of other founders who are all going through this journey. We often get together and swap tales and help each other out. And that's been the biggest source of growth."

How DO you deal with failure?

"Things often don't go to plan. And I think sometimes, in one day, you can have a failure and a huge success. That's just the journey of an entrepreneur. So it's just keeping it in perspective. Oftentimes, you get your greatest successes after what seem to be the greatest failures. So just understanding and keeping that perspective that nothing is ever as bad as it seems and nothing's also as great as it seems. Having that perspective will get you through anything."

LISTEN to Jing's episode to find out about her experience in a tech accelerator, the way she got her products into retail, and the best places to eat in China.

24

BIGWIGS

JORDYNN WYNN AND SHARON PAK: HOW TWO BEST FRIENDS ROCKED THE WORLD OF WIGS

Jordynn Wynn and Sharon Pak are best friends and cofounders behind the coolest wig company you will ever meet: Insert Name Here Hair (or INH Hair for short). It's inspired by pop culture, celebs, and trends. INH Hair produces premium quality ponytails, wigs, buns, and extensions full of sass and so much bounce. Jordynn and Sharon were early members of the beauty startup ColorPop.

After a few years of learning the ropes at the wildly successful business, they decided it was time to get out of there and do their very own thing. The pair connected with their third cofounder, Kevin Gould, and soon realized they had a really great idea in mind. Next, they got to work developing and launching INH Hair. When I was chatting to Jordynn and Sharon, we talked about everything from their current marketing approach to which initiatives are driving a projected $20 million in sales in 2021—and that time Ariana Grande wore their signature pony.

Jordynn and Sharon shared a dorm at Pepperdine University. After graduating, Jordynn interned at a cosmetics company. Sharon soon joined her. Together they worked at ColorPop cosmetics, one of the fastest-growing online beauty companies in the world. Jordynn and Sharon discovered their complementary skill sets (including being able to fight really well together, they tell me). Soon, Jordynn and Sharon set out to start their own enterprise. They considered everything from sofas to Tupperware®, but it was wigs that got them excited.

TAKEAWAY #1: Create a Sticky Community

For startup entrepreneurs, work experience at another successful startup is a major advantage (especially if it's in the same industry as their venture). It's true that almost all startups across different industries have similarities. Jordynn and Sharon worked at ColorPop, which was not only a startup but also a hugely successful one. They shared one of the powerful lessons they

learned there, which was the power of creating a "sticky community." This involves creating content that keeps customers returning to your website—in effect, creating a genuinely involved and regular following.

"The biggest thing we learned was the community aspect of the brand. Having a community is so incredibly powerful (especially a group that's going to go beyond the product), and with ColorPop, they have this insane avid fan base who's just talking about ColorPop all day, every day. Like it's beyond the actual product itself. They're finding connections and relationships with one another through a brand and a product—and that was something that we needed to replicate. Customers are going to go and evangelize for you, for the brand. It makes things so much easier."

·   ·   ·

TAKEAWAY #2: **You Don't Need to Start with Perfection**

INH Hair launched their first range of wigs ahead of Halloween, hoping to capitalize on big spending over the holiday. One of the early challenges entrepreneurs face is the question of perfectionism. Of course, we all want to launch that absolutely perfect product from the get-go, but many successful entrepreneurs suggest otherwise. It can be best to trade perfection for momentum. I asked Jordynn and Sharon how they got the word out there about their launch.

"It was friends and family, but we were slightly disappointed because you're building to that starting line and you just want to go. And when you get to the finish line . . . you get there, and you're like, 'Oh, wait. Nobody knows about us.' I don't even know why we spent so much time to just get it so perfect. One of our biggest tips to entrepreneurs is don't be a perfectionist when it comes to launching a brand. Because there's just so much that needs to happen once you get to the finish line anyway, so it doesn't really matter as much. Don't get hung up on it. So many people are like, 'I need the perfect unicorn. I need the perfect PR.' I'm like, 'No one's going to read it. You're not going to have enough people to even send it to.' Don't worry about it."

TAKEAWAY #3: **Interact Personally with Your Customers**

Jordynn and Sharon mentioned sticky communities to me. Professionals in advertising and marketing call memorable campaigns sticky because they remain (or stick) with audiences long after they've been exposed to the advertising. Jordynn and Sharon developed their sticky campaign with a personal touch.

"It's the nitty-gritty of actually getting in there and doing it yourself. A lot of people think there's a shortcut for sharing. I respond to a ton of comments. We're constantly going through and looking from our personal pages. . . . Like, anybody who talks about us, tags us, even likes our stories. . . . And I think that in the very beginning, with that one-on-one interaction, not only are you going to really learn and understand the customer, but they're going to feel like they know you because you have been so hands-on with them. And I think that that's one of the biggest mistakes of a lot of brands. They don't have that direct touch with their customers because it does take a lot of work and it is difficult to scale. But I think it pays itself back, like, tenfold. It's 100 percent worth it."

TAKEAWAY #4: **Have Multiple Touch Points**

Researching INH Hair, I was struck by their thorough and multilayered marketing approach. Successful marketing in today's world demands an omnichannel approach—reaching out to (and listening to) audiences on *all* the different platforms. Jordynn and Sharon shared some advice.

"Today you have to take an omnichannel approach. You need email. You need SMS. You need all these funnels running performance, marketing. Without any of those moving funnels, you really can't have a brand. For us, it's just been going hard on every single funnel and capturing the audience on every level. There is so much noise in the world right now, and you're just getting pushed so much content in your face all day, every day. So you have to have all these multiple touch points to make it work."

TAKEAWAY #5: **Start with Social Media**

Omnichannel marketing can be pretty overwhelming for the novice entrepreneur, especially if you don't have a digital marketing background. I asked Jordynn and Sharon, Where do they think is a good place to start early marketing?

"I think that people truly need to hear about the brand, especially these days when the barrier to entry of launching a brand is so low. There are new brands every single day, popping up like wildflowers. If you're just getting started, a good thing to prioritize is social media, which is really important and really easy. You don't really need to have a crazy skill set to get started, and especially if you have this touch point on your customer, it really is a learn-as-you-go process. And then getting your attention on your email capture when people land on your website. Even if you don't have a really elaborate email or SMS platform built out, it's just important that you're at least retaining all of that information so you can reach back out to these people later."

Takeaway #6: Get Your Product in the Hands (or Heads) of Celebrities

For Jordynn and Sharon, the magical moment for INH Hair—when they started to gain confidence that they were on to something really big—was when their product was used publicly by an A-list celebrity. It's not always easy to connect to a celebrity for endorsement, but it can be a worthwhile strategy to tackle as it can pay off big time.

"Ariana Grande wore our pony in her 'In My Head' music video with *Vogue*. And it was really cool because we worked with her hairstylist and worked with *Vogue*, and they asked us for hairpieces. But it didn't sound like it was guaranteed. So we sent it, and then we didn't hear back from them for months. And then one day, her video goes live, and we're in the credits. And everybody started sending it to us. And we were like, 'Oh, my gosh. This is crazy!' So that was a really big moment for sure. If Ariana Grande is wearing us, we got this. We're, like, the pony queens."

THREE QUICK QUESTIONS

WHERE DO you hang out to get smarter?

[Jordynn] "I try to hang out with smarter people just generally. My boyfriend has a ton of really smart friends—and we also reach out a lot to other founders or other businesspeople. Just cold turkey to see if they'll be our friend. Talking to other people in the space is the best thing you could do."

HOW DO you win the day?

[Jordynn] "One of my biggest things is taking time to go on a walk in the morning with my dog. A big part of that is because then she'll be chill for the day, so I don't have anxiety. But then also having a cup of coffee. If I did not have my coffee in the morning, I'm like a zombie throughout the day. And then the whole day, I'm thinking, *Why do you suck?*"

HOW DO you deal with failure?

[Sharon] "I don't really deal with failure because I'm a constant fixer. It's my toxic but also positive personality trait and is extremely exhausting for the people around me. But I'm constantly fixing, making better, optimizing. So there's no such thing as failure. For me, it's just a learning curve. You get on with it. And also, hot yoga has been my personal therapy where I get to talk through a lot of my emotions and feelings with myself."

LISTEN to the podcast with Jordynn and Sharon to discover why they think partnerships are important, how they created a team of baby entrepreneurs, and what the upsides are of being shameless.

Since the brand tempted us to insert a name, here are three ideas (laugh cry emoji!):

Wiggy Smalls
TWL (The Wig Lebowski)
CIWIYYC (Can I wig it? Yes you can!)

25

CHANGING YOUR SPOTS

JU RHYU: HOW AN ENTREPRENEUR GAVE THE GIFT OF SELF-CONFIDENCE

Ju Rhyu is the founder of Hero, a forward-thinking cosmetics brand that makes superpowered skincare products to help customers get in control of their skin and gain confidence. Hero is perhaps best known for their "Mighty" acne patches, which have been described as having a cult following. I love fun facts, so here's one: Hero sells a box every fifteen seconds, with over two million boxes sold in over 8,500 retail stores. That's pretty darn Mighty, right? I discussed all sorts of things with Ju—from how she launched her brand exclusively through Amazon to how she found a manufacturer in South Korea and how she goes about driving crazy growth.

TAKEAWAY #1: See What Works in a Foreign Market

Ju always wanted to follow in her father's footsteps and be an entrepreneur. However, she began her career in corporate after getting an MBA at Columbia Business School in New York.

Ju worked for many of the world's top companies,

including American Express, Kraft, and Samsung. Her stint at Samsung meant a relocation to Seoul, and in Seoul, she discovered acne patches. It was a product she had never heard of before, and its popularity was evident in how many people she saw on the street wearing them. So she tried it out herself and was amazed at how well it worked.

The world is full of endless products, and there are plenty of opportunities for entrepreneurs to introduce a new product to their home country. Going down this route has its advantages, as an already existing product in a foreign country has a proven track record and a business model to follow (or to use as a starting point to innovate).

"I started wondering why I was learning about it at that moment and not fifteen years ago and why it wasn't more readily available in the US. And then that gave me the spark of like, 'Hey, this could be a business idea!'"

TAKEAWAY #2: Research Straight Away and Follow the Breadcrumbs

Once the idea popped into her head, Ju did what every successful entrepreneur starts with—research! She searched on Google and looked at Amazon to see if there were similar products available in the US.

"I discovered the product did exist in the US. There were maybe one or two brands that had acne patches, but they weren't beauty brands—they were more like medical brands. This made me think that the opportunity lay in introducing this product as a beauty brand."

Next, Ju started researching manufacturers. It can be a daunting task to track down manufacturers, but Ju had the help of Korean packaging requirements.

"In Korea, cosmetic products have to put the name of the

manufacturer on the back of the box. Perfect! So I went to a pharmacy and bought up all these different types of acne patches and took note of the manufacturer names. I Googled them. I called, I emailed."

Putting in the leg work and contacting many manufacturers paid off for Ju.

"Most didn't reply. They probably thought I was just after free samples. But a few did, and one of those, we still work with today. They make the best quality patches in Korea in my opinion."

Takeaway #3: It Takes Twelve Months to Launch

Many startup entrepreneurs are unsure of how long it will take to get from concept to launch. It's a process we sometimes want to rush in the excitement of racing to launch, but that period of researching, developing, and planning can be vital to a company's success. In Ju's case, it took a full year before she launched her brand in September 2017.

"I've noticed that launching new products does take about twelve months. So I think that's a good rule of thumb in terms of if you're thinking about launching a product; that's roughly how long it will probably take."

Takeaway #4: Bootstrapping Puts Focus on Profitability

Together with her two cofounders, each partner put personal capital into a dedicated bank account to get the business going. Many startup entrepreneurs find that having limited capital can prove to be a blessing in disguise. Having a tight budget forces you to think twice about every move and be resourceful and creative. Further down the line, showing an investor that you've gone through this process and made it to the other side can be seen as a big plus for credibility and set a higher valuation for the business.

"Bootstrapping was good because it forced us to really focus on being profitable from the very beginning. We couldn't pay ourselves fancy salaries or spend too much on PR firms and those kinds of things. So it was 'boots to the ground,' which means being really resourceful. That actually makes us more attractive as a business to investors."

TAKEAWAY #5: Start with the Quickest, Easiest Route to Market

Ju considered how to get her products to market in the most efficient way so she could see the market's response as quickly as possible. Not having the capital to set up a DTC business, she decided to exclusively launch through Amazon. Amazon provides an excellent platform for startup brands. It's simple to get started and has incredible reach.

"It's really easy to sign up for a seller's account. You create a product page, you put your images on there, you put your content on there, and you make sure all your copy and descriptions are optimized. You can even send your products into the Amazon fulfillment center so that they do the fulfillment for you."

Within three months, Ju had sold ten thousand units—her entire inventory!

TAKEAWAY #6: Work Out Your Marketing Strategy Early on and Don't Spread Yourself Too Thin

As the product was exclusively sold through Amazon,

this allowed Ju to focus her marketing strategy and use all the avenues available through the platform. Sometimes startup entrepreneurs are eager to have their products on as many platforms as possible, but it's often a better idea to have fewer platforms, even just one, and take full advantage of what it has to offer. Understanding and implementing all the opportunities each platform offers can take a lot of focus and time.

"Amazon has their own paid media platform that you can leverage to boost awareness of your products. The other thing that you need to do is focus on organic content so you can focus on things like the product titles, the copy, and the description. Also having the right keywords, so that when someone's searching for a similar product, your product shows up in search results."

Takeaway #7: Start Planning Ahead Early On

Around nine months after their Amazon launch, Hero had enough resources in the bank to start setting up their DTC operation. This included creating a website and finding a fulfillment solution. Even though going the DTC route was always Ju's plan, she didn't waste any time in also approaching retailers.

"After launching on Amazon, I immediately started pitching to retailers. Anthropologie was the first retailer to take us on in January. That pilot had gone really, really well. So they launched this nationally. And then as we started, I started focusing on PR, and I started getting a lot of inbound requests from retailers."

Amongst Ju's requests were several major retailers, including Neiman Marcus and American Eagle.

. . .

Takeaway #8: Offer a Real Solution

Ju attributed her success with retail buyers to her ability to provide an actual solution to a real problem. If you get that right, you'll be sure to catch the attention of buyers.

"Buyers are very trend savvy; it's their job to spot what's new and to create things that they think their customers would want. So I think acne patches were seen as an emerging trend. But, at that point in time, the only options were Korean brands. I think they liked the idea that there was an acne patch made specifically for the American audience with a company that was really going to support it with marketing and education. Acne is unfortunately something a lot of people struggle with, and everyone's still looking for that magic bullet. We were offering a real solution."

Takeaway #9: New Products Bring New Customers

Having secured their place in the market with a product that reached "cult" status, Ju worked quickly to develop and launch new products to expand the range. The new products offered solutions to other skin issues, and the hope was that they would be popular with their loyal customer base. But it turned out to actually attract a whole new set of customers—a testament to the power of taking swift advantage by expanding a range that's already proved popular.

"I thought 70 percent of the customers who would buy these new products would be repeat customers that know our brand. To add to their skin routine. But I was very pleasantly surprised that over 70 percent were in fact totally new customers to the franchise, which I think is awesome."

THREE QUICK QUESTIONS

. . .

WHAT'S YOUR "WHY"?

"I love to create. I love to bake, and I love to cook because I love making things. And so, for me, my "why" is that I just love the art of creation. And starting a company is such a great example of that—like starting from nothing and then creating a fifteen-to-twenty-person company with a product that sells every fifteen seconds. I get a lot of satisfaction from that."

WHAT'S **the number one marketing moment that made your business pop?**

"I think one of the key pivotal times was early on when I was emailing editors and people in the press. Our first few feature articles drove our sales pretty significantly on Amazon."

WHERE DO **you hang out to get smarter?**

"I read the Wall Street Journal every morning. Also, my favorite podcast is *Pivot* by Kara Swisher and Scott Galloway. Those are probably the two biggest things that I do."

LISTEN **to Ju's episode to find out what working at Kraft Foods taught her, how she plans to spend now that she has the capital, and how she deals with her unusually long commute.**

26

WHO RUNS THE WORLD? CURLS

JULISSA PRADO: HOW AN ENTREPRENEUR ROCKED THE WORLD OF CURLS

Julissa Prado is the founder of Rizos Curls. Founded in October 2017, Rizos Curls is a clean hair care brand that celebrates the beauty of curls, kinks, and waves everywhere. The Latina entrepreneur launched Rizos Curls in 2017, shortly after Hurricane Maria hit Puerto Rico and disrupted the daily beauty routines for its women with nationwide electrical shortages. In just under three years, they've amassed a global following of more than 300,000 followers on social media and ship their products to fifty-seven countries. Julissa shared her inspiring and deeply personal story, covering the origins of her business and her journey of creating her own potions and formulas since she was in the ninth grade.

Julissa had been attracted to hair since she was a teenager. In fact, in ninth grade, she had a hairstyling operation in full swing—sourcing her clientele from among her "sixty to seventy first cousins just in LA!" During that time, she switched from straightening her own hair to celebrating her natural curls. With some inspiration from her grandmother, she began experimenting with her own hair care concoctions, which included natural ingredients like aloe vera and flaxseed oil.

Despite her busy teenage hairstyling hustle, Julissa never considered the idea of hair as a career. She did her undergrad at UCLA and then got a master's in business, thanks to a PepsiCo scholarship. Her dream at the time was to become a lawyer.

Although Julissa was deep into the corporate world, hair remained a big part of her life, and she found herself regularly helping other girls who would compliment her on her hair and ask for advice. Over time, this got her thinking about hair care as a career possibility.

"By the time I decided I want to make this professional, I still didn't think that it was going to be enough for me to leave my corporate job. But I just thought it was very inconvenient every time I was helping these people, which I was doing all the time. It would be easier if I didn't have to write down all these instructions. And I thought, *You know what, this is a big risk. But, like, worse comes to worse, I have a lifetime supply of hair care products for me and my huge family.*"

Takeaway #1: Save Money as Early as Possible

Entrepreneurs often have to rely on their personal savings as startup capital. Putting savings away from a young age can really pay off; one doesn't need to wait until you have your business idea.

From a young age, Julissa made incredibly wise entrepreneurial decisions for her future, even though at the time she hadn't recognized the idea that she could start a business and hadn't yet viewed herself as a startup entrepreneur. Describing herself as a "big saver," she took steps at fifteen years old to put away half of her earnings. By the time she decided to have a go at her new hair care venture, she had saved up around $80,000, which she used to self-fund her business.

Julissa invested her savings into funding her formula development. The process took her around four years before she settled on a formula she was happy with.

Working with multiple chemists, she was relentless in her pursuit of finding the perfect formula. It finally paid off, as she explained, "I think the reason why, when I did launch, it did so good is because it actually works."

Takeaway #2: Stick to Your Guns

Something that's come up on the show pretty regularly is that founders' stories start with manufacturers telling them that their vision can't be done. And it's all the more reason why, as an entrepreneur, you need to stick to your guns and trust your conviction that your idea is possible.

"I was very, very focused and knew exactly what I wanted. And no chemist, no big fancy lab could sway me in a different direction. I remember the first lab that I was trying to go with. . . . They were like very fancy, big time. And then they kept telling me, "This is how you should do this." And I was like me, with no experience, this little twenty-one-year-old girl like, 'This is going to work,' you know, like, who am I?"

Takeaway #3: Emotional Connection Is Valuable

Working with manufacturers can be a difficult obstacle at the startup stage, especially with high minimum orders and needing to convince a manufacturer to invest in a relationship with you. Julissa didn't have hard data to back up her ambitions. But what she found was that her ability to connect with others on an emotional level resulted in out-of-the-ordinary cooperation. It's a testament to how important developing relationships and having the right attitude are.

"I was born with a Pisces gift of being able to relate and being able to really connect with other humans and being able to have a really strong sense of empathy and how others empathize with myself as well. And so many of these people that I was meeting along the way, they would literally tell me, 'I've never done this before, but I believe in you. I believe your story. I want to support you. Like, I would never lower my minimums like this, but I believe in you, and I want to support you.'"

Although Julissa didn't have hard data to present to her manufacturers, she did have years of personal data, which she explains "just came in a different way than numbers on a spreadsheet."

Growing up in a predominantly Latino neighborhood, Julissa realized that the natural hair movement was missing so much of the Latino community because of the language barriers. In general, the market didn't seem to understand that Latino women really care about natural and high-quality ingredients. Organic is very much part of Latino culture.

TAKEAWAY #4: Create a Solution to a Problem—A Really Good One

The most powerful startup ideas, and the ones that are most likely to succeed, are those that create a real solution to a real problem. Although big companies throw large budgets at market research, there's nothing more powerful than personal experience in your own community.

"One thing that I know is my culture, my community, my people, and I know what they want, and I know what the market is lacking. And that's one thing that I tell everyone that wants to go into an industry that they are unfamiliar with, or they feel like it's too saturated, or they feel like they are the super underdog. What I tell them is you don't just create a business; you create a solution to a problem. And if you have the solution to a problem, and you're looking around, and there are all these people that also need that solution, your knowledge is worth what other companies will need millions of dollars to do in market research. That is knowledge that's unmeasurable. And if you have that, the world is going to help you get that solution out to people."

THREE QUICK QUESTIONS

WHAT'S the number one marketing moment that made your business pop?

"One really big moment, that I didn't expect to be so big, was that Patty Rodriguez highlighted my small business on her radio show, together with Ryan Seacrest. Following that, our sales and our inquiries were just insane. And I think that was like the first step toward a mainstream audience seeing my little business."

IF YOU ONLY HAD $1,000 left in your business bank account, where would you spend it?

"I would just get more product or new product, as many

units as I can afford with that $1,000. I would tell people about it and make a really fun video on TikTok. By the way, anyone who is starting or growing a business: do not sleep on TikTok. TikTok is the future."

How do you deal with failure?

"I'm grateful. I'm grateful because what is better for you will always be for you. And when a door closes, it's because that door wasn't there for you, and the universe and life has a plan for you. So when something closes, don't be upset. Be grateful that you didn't go in a direction that wasn't going to serve you."

Listen to Julissa's episode to find out how she made a million dollars' worth of sales in her first year, why there's no such thing as bad luck, and what's more important than a really dope PowerPoint deck.

27

ALL IS HAIR IN LOVE AND WAR

KAILEY BRADT: HOW AN ENTREPRENEUR
TOOK THE WATER OUT OF HAIR CARE

Kailey Bradt is the founder of Susteau (formerly OWA Hair Care), an innovative, clean beauty brand delivering concentrated, effective formulas. Their first-of-a-kind water-activated powders deliver everything you need and nothing you don't. We discussed how Kailey decided to reinvent the wheel with a powdered shampoo, how she got the money she needed to get started, and why she decided to make a name change.

Her interest in sustainability goes as far back as her school days, when she started an eco-club with her chemistry class. Kailey struggled with deciding what career path she wanted to take. On one hand, she was creative and wanted to use that creativity, but on the other hand, her academic strengths lay in math and science. She decided to take the direction of chemical engineering, something she considered a "good backup plan," although she still dreamed of doing something more creative.

. . .

TAKEAWAY #1: Find a Solution to a Problem

Like all startup entrepreneurs, there's a story of the "aha" moment. Often, the seed of an idea comes from an actual problem encountered in daily life or through work. Kailey explained the problem she came across that needed a solution.

"One day, I realized that I was packing all of these little, tiny bottles, and they would always explode. And then I was like, 'OK, what's actually in this?' Because everything has water. It's the first ingredient for shampoo, conditioner, body wash, my styling products. . . . I thought, *What if I could eliminate the water?* So with my background in chemical engineering, I started digging into these formulas and realized it wasn't like 40 percent water; it was more like 89 percent, 95 percent water. And so that was really the moment where I was like, 'Oh my gosh, I think I have to do something about this.'"

TAKEAWAY #2: Think like an Engineer

Kailey used her engineering background to develop her idea further, which ultimately led to the idea of using powder. It's a testament to the saying that no education is wasted. Often, startup entrepreneurs will find that their skills from another industry end up giving them an advantage.

"So it might be a gel, it might be a cube, it might be anything. I think my perspective on product development is unique in that way, as I think like an engineer. And so I think, like, what does something need to do? Not what does it look like, how does it need to feel? And so I really just wanted something that functioned like a liquid, but I wanted to eliminate the water. The idea of a powder was definitely there, but I didn't know if it was the answer until it was fully vetted a couple of years later."

TAKEAWAY #3: Research before Diving In

Kailey began to think about patents and did thorough research before moving forward with her idea, a step she highly recommends.

"The first thought I had was somebody has to have a patent on this because I can't imagine that I'm going to do this and not get sued by someone that already had this idea. But when I started looking around at patents and doing more research, I really couldn't find anything that was like a powder format or even a concentrate, aside from shampoo and conditioner. I always recommend, to anyone, to start talking to friends and family and literally just get on Google and see what you can find before you dive in and invest yourself in something."

So many startup entrepreneurs that we've had on the show reminisce about the time they started their product development in their kitchen. Kailey's story was similar, except it was in a different part of the house.

"I got started literally on my bedroom floor. I was ordering ingredients. And luckily, I didn't start with kitchen-grade ingredients because of my background. I knew how and where to get cosmetic-grade ingredients. So I was able to take a very scientific approach to the product development process and buy myself some time.

During this time, Kailey continued her experimenting as a side hustle while she enrolled back in school and got her master's in product development.

. . .

Takeaway #4: Many Iterations Make Things Right

From speaking to previous entrepreneurs who've had to come up with formulations, I've always found it interesting how many iterations they had to go through before finding the perfect one.

"I always tell people there is a lot you can kind of get from just doing your research and talking to people, making phone calls. And what I realized was I wasted an entire summer in 2017 getting the formula to a point where I thought it was really good, and I wanted someone to finalize it for me. And pretty much all of the labs and manufacturers I spoke to just told me, 'no.' I'm like, this isn't possible! I just want somebody to check it over for me, make sure it's OK! This is why I'm so crazy with research. One of the main ingredients I was using actually stopped being manufactured. And so I had to completely reformulate. It took about fifty formulas and two years in total to get that final formulation for what is now Moondust hair wash."

Takeaway #5: Invest with Your Time

Getting a startup off the ground is not all about having the cash. To a large degree, the most important investment you can make is your time—what they refer to as "sweat equity."

"In terms of funding, it was literally me, and your time is so valuable, right? I had the experience that I was able to do fifty different formulas. If you went to a lab and needed to change this ten more times, it would probably cost you five to ten thousand dollars. I was able to do whatever I wanted because it was my time, and I really put that investment into the business."

. . .

TAKEAWAY #6: Raise Money with Pitch Competitions

While juggling studying and side-hustle product development, Kailey was short on finances and needed a plan. There are many ways to get financing for your startup, and one of them is through pitch competitions. Kailey took advantage of the many student pitch competitions, realizing there were more opportunities than she originally realized.

"I was still working a little bit on the side. But I was actually able to do these pitch competitions, and there was an opportunity to win money. And I was like, 'OK, this is great.' So I threw together a paycheck. I actually have some photos of me presenting this. And let me tell you, it is really embarrassing about why."

I couldn't resist the temptation of asking why!

"I was calling friends and coworkers and was like, 'Can I put you on a paycheck as part of my team? Because I don't have one. And I need to look like I can do this, and I think I can do it. I just have not prepared for this. But, you know, I could win $100,000!' And people are like, 'Yeah, take the photo from my LinkedIn.' And then with a student competition, I won $10,000, which, in the grand scheme of things, is not a lot. But it was a lot to me as a grad student living in Rochester, New York, with little to no income and now all these student loans for school."

TAKEAWAY #7: You Can Do a Lot with a Little

With the prize money, Kailey spent a few hundred dollars on incorporating the business and $1,000 on filing for a provisional patent. Next, she put up a simple website using Squarespace—just a landing page with an email sign-up. The remainder of the $10,000 lasted Kailey all of 2017 and got her to the point of doing her first pitches, for which she used some of the money to cover travel costs.

For many startup entrepreneurs, it's vital to be savvy with the little capital you have and be super lean with your costs. The early days call for good old-fashioned elbow grease and calling in favors so you can save as many dollars as possible.

"So honestly, you can do a lot with a little as long as you're putting your time in. Our first round was about $475,000, and that got us to launch the company. It got us to launch our first product. But things get very expensive very quickly, as you can probably imagine. And we're based in New York City. So that also is very costly. But you know what? You can make it work. And I think there's so much you can do without having to spend a lot as long as you put the time in. And so to get to where we are today, we've raised about $3.3 million total."

Takeaway #8: It's OK to Just Start Somewhere

Kailey's launch faced two challenges—one being the start of the global pandemic and the other being that she found raising capital takes a lot longer as a female founder. She ended up having a soft launch—one that she described as being "scrappy." She didn't have any PR and hired a few friends to help out. One of the takeaways here is that where you start isn't where you finish—everything is an evolution, and you build on things over time.

"It's OK to just start somewhere. And I think what's really important is you have to try everything. And so that's what we did, called and emailed press, sending out product to influencers, even sending out products to friends. I mean, my mom's friends are still some of our best customers, you know, so don't underestimate your closest family and friends to really help you get out there and spread the word. It's not just about a big launch."

TAKEAWAY #9: Don't Do What Everyone Else Is Doing

Kailey eventually got to do the big launch that she envisioned with her second round, launching the renamed brand as Susteau. Sometimes as a startup entrepreneur fighting for your space in the market, it takes out-of-the-box thinking when it comes to your marketing. It can be a powerful move to approach your marketing with a fresh lens—pinpointing where your customers are but your competitors aren't. That could sometimes mean new platforms or finding new and innovative ways to take up space on the go-to platforms like Instagram and Facebook.

"With the launch of Susteau, we got to do all the traditional influencer marketing, press podcasts, all the fun stuff. I love doing interviews! I love doing digital and Instagram live and super fun Clubhouse. I'm doing my first Clubhouse. So it's like there is a lot that's happening that I just think there's so much opportunity. Just don't do what everyone else is doing is probably my best advice around that because there is always a new platform. There's always something new to experiment with."

TAKEAWAY #10: Don't Limit Yourself with Your Brand Name

After the launch, Kailey immediately set out to fundraise. It took longer than she expected, which she attributes to the challenges of being a female entrepreneur.

"Less than 2 percent of the capital last year was to female founders. And so I know that's part of why you have this podcast and you're so supportive. And it's amazing because everything helps."

A few weeks after closing her seed round, everything started shutting down due to COVID, which presented a big challenge—specifically in getting packaging made. However, looking back, the challenge steered her in a valuable direction.

"The silver lining of this is that I was accepted into an accelerated program. As one of thirteen women from around the world, I had all these amazing boot camp classes. We went through branding, marketing, retail strategy, PR, all of these things. And I had an amazing mentor who gave me so much advice. I realized that I really wanted to take this brand global. I really wanted this more sophisticated brand. And so where Susteau came in is that it really had more meaning and more alignment with what I thought the brand could be doing."

Part of Kailey's thinking around the name change had to do with removing the limits to what kind of products she could incorporate.

"It was also not limited to hair care. I have so many crazy plans that don't just include hair care. So the name comes from sustainability—the *sus* for sustainability and then the *eu* is water in French. And so bringing that together, you have this sustainable water story. And that's really what we're about."

THREE QUICK QUESTIONS

.   .   .

WHAT'S YOUR "WHY"?

"I want to create change beyond what I am capable of as one person. I feel like, OK, I can make these improvements; I can do this small thing, this small change. But I really want to help people do that in their lives, do it in a greater capacity, and also make it fun. So really getting people to rethink what their personal care routines look like and feel like. Like maybe it's fun to wash your hair now, and you're also doing something that's better for the planet."

WHERE DO you hang out to get smarter?

"I am very much in my own head, and I'm very much an ideas person. My best thing for getting smarter is for me to sort everything out, which is actually getting away from anything, especially my phone and my computer. So that means going for a walk or a run or a hike, definitely out of my apartment. I just have to get into a new space so I can sort out what's going on and get into a mindset that gets me ready to go. For me, it's not about watching what other people do because I feel like that influences you to fit in rather than stand out."

HOW DO you deal with failure?

"I say, "Bring it on!" If you don't fail, and you don't take risks, and you don't kind of just see what happens, you're never going to learn. And if you don't learn from failure, then you know that's the problem. The biggest thing is to learn from it and let it happen. Failure is totally normal, and it brings good change."

· · ·

LISTEN to Kailey's episode to find out how she manufactured her first order, who her first employee was, and what needs watering.

28

HINT OF GENIUS

KARA GOLDIN: HOW A MOM TOOK ON THE WORLD'S BIGGEST BEVERAGE BRANDS AND WON

Kara Goldin is the founder of Hint—a healthy lifestyle brand perhaps most famous for its flagship product, Hint Water. Hint Water is a delicious unsweetened flavored water. I'm not saying it's delicious because it says so in a press release. That's from the kazillion five-star reviews online. Fifteen years after it was founded, Hint is the largest nonalcoholic beverage in the US that doesn't have a relationship with Coke, Pepsi, Dr. Pepper, or Snapple. Mind-blowing stuff!

Founded in 2005, the company has grown beyond water to offer products for better, healthier experiences. My interview with Kara was in fact our one hundredth *Female Startup Club* podcast episode, and meeting with such an inspiring female entrepreneur was fitting for the occasion.

Before Hint, Kara had a fascinating career that included working for CNN, Apple, and AOL. After putting her career on pause, she decided to start her own venture (brave with three children under the age of four). The idea came to her after she found that her Diet Coke addiction wasn't helping her weight or health—with sweetener being the culprit.

TAKEAWAY #1: If All Else Fails, a Roll of the Dice Makes a Great Story

Every female startup story begins with the same challenge—a point at which a leap of faith is required. Kara chose to see it as a roll of the dice that would, at worst, show her passion and inspiration to those around her.

"I thought I should just try because if nothing else, it would be a great dinner conversation. They'd say, 'Hey, Kara, what have you been doing since leaving tech?' What if it failed? I thought, *Who cares?* Instead, I could tell people why it inspired me, why I wanted to work on this every day."

TAKEAWAY #2: Find a Product That Impacts People's Lives

Kara's idea started with making an early version of her product at home in an attempt to help her enjoy drinking water more. After being personally satisfied, she began to put the word out there and offer it to others. It's always a brave step because it's that make-or-break moment of truth. But what she found was that she was helping people in an even more meaningful way than she had intended.

"A number of people were saying, 'Your product is helping me control my type 2 diabetes,' which was around 2 percent of the population in the US at the time. Today in the US, forty to forty-five percent of the population has type 2 diabetes or prediabetes. It's not a pandemic. It's an *epidemic.*"

TAKEAWAY #3: Don't Let Anything Get in the Way of Selling

Kara explained in great detail one of the most incredible "go get 'em" entrepreneur stories I've ever heard. It's well worth hearing the full story on the podcast. In brief, Kara was on her fourth pregnancy and was about to have a planned C-section. Her first batch of products arrived two weeks late and were filling up the little space she had in her garage. On the morning of her planned C-section (which was scheduled for 2:00 p.m.), her husband asked her what she wanted to do with her morning. Her reply was as entrepreneurial as it gets.

"I would like to go to Whole Foods and see if we can get our product on the shelf."

After her sales pitch, she went off to the hospital. Later, she received a phone call from the flustered store manager:

"The product is gone . . ."

"What do you mean it's gone?"

"It's sold. You guys need to get some product back in here because I'm going to get in trouble with my boss unless there's more product."

"You sold ten cases overnight?"

"Yeah."

Soup for the Female Entrepreneurs Soul. A pun that would definitely be fitting here is around the importance of hard labor.

TAKEAWAY #4: Figure Things Out Yourself

Despite her initial success, a bumpy road still lay ahead for Kara, with many problems such as how to prolong the product's shelf life. She explained the importance of looking ahead and staying on course. A mindset, or perhaps even a skill, that can be very useful for startup entrepreneurs is to be able to cut out the noise around you and make your own decisions.

"People have said stuff to me my whole life. At the end of the day, you have to figure out if it matters or not. I've had failures along the way. But if you just figure it out instead and be driven by your curiosity and listening to your customers, that is the most important thing that you can do."

TAKEAWAY #5: **Experience Isn't Always Necessary**

Before starting her business, Kara was of the opinion, like many, that one needs to have experience in the industry they are approaching. But after starting, she soon changed her mind.

"So often, it's the people that are curious like me that come into it from a consumer perspective, trying to solve their own problem. And those are actually the people that succeed."

LISTEN **to Kara's episode to find out how she lost weight, why she wrote a book, and what happened that one time she was called "sweetie."**

Talking about being called "Sweetie," here are our
**Top five condescending names that female entrepreneurs
get called:**
Sweetie
Love
Darling
Buttercup
Treacle (UK)

**Top five condescending names that we'd love to answer
with:**
Babycheeks
Mr. Grown-up
Boobywoobybear
Clark Kent
Hot Buns

29

ELECTROLYTES, CAMERA, ACTION!

LAUREN PICASSO: HOW AN ENTREPRENEUR REHYDRATED A MARKET

Sports drinks are a serious business in the US. The once rapid growth has since slowed, and analysts link this with a decline in soda consumption due to health concerns over sugary drinks.

Lauren Picasso is the founder and CEO of Cure Hydration. Cure Hydration is an all-natural, organic electrolyte powder. It has four times the electrolytes of sports drinks but no added or artificial sweeteners. Cure Hydration is based on the science behind oral rehydration solutions, originally developed by the World Health Organization. It's proven to hydrate as effectively as an IV drip (hence the name)!

At the time of our interview, Cure Hydration was sold in more than five thousand stores. Lauren shared her business journey from its beginning to how she validated her idea—a crazy go-to-market launch strategy that landed her thousands of emails—and the top lessons she's learned along the way.

Lauren's father was an entrepreneur who inspired Lauren early on to start her own business. "Especially one that does good," she added. Most of her career was spent in e-commerce and retail, working for successful companies such as the subscription-based fashion rental business Rent the Runway and Jet.com. I wondered how Lauren came across the World Health Organization (WHO) oral rehydration solution and why she decided that was the basis for creating a business.

TAKEAWAY #1: Research the Origin of Trends

Lauren was training for a triathlon and couldn't find a product to replace electrolytes without added sugar. She explained that the average sports drink has thirty-six grams of sugar—gulp!

"I discovered Pedialyte. It was originally made for children, but it was really taking off for adults as an underground hangover cure! That made up about 50 percent of sales . . . And so I started researching effective hydration solutions, stumbled across medical-grade products like Pedialyte, and then started learning about this term *oral rehydration solution*. And that's how I discovered the WHO formula, and there was tons of literature online about the science and all of the key components of the formula that make it effective."

TAKEAWAY #2: Experiment with Your Own Formula

Now that Lauren had done her research, I was curious if she thought the solution needed improvement. If so, how did she go about making that happen, and did she experiment on her own or reach out to a professional?

"It was really about getting that minimum viable product (MVP). I knew I wanted to take the science but replace it with premium and organic ingredients. My original concept was coconut water and pink Himalayan salt. I started mixing these ingredients at home, and I found that the product really worked. But it tasted terrible. So the next step was to find someone who had experience in food science. I experimented with different powders and organic flavors to make the product really pop. Because, at the end of the day, if something doesn't taste good, we're just not going to get consumers to buy it."

Takeaway #3: Be Scrappy

After about a year of developing her formula and getting feedback from people, Lauren decided to leave her nine-to-five and focus on launching her business. I wondered what she learned from her dot-com experience that was mega valuable. Did it carry over into her new venture?

"Absolutely! At Rent the Runway, it was really about being scrappy. Scrappiness was a virtue. When I first started at Rent the Runway, we didn't have a way to actually track our dresses. So we ordered these labels that could be pressed onto the dresses, but we couldn't actually afford to buy an industrial machine to do the pressing. So we had all the girls in the office bring in their hair straighteners, and we sat around pressing twenty thousand labels on dresses. That's just a mindset that I've taken into Cure Hydration—and especially in the early days where we had bootstrapped the first nine months or so."

That is what startup entrepreneurship looks like.

Listening to Lauren reminded me about my own scrappy experience. When I started out in social media marketing, I worked for an online fashion startup in Australia that is pretty big now. In the beginning, our building didn't have internet so we simply used dongles. It was such a funny contradiction: we were running this internet-based business using dongles because we didn't have Wi-Fi. Experiencing these things builds character (and scrappiness).

TAKEAWAY #4: Find Customers through Referrals

Every startup entrepreneur reaches the point where they have to find their first customers. Sometimes this takes creative thinking, and on the show, we've heard many different approaches. In Lauren's case, she focused on a referral strategy.

"We did a prelaunch referral campaign where a user would come to our site, and they were encouraged to refer friends. With each referral, they would unlock prizes. Depending on how many people they would refer, they could win free product lifetime subscriptions, all the way up to our grand prize, which was a Peloton bike. We actually acquired thousands of initial customers that way. And so that cost of the Peloton bike, which is a big bite to chew, ended up being a great ride!"

Word on the street is Viral Loops is a great solution for referral programs—and it's easy to use.

TAKEAWAY #5: Build Momentum Ahead of Fundraising

Lauren's business required quite a bit of capital to get off the ground. Looking at her timeline, I realized she would have to raise capital during a global pandemic, after the outbreak of COVID-19. No pressure, right? How did she do it?

"It's really important to build momentum ahead of your fundraise. It was challenging for us because we needed investment at the beginning of the pandemic, and investors were unsure of what was going to happen. We got funds raised by an alternative capital because we were about to launch in 2,900 stores. We had guaranteed sales, so it was just a matter of time before getting paid by the retailers. I was able to find a debt financing solution, which was a great intermediate. We essentially found a fund that would purchase our invoices from us and that gave us liquidity. So we were profitable. And a lot of investors—especially in this climate—were looking for companies that were self-sufficient and profitable, and that ended up being something that was really differentiating for us."

THREE QUICK QUESTIONS

WHAT'S the number one marketing moment that made your business pop?

"When we announced our seed round of funding, which we waited a few months to share. We wanted to wait until after the election to make sure the news cycle wasn't as crazy as it had been in 2020. And we coincided that with Cyber Monday and Black Friday. So we made the announcement on the Monday before Thanksgiving. And that coincided with a lot of marketing offers and initiatives that we had lined up for that week. We had this big surge of traffic when the press came out. But we also had a lot of really compelling offers. We ended up having the biggest month we've ever had on our website since launch."

WHERE DO you hang out to get smarter?

"I had interpreted that literally and thought, *Where do I hang out right now? At home!* But I will say I've worked alongside my partner now for ten months (since we're both working from home), and I actually think that's made me a lot smarter. I basically got to shadow somebody in an entirely different industry, finance specifically, and I feel like I have a much better understanding of his industry and what he does."

IF YOU ONLY HAD **$1,000** left in your business bank account, where would you spend it?

"I would apply for a business loan, and I would use that $1,000 for the due diligence fee. Often, banks will have some sort of fee associated with giving you a loan for any sort of diligence they have to do. And I think that would be a great way to turn that $1,000 into potentially a much bigger number!"

LISTEN to Lauren's episode to find out how she built her team, what her father taught her about business, and what happened to the lucky customer that won that Peloton bike.

30

A LIL MAGIC

LIL AHENKAN: HOW AN ENTREPRENEUR STARTED BIG CONVERSATIONS

Lillian Ahenkan (aka Flex Mami) is Australia's favorite woman. It's a big title, but many would agree. She's something of a millennial entrepreneurial whirlwind. She's so many things at once—startup entrepreneur, TV presenter, reality TV star, DJ, author, DIY guru, social commentator, media influencer, and podcaster. Whew!

Lil is the CEO and founder of Flex Factory. And FF houses the super popular conversation card game ReFlex, which represents her passion for promoting conversations around mental health, identity, and intersectionality. She's not shy about using her platform to tackle taboo topics—everything from body positivity and sexual liberation to identity and critical thinking—all in the name of giving her followers the tools to be their best selves.

Her efforts have earned her many awards—from being crowned Instagram Young Entrepreneur 2020 to winning E Online's People's Choice Award for Influencer of The Year 2020.

These are the key takeaways from our conversation

around her rise to success and how she built her business, Flex Factory.

Takeaway #1: Introduce Yourself (Loud and Clear!) in Context

Many entrepreneurs wear many hats, and Lil is a prime example of that. It can make an elevator pitch quite complicated. Do you run through your long list of achievements? Do you edit? Lil advises adapting how you describe yourself based on the context of who you're talking to.

"If I'm in a creative space, I'll stick with DJ and MTV Presenter. If I'm meeting someone in an older demographic, I'll just go with, 'I run a business.' It's obnoxious to go through the whole list of slashes, and it just never goes well. It sounds like I'm gloating, and I think when I go through everything I do, it sounds as though I do a lot of things poorly, when in reality, I am very good at all the things I do."

Takeaway #2: Raise Your Children with Positivity

With Lil's undeniably impressive go-getter attitude, she explained how she was influenced by being brought up by a single mom who affirmed unwavering positivity and a sense of gumption (Lil's choice of word). This isn't something we can choose as entrepreneurs, but it is a useful takeaway when it comes to raising confident daughters.

"Growing up in a single-parent household made me aware quite early of the value of money, how I wasn't going to do certain things because of the resources we had or that we didn't benefit from nepotism. But in contrast, my family really instilled a lot of ego in me. They would call me 'princess' and 'boss,' and I just felt a lot of respect in my household. My family always went out of their way to make me feel validated and appreciated."

Lil's mother went to incredible lengths to make her feel special. Lil told me about a time as a child when she felt self-conscious about the large gap between her front teeth. Her mother told her that it was a sign of wealth and beauty in Ghana. Lil wasn't quite convinced, so her mother went to the dentist and had a gap shaved between her front teeth. "It wasn't even about you," she told her daughter, "It's because I really think it's pretty."

Takeaway #3: Differentiate Yourself, Girl!

Around 2018, Lil was enjoying a successful career as a DJ and MTV presenter. But she began to look to the future, wanting to transition to a career less reliant on hype and trend. She looked toward the fast-growing world of social media influencers. Lil's approach is an inspirational one as she wasn't deterred by not fitting into the typical influencer mold of bikini bodies and inspirational quotes. Instead, with that infectious "Lil confidence," she created a space for herself.

"I don't like to compete where I don't compare, and there was a very specific look for an influencer that I didn't have, and so I was like, 'I need to make my own land. I need to do something completely different.'"

Considering her strengths, Lil realized that she had always been the type of person that likes to have big conversations. She enjoyed asking hypothetical questions and was interested in the way people think. So she began posting daily questions and would share the responses.

"It would start this huge dialogue, and it was so cool to me because I noticed that what I had that my other peers didn't have was an audience that humanized them. I wasn't just a body and entertainment. I was a person with thoughts, and I was a facilitator of something far bigger than this discussion. I was helping people build their understanding of the world."

Takeaway #4: Test and Then Validate

Lil wanted to produce a physical product to sell but knew that she didn't want to do the typical DJ thing and make T-shirts and hoodies. Her best friend (and future business partner), Grace, suggested the idea of turning her popular questions into a card game. Without too much pressure or ambition, they gave it a go. With good old-fashioned startup scrappiness, they printed one hundred sets at a local printer, sorted and packed the cards in their living room, and put them up for sale on the online selling platform Big Cartel. The cards sold for around ten dollars, and with the low production quantities, there wasn't a profit to be made. But it was an exercise in validation.

The cards were an instant success and sold out overnight. Finding the home production, hand packing, trips to the post office, and little profit tedious, Lil resisted producing more. But there was an instant backlash from her audience, who were desperate to get their hands on more product. Seeing the business potential, Grace agreed to take on the daily slog herself.

Takeaway #5: Sometimes Your Winning Idea Is Easy

For a while, Lil took her hands off the card business, feeling that she had already gotten the validation from it that she wanted. But its success made her pause and think about whether this was something she should focus on.

Grace offered Lil some really insightful advice, and it can be useful for other entrepreneurs to think about. Entrepreneurs often try their hand at many different ventures and ideas. Typically, most require great effort, but sometimes the idea that ends up being the winning concept happens surprisingly easily. And sometimes we feel guilty or unworthy of that success.

"Grace was like, 'I think this is what you actually want to do. I just don't think you like the fact that you didn't work very hard for it. I think you're fighting against this fact that it was simple and easy.' And it's true because my therapist would say the same thing: 'You like the struggle; you like to break your back a little bit so everyone can see how hard you worked and that you suffered.' And this just felt too easy."

After that realization, Lil and Grace got serious about turning their card game venture into a business. They rebranded their packaging and renamed their product to ReFlex, as the idea was to answer the questions on reflex. They pulled apart the numbers while also considering their manufacturing options. The next thing they did was create a website that they called "Flex Factory," where they talked about their values—creating connection through conversation.

Takeaway #6: Go to Market, the Organic Kind

Rather than spending on paid advertising, Lil used every opportunity she could from her exciting platform to market the game.

"It just became this circular marketing exercise. The

more I just maintained my profile, the more I talked about the game, the greater audience share we'd have just by existing."

In the first year, the pair did $800,000 worth of sales.

THREE QUICK QUESTIONS

WHAT'S YOUR "WHY"?

"I'm sick of having conversations I don't care about, and I think that issue was only exacerbated by the fact that I interact with strangers on a daily basis and the quality of those conversations was not improving. So this was my solution, which I recognized as a greater issue on a far larger scale, and I just want us to remember that the only thing stopping you from getting what you want, improving your life, whatever, is a conversation."

WHERE DO you hang out to get smarter?

"There's this newsletter called the Growth Marketing newsletter by Julian Shapiro. They basically give you all these really actionable, easy, insightful tips on how to grow and market, but they put case studies and results and links to other resources, and they're fresh tips. Also, I love the Shopify blog. I think it's very underrated. I get so much information from there."

HOW DO you win the day?

"The only way I can properly win the day is if I action off one priority from every business I have. So it means that everything gets care, and I don't feel like I'm neglecting everything, but I don't put pressure on myself to have a game-changing moment every day. And I also know there are not enough hours in the day for me to resource everything equally. So allowing myself to create just small priorities."

LISTEN to Lil's episode to find out what her biggest marketing trick is, why she decided to manufacture locally, and why you shouldn't sell a T-shirt.

31

TAKING A BITE

LINDSAY MCCORMICK: HOW AN ENTREPRENEUR IS CHANGING HOW WE BRUSH OUR TEETH

Lindsay McCormick is the cofounder and CEO of Bite. Bite is on a mission to upend the oral care industry with innovative products that are made with the planet in mind. Former TV producer Lindsay started the company with two questions in mind: Why does toothpaste come in plastic tubes? And what exactly are we putting in our bodies when we brush our teeth?

Bite scored more than $3 million in revenue in 2019. Lindsay received many investment offers, famously including one Mark Cuban on *Shark Tank*. Lindsay and Asher Hunt, cofounder and COO, have managed to retain 100 percent ownership, enabling them to put the environment first when making choices. We discussed how Lindsay started her business in her living room, taking online chemistry classes, and Googling "how do people make drugs."

Lindsay was a successful TV producer, which meant plenty of traveling. As someone passionate and mindful about the environment, Lindsay noticed that—unlike with her refillable shampoo, conditioner, and mouthwash—she was constantly throwing away little toothpaste tubes.

"I was thinking, *This feels so wasteful. I feel like I've done so much with the rest of my stuff, so why can't I figure out tooth-paste?* I started looking into alternatives like tooth powder and tablets that were on the market, but they were all in plastic. And so that was the beginning of this process for me. It was like, 'OK. I want this so I can take it on shoots for my job. I'm going to start making it.' I started looking into the ingredients of most toothpastes, and I thought, *Wow. There was a bunch of stuff in there that I didn't want in my body every day.*"

That really gave me food for thought or something to chew on. It's amazing how much care we take looking at the back of the box or bottle, scanning the label for ingredients in other products! I had never thought of checking out my toothpaste.

Takeaway #1: Take a Course

Lindsay set about educating herself. She is a living testament to how we can take control and teach ourselves about a new trade. Even if we have absolutely no experience, there are plenty of courses to close the gap. There are more accessible and budget-friendly options to study than ever before thanks to online learning. You can also connect with and talk to a range of professionals, who are often more than happy to share their knowledge.

"I started taking online chemistry classes and talking with dentists and dental hygienists. I started making the first iterations of what Bite was in my toaster oven at that time! So that's how it all started. And I definitely did not set out to make a business, but after I started investing in machinery

and time, I was like, 'Well, I might as well sell this on Etsy
and Shopify and see if other people want it.'"

Takeaway #2: Invest in Proper Machinery

Lindsay started humbly, working at home with basic
household tools. It was a good place to start and an inexpensive way to work out what was needed.

"At first, it was just me in my—I say, lab–dining-room—
and I would just sit there all night and research different
ingredients. I'd buy things from Whole Foods, Amazon, and
a website called Chemistry Connection. I needed a tablet-
making machine, but they are complicated and expensive.
So I bought a pastry kit, and I was trying to take the powders
and pipe them out of a pastry bag. I was like, 'Maybe I could
do this, and I can bake it?' And I set my toaster oven on fire,
and I was like, 'OK. I can't bake it.'"

After playing around with home solutions, Lindsay realized she needed a more industrial machine. Many startups
require some initial investment, and it's important to put
that into perspective. What may seem like a big personal
expense at the time is relatively small or justified when
framed as a business investment.

"And so then I thought, *OK, fine. I have to invest in this
machine.* It was $1,000, which now, looking back, was
nothing to start a business. To find out what kind of
machine I needed, I had to spend time in the deep holes of
Reddit. And I was actually looking up how to make drugs.
There is for sure an FBI watch list of my search history
because I was Googling, 'How do you make tablets?'"

Takeaway #3: Start with a Simple Website

Lindsay surveyed family and friends, who gave her invaluable feedback for developing the product further. She started with an Etsy page, choosing to start simple and get her products online in the quickest and most inexpensive way. By simply getting started somewhere, you create an opportunity to establish what is the best next step through experience.

"I actually took it down from Etsy and put it on Shopify because there I was able to make a site. I don't have a tech background. At first, my Shopify site was literally photos from my iPhone of my product. Like, on a template. It did not look great, and most of the people who bought from me at first . . . I recognized every single name."

TAKEAWAY #4: Don't Be Facebook Shy

For some female startup entrepreneurs, putting yourself out there and posting regularly about your product can feel forced, even unnatural. In our personal lives, we may choose to be humble and private, to say less. But it's important to realize that being outspoken in business marketing is not a reflection of how we conduct our personal lives.

"I'm not necessarily a shy person, but I'm not a very big 'this is me and what I'm doing' person. So I had to get over that, and the way that I would think about it was that I didn't want to post on my Facebook, but I saw it as something that's so important to me: the billion toothpaste tubes that end up in our landfills every year. And just being so motivated that I was like, 'This is my job, and I need to get over my shyness and just post.'"

It can feel disheartening when your initial audience is exclusively family and friends. But that's often an early launching pad and not a sign it's already time to give up.

"The first customers were all friends and family. And I still remember the first time where I saw someone's name, then I looked on Facebook, and I was like, 'No! I don't know that person.' I thought, *Oh my gosh! How? How did this happen?* So I still remember when it started to cross that chasm."

TAKEAWAY #5: Go Viral

OK, not the most useful takeaway because we'd all go viral if we knew the secret formula, but Lindsay made a video that went viral. It garnered over two million views in two days! The previous year, she brought in about $6,000 worth of sales. Within the first few days of her video going viral, she had generated over $200,000 in revenue!

TAKEAWAY #6: Go Local with Your Manufacturing

Although startup entrepreneurs often seek out foreign manufacturers, there can be wisdom in keeping things local —both in having more control and the ability to meet face to face, as well as supporting other local businesses.

"So there's the beginning of the business when you're doing it all yourself in your living room (which I'm sure so many people are in), and that's such a great space. I was so happy, and I was really in love with the process. Then, once that happened, we now have customers and expecta-tions, and we need to become a business. I want the busi-ness to make things better for people. So I was like, 'I want to stay in the LA area. I want to support the community that I'm in.' That meant finding manufacturers that I could go in and meet and know and support other small businesses. So that really significantly cut down who I could work with, but it also made things really easy and simple."

THREE QUICK QUESTIONS

What's your "why"?

"Wanting to protect the planet. When I first started, I would watch the documentary *Plastic Ocean* whenever I felt really discouraged. It's a really sad documentary, but I would watch it, and then I would cry my eyes out, and I would be like, 'OK, back to work!' And it's the idea that we really do need to make some changes. It really will be the outsiders. The girls who are learning chemistry in their living room are the ones who will take on these problems."

IF YOU HAD $1,000 dollars left in your bank account, how would you spend it?

"It would definitely be on ads because it puts more money in your bank account. So I would say probably Google because things have been really crazy on Instagram and Facebook. Especially with the elections, our ads were being taken down as "political" because apparently plastic is political, which doesn't make any sense to me. There are actually quite a few other brands that are in our space that I've been talking to, and the same thing happened to them. But you want to make sure that you're really building a solid foundation on Facebook, Instagram, Google Ads, TikTok, YouTube, influencers, everything."

How DO you deal with failure?

"Failure is great. That's what is going to get you to where

you want to go. It doesn't feel good at the time, but every single time you fail, you can look back, and you've learned a lesson. Failure makes you stronger, and that's 100 percent true. So you want to fail a lot. You want to fail fast. You want to learn from your failures and embrace that part of the process."

LISTEN to Lindsay's episode to find out her thoughts on *Shark Tank*, the ways she kept up the momentum after going viral, and the power of vegans.

32

SKIN IN THE GAME

LINDSEY MARTIN: HOW AN ENTREPRENEUR ADDED JOY AND WHIMSY TO SKINCARE

Lindsey Martin is the founder and CEO of Kiramoon, a skincare brand that's challenging the way effective skincare can be delivered. Their holy-grail, science-backed products are infused with the joy and whimsy of super cute packaging, and the brand has quickly gained a cult following on social media. When I spoke to Lindsey, she explained how she started her brand, from finding the manufacturer to branding, her influencer strategy, and their epic launch.

Like so many startup entrepreneurs, Lindsey was inspired by growing up with an entrepreneurial parent. She witnessed the highs and lows of her father's journey as an entrepreneur, and seeing how rewarded and fulfilled he was when his business was successful planted the seed of entrepreneurial spirit in Lindsey from a young age.

Now thirty-five, Lindsey started her entrepreneurial journey at around thirty. Prior to that, she had a successful corporate career working for a large software company. Looking to the future, she wondered whether working her way up the ladder to becoming the CEO of a software firm was what she really wanted. She decided that her real dream would be to have a company of her own, which got her thinking about what she might do.

During her stressful years of corporate work, she highly valued her skincare routine as a time of relaxation and personal reward. With her eyes open to possible startup business ideas, Lindsey considered the skincare products that she loved and noticed something missing:

"I looked at the packaging, and it felt like it was really only catering to one aesthetic. It was very clinical, and it was white and black and cream. And I just thought to myself, *We can do better. These are magic potions that put a smile on my face. Why is the packaging kind of lackluster?*"

Takeaway #1: Consider What You Want Your Life to Look Like

When Lindsey was considering her options, she had an important conversation with a girlfriend. Her friend posed the question: "If you could do anything, if money was no object, what would you do?" It's an important question for everyone to ask themselves at some point in their career (and life).

"There's this sort of momentum of life that we're pushed through. You go to school, and you decide what you want to be when you grow up, and then you're supposed to work and maybe become a manager. And I think it's so important to have the courage and honesty with yourself to stop and say, 'Am I happy?'"

Lindsey admitted that it's a scary question to ask because it may cause a realization that can't be undone. One of the obstacles she faced, and I imagine this is a common one, was the intimidating choice to let go of one's career identity.

"For a lot of women and men who do a career shift in midlife like I am, I think you lose a part of your identity. I really identified with the career that I had before. So much of my confidence came from that career. But I knew I had to take a few steps back and start over to get to a greater long-term outcome."

TAKEAWAY #2: Make Sure Your Brand Name Is Available

Often, the first step of creating a new thing is picking a name for your brand. It's vital that you do your research to find out if the name is available—both in terms of incorporation, online domain availability, and trademarking.

"You need to pick a name. Make sure that you're not infringing on anyone's IP. Make sure the domains and social handles are available. I made the mistake early on of picking a name before I checked with an IP attorney, and I got kind of far in the development and then had to pivot."

TAKEAWAY #3: Sell Yourself to Manufacturers

Lindsey found that her biggest obstacle to getting started was finding a manufacturer that not only was trustworthy but also had minimum starting orders that she could afford. Entrepreneurs looking to manufacture often have this obstacle around minimum orders, and it can take a lot of cold calling and research to find the right fit. Lindsey contacted over fifty manufacturers, and what she found was that she had to put effort into selling herself to them—most simply replied with an automated email, explaining the minimum orders in an effort to weed people out. In hindsight, Lindsey suspected that many manufacturers ignored her inquiries because she was emailing from a personal Gmail account.

"To anyone listening that wants to start a beauty brand, that is something you're going to come up against. You have to sell yourself. Let them know why they should take a risk on you. Why is your product different? What hole in the market are you filling?"

TAKEAWAY #4: Prioritize Investment in Branding

Lindsey realized that getting the right visual branding for her business was vital. Perhaps more than ever before in history, because of the power of social media, visual branding can make or break a new brand.

"I knew that branding was going to be such an important part of Kiramoon. It needed to be shareable. I wanted it to have that 'take it out of the box when you buy it and immediately want to take a photo of it.' So that's kind of the North Star for everything that we do."

Lindsey Googled and searched on Behance and eventually found a top-tier branding agency that she loved. They took care of the full brand identity, including packaging, photography, website, and social media, and it ended up costing Lindsey around $30,000. Lindsey explained that for a self-funding startup, this was a scary leap to make, but she found it invaluable to her success.

"I think that investing in the branding and making sure you picked the right partner is so important. And I just feel really lucky that I got it right the first time."

TAKEAWAY #5: Build an Online Community as Early as Possible

Often, entrepreneurs will only start considering their online presence once they have their product ready, but Lindsey found that building an online community far before her launch was fundamental to her success. She started her social media campaign around a year before launch, but she admits that this wasn't an intentional strategy as she thought her products would be available a lot quicker.

"I think leading up to the launch, the thing that really helped us was community. We built a community early on; I was very open with them, transparent about what I was doing, what I was working on. I sent out our little promo item, and then I did a lot of teasing and hype type posts. So that was all, like, the magic potion that together led to a really successful launch."

Takeaway #6: Target Realistically Sized Influencers

Prior to launch, Lindsey had a promotional product—an iridescent makeup bag called "The Magic Pouch." She contacted one hundred influencers, each with followers ranging from two thousand to eighty thousand. Lindsey was nervous about how influencers would respond, but she found that her bravery paid off. While we often think of celebrity influencers as being the holy grail, Lindsey's strategy proved that more realistically sized microinfluencers are where you can generate some real buzz.

"I wasn't reaching out to Kim Kardashian. It was nano- and microinfluencers, people that I knew weren't just going to ignore me. Every single person replied, and I got their information, and I sent the pouch with these little postcards I got made on Vistaprint that had some cute branding. It wasn't very costly; I think with shipping and packaging and

everything it was maybe five dollars each. I think the important thing is that you're targeting realistic influencers and
don't be intimidated."

THREE QUICK QUESTIONS

**What's the number one marketing moment that made
your business pop?**

"The traffic that I've gotten from TikTok. I think most of
the buyers that have reached out to me found us through
one of my viral TikTok videos."

WHERE DO you hang out to get smarter?

"I used to hang out listening to podcasts before I had an
amazing group of founder friends. I really loved *Second Life*,
which is a podcast that interviews women who have made a
career pivot and have gone on to be really successful in their
second life, similar to some of the people that you speak to.
Now I have such an incredible network of beauty brand
founders that have become like my family and my best
friends. And I learned so much from them, and I hope vice
versa."

*Find out more about Hype Club, our own private network for
female startup entrepreneurs, which we launched after hearing so
many people credit their network as invaluable support. Details
at the end of the book.*

HOW DO you win the day?

"My newest habit that's been really helpful for me is, in
the morning, I write down a list of five or six things I have to
get done during the day that are the most important. That's

been so crucial to me because as a solo producer or even as a founder with a partner, the early days in a business are so chaotic. You're doing so many different things, and you're constantly getting DMs and emails and phone calls, and it's very hard to stay focused."

LISTEN to Lindsey's episode to find out how much it cost her to self-fund her venture, what gave her the confidence to quit her day job, and how important it is to make customers smile.

33

CURL POWER

MAEVA HEIM: HOW AN ENTREPRENEUR BROUGHT HAIR CARE TO AN OVERLOOKED MARKET

Maeva Heim is the founder of Bread Beauty Supply (or just Bread for short). Bread is a hair care line for curly hair that aims to simplify hair care for those with 3A–4C curls. A recent article I was reading about Maeva said it perfectly: "This new hair care line wants to make 'lazy girl hair' an option for Black folks too." I actually met Maeva by chance in 2019, when I was in Melbourne visiting a girlfriend, and I randomly recognized her voice from a podcast that I'd listened to her speak on before! Maeva stepped me through how she launched exclusively with Sephora, what she's learned so far on her entrepreneurial journey, and what things resulted in a few giggles along the way.

Maeva's journey to being an entrepreneur was a long one that started with her entrepreneur mom; her mom had a hair salon "in a tiny, little garage at the back of an Italian restaurant." Maeva worked for many years in the corporate world, including within the beauty industry for brands such as L'Oréal. It was there that she spotted a problem she wanted to find a solution for.

"I just got to a point where I was really fed up with the beauty industry. I was behind the scenes of this enormous corporation, working on some of the biggest brands in the world. And I didn't feel like those brands were talking to me. There weren't many foundation shades in the market for women who look like me and women with darker skin tones. I really saw that as, one, a huge problem and, two, an opportunity to potentially start my own brand."

TAKEAWAY #1: You Don't Have to Be Powerful to Make an Impact

Although Maeva had spotted a problem, she initially felt she had to be a powerful industry leader to really make an impact. But her story, like so many others I have heard, proved that theory wrong.

"I felt like you have to be in a position of power in order to really have the effects trickle down into the market. And I remember complaining about this to my partner one day and saying there aren't enough female founders in beauty that have massive companies. There aren't enough Black women CEOs of these big companies that can make decisions to impact the market."

Her partner gave her a push in the right direction:

"He was like, well, what are you going to do about it? And it was kind of that moment that I was like, oh, well, I guess I could do something about it."

TAKEAWAY #2: Picture Your Customer

Maeva's original plan was to start a makeup company with one hundred different shades. Then, on a trip to Colorado, her hair-straightening product exploded in her bag, and it got her thinking how unhealthy these chemicals were. That led her down the rabbit hole of considering hair products for African American hair types, and she realized that the market was seriously lacking innovation.

In crafting her brand, Maeva put a lot of emphasis on being relatable to her target market. Being relatable and accessible in your brand's tone of voice has proved to be an effective strategy for many successful startups.

"I think that a lot of the brand and the vibe and the aesthetic has been driven by this woman that I was seeing online who wasn't being spoken to by other brands in this space. And so I was looking at these brands. A lot of them were heritage brands with a look and feel that was very polished and glossy. The way this woman presented herself was completely in opposition to what you would see in the market. I thought that there had to be room for a brand like Bread, to be a product that you'd be really proud to have on your bathroom shelf and that aligns with her identity."

TAKEAWAY #3: Stick to Your Vision

So far, Maeva hasn't found it all that easy to translate her vision through a team. It's true that no one else will have quite the same understanding of the vision as the founder. This can be a stumbling block, and part of the founder's job description is to ultimately relay their vision effectively to a team. But nevertheless, there's no substitute for being hands-on.

"I worked with multiple different people to bring it all together. But I think, in the end, a lot of it was my gut. That has probably been one of the most difficult pieces of building this brand. Because when you have an idea in your head and you know what you want something to look like, it can be very difficult for somebody else to translate something that exists only in your mind. And, of course, when you're working with designers, designers want to design. But if you already have a strict idea of what you want, it can be really difficult to rein people back and be like, 'No, we don't need new concepts.' And we're still on that path of finding a team who can really translate that vision into tangible things because a lot of that work I still do myself."

TAKEAWAY #4: Validate Your Idea with Data

Maeva's first step was to validate her idea by gathering data. It's one thing to have an idea in our heads of what we think the market needs and wants. But it's vital to gather data and find out if our thinking is correct.

"It's so funny because I was in this phase for so long of listening to all the podcasts, going to all the conferences, reading all the founder stories. And that was always my one question: what is the first thing that you did? Because I felt so stuck even when I landed on this concept and even though I knew that this was what I wanted to build. There was still so much push and pull about 'What do I do first?'

The first thing that I did was figure out if other people would agree with my thinking. I was scraping the internet, any kind of market research that I could find for free that would validate that there were other people that would need this. Just getting that data and getting those insights made me feel really confident about the direction and made me really feel good about how we would position this story to investors or to retailers or whoever it might be."

TAKEAWAY #5: Network at Conferences

Maeva's vision was to impact the market, and to do that, she knew that she would have to go large. She set her sights on the mega-retailer Sephora, and her next challenge was how to connect with them. Cold calling sucks even though it does the job half of the time, IMO, but in most cases, there's nothing more valuable than a warm introduction or, failing that, a chance to introduce yourself face-to-face. Networking at conferences can be a great way to do this.

"Going the traditional route of finding someone's email and sending an email to a buyer is probably not going to get you through. I knew that there was an opportunity to potentially speak to a Sephora executive at events. That's one way that I've been able to meet different people and build relationships. So I ended up going to this conference in LA, and I knew that there was going to be a Sephora representative speaking. She kind of went off to get some lunch and was just wandering around, and I approached her, and I just introduced myself, said, 'I'm working on this brand. What is your advice for being able to get a meeting with a buyer?'"

Maeva had success, and the Sephora representative was open to finding out more.

"She was like, 'Do you have product samples?' And I had some really early product samples at the time. I said, 'Yeah, I've got some samples, and I've got a brand.' And she said, 'Well, here's my card. Email me the deck, and I'll get it to the right person.' How easy was that? I thought, *Was that too easy? I don't know. I just asked for advice. And now you're going to connect me with the buyer!*"

THREE QUICK QUESTIONS

. . .

HOW DO you win the day?

"I think one of my big things is my dog—just having her there and being able to take that break in the middle of the day [to] take her out to the dog park and watch her run around. It gives me so much joy. Aside from that, creating a workspace that feels really aspirational and looks amazing makes me feel so much more legitimate and encourages me to work hard and bring everything to fruition."

WHERE DO you hang out to get smarter?

"When I was working at L'Oréal, I would walk to work every day and have an audiobook in my ear. I was listening to books like *The Magic of Thinking Big* and *The Hard Thing about Hard Things* and all of those kinds of startup classics. Also, books by Eckhart Tolle. But right now, the main place that I am learning new things is Twitter. It's often the first place that I find things out, whether it's news, whether it's industry, whether it's insights on consumers and what other brands are doing. I feel ahead of the curve because content on Twitter filters through to Instagram etc, but it generally starts on Twitter."

HOW DO you deal with failure?

"My approach to failure is almost like a disconnect from failure. I think a lot of that mindset has been driven by reading books by Eckhart Tolle and understanding the ego, and also understanding that everything is malleable and changeable and that you don't always have control over things. And so, when there is a failure, it's not necessarily like a denial of reality. But I do have this sense of, OK, . . . the failure happened. You can't go back in history and change things. There's absolutely no point in exerting energy on that. The only thing you can do is think about what's next and the possibility of something new. You can't have happiness without sadness. You cannot have success without failure."

LISTEN to Maeva's episode to find out how she got funding for her business, how she worked with influencers, and what cliché turned out to be her best advice.

34

CHAPTER AND VERSED

MELANIE BENDER: HOW AN ENTREPRENEUR MADE CLEAN BEAUTY ACCESSIBLE TO ALL

Melanie Bender is the founding general manager of Versed. The skincare brand launched as the first community-driven mass beauty brand and the first clean skincare line to debut in over 1,850 stores as part of Katherine Power's Who What Wear fashion empire. Known as the cleanest drugstore skincare brand out there, Versed prides themselves on selling at drugstore prices while still containing high-end ingredients such as squalane, vitamin C, and glycolic acid. Within their first nine months, the brand was outselling mega brands such as Burt's Bees and Olay.

Driven by a team of skin experts and a community of sixteen million people, their mission is to make clean products for all (planet included). Melanie explained the importance of gathering data to drive forward brand building and keeping creativity as a core focus, as well as what's driving the brand's growth today.

Takeaway #1: No Education Is Wasted
Melanie explained that she was always someone who

was incredibly curious. She loves learning different things, learning how things connect with people, and understanding how they're interacted with. She studied aerospace engineering and global environmental science—a pretty far cry from the beauty industry, but maybe not entirely.

Many entrepreneurs have found that previous education in a sphere that seems completely different ends up being invaluable. An example that comes to mind is Steve Jobs taking a summer course about typographic fonts. While seemingly far from computers, it ultimately helped with Apple's enviable UX design. Melanie found her education came to her benefit too.

"I clearly had no idea I wanted to get into beauty. But it gave me this really awesome foundation for scientific theory and thinking, forming hypotheses and testing them from a really strong engineering perspective, and understanding operationally, 'How do you put things together?'"

Takeaway #2: Communities Are Great for Gathering Data

Melanie had a successful career in marketing, which led to her giving an industry talk. This is where she met panelist Katharine Power. I'm a big fan of Katharine, but for those of you who haven't heard of her, she's an American entrepreneur that cofounded Clique Brands (including "Who What Wear"), which produces trend reports, celebrity style guides, wardrobe how-tos, and fashion news, as well as a line of fashion apparel and accessories with Target. Impressed by Melanie, Katherine quickly offered her a job in marketing. Shortly after getting started, Melanie heard that Katherine was interested in new product development, and she quickly put her hand up.

"She gave really incredible direction as to the vision for

the brand that she wanted to see. Something that was very digitally driven, that was in beauty, in this really growing, exciting industry that was powered by the community that she had built."

Melanie harnessed the power of building a community around the brand. Besides the opportunity to build a loyal following and gain word-of-mouth marketing, communities can be very useful as a way to gather data.

"The community continues to be the beating heart of our brand, and where other brands are found or driven or influencer driven or even retail driven, we're driven by our community. It just was like this explosive experience of having so much information, so much depth, but also so much connection. It's connected to the people using our products every day. We have a private Facebook creation group, which now has over sixteen thousand people. We do surveys that reach two thousand people, and it's in knitting all those data points together that we really navigated each step of the journey."

Takeaway #3: Democratize a Trend

I've seen so many successful businesses with a similar objective—to break down the barriers to a trend and make it accessible to the mass market. Trends are often first marketed to the elite consumer at expensive price points, but once the trend has taken off, there is often opportunity to bring it to the masses.

"Many consumers saw the clean movement happening around them. But it felt like it wasn't for them. It was for people with access, with income, with the right connections. And that was what was really the exciting moment for us, this opportunity to take this movement that we so believed in and were already benefiting from and make that something for everyone, really democratizing the access to it."

Takeaway #4: Make Your Brand Relatable

One of the first steps in making a trend accessible to the masses is helping them understand it. Trends come with plenty of new jargon and new concepts to grasp, so explaining and educating in a relatable way is vital.

"Price point is a huge barrier. How it's distributed is a huge barrier. But also just making it easy to understand, not treating it like it's rocket science. The biggest outcome of creating with our community is really the breaking down of those barriers."

Takeaway #5: Be Transparent with Your Customers

Melanie's approach with marketing to her community was based on full transparency. Many brands hide behind a glossy veneer with slick marketing. But consumers can really appreciate when they feel a brand is being transparent and honest. It engenders trust and results in customer loyalty.

"Connecting with our community gave this desire and even imperative for transparency. And when there's transparency, you're held accountable to everything you're doing as a business. From how you're sourcing your products to the claims that you're making, the imagery you're using, and who's on the team around you. I think that's been to us something that's beautiful (and scary at times too), to really prioritize transparency because there's nothing to hide behind, like your airbrushing and your luxurious imagery, your beautiful merchandising displays . . . But for us, it was really about building this entire brand for the community that we were serving ultimately."

Takeaway #6: Spend Where It Counts Most

Melanie faced a challenge in seeing her vision through, which was to have the high-end active ingredient of the luxury competition but still have an affordable price point. There were two strategies she had to achieve this. For the first, Melanie reaffirmed what my mother (and probably yours too) had always said, which is that "it's what's inside that counts." Instead of weighing down the product cost by producing expensive packaging, she prioritized the ingredients.

"The biggest cost between a mass product and a prestige product is the packaging. When you see a beautiful prestige product, and it's got that custom jar or bottle that you don't see anywhere else, you're paying a lot for that. That's a custom mold. It probably costs more than what's going inside of it. So we made some very deliberate decisions about our packaging."

Melanie's second strategy was to focus on using the right ingredients. She steered clear of the latest trendy ingredients that were still in the phase of being overpriced.

"There's something that I learned from my time in beauty manufacturing. There's this practice of using 'marketing ingredients.' So you put just enough of something on-trend in there. It's something to talk about in the packaging, but it's not in there at an active level. So it's not going to benefit your skin, but it's still adding to the cost profile of the product. We focused on the most readily accessible, active ingredients. Instead of the buzzy new ingredient that everyone was pushing out this season and next season, we focused on the tried and true. These ingredients are a lot more cost efficient because so many people are buying into them."

THREE QUICK QUESTIONS

WHAT'S YOUR "WHY"?

"I love the alliteration "People Planet Profit." People, because ultimately, in everything I've done, I really strive to have an emotional connection. Planet, because everything we hold dear in life is supported by this incredible planet that we're on. Profit, because by building a thriving business, I can do more of the first two P's."

WHAT'S the number one marketing moment that made your business pop?

"It's all about people talking about us. It starts with values—creating something that you think has an impact, that you think is worth something. Twenty years ago, you might have paid someone to host a press conference for you or a celebrity to star in your campaign. That's not what people care about today. So, for me, the best marketing is the values that we've built into the brand and really inviting people in to be a part of them."

WHERE DO you hang out to get smarter?

"I'm a total podcast nerd. I love podcasts for going deep into a topic. I love *Freakonomics* and *Planet Money*. *How to*

Save a Planet is really incredible too. I also still subscribe to the *New York Times*; we get the paper in the mail."

LISTEN to Melanie's episode to find out how she launched her brand with Target, what she thinks about airbrushing skin, and how she wrote herself a new job description.

35

I'LL DRINK TO THAT!

MELANIE MASARIN: HOW AN ENTREPRENEUR MADE A NONALCOHOLIC APÉRITIF COOL

Melanie Masarin is the founder and CEO of Ghia—producing the hottest new spirit-free apéritif on the block. Their social tonic is inspired by the Mediterranean *aperitivo* culture, and it's made entirely from botanical extracts (I found myself taking a guilt-free sip at 11:28 a.m.) Melanie bravely launched the brand earlier this year, during the COVID-19 pandemic. I spoke to her about her light bulb moment and her step-by-step lead-up to the launch.

Although she fondly remembers lazy days in the Mediterranean and her grandmother's famous limoncello, Melanie had stopped drinking altogether because of a troubled stomach. Not drinking led to constant "you're boring" comments, and Melanie wondered what she could replace alcohol with in social settings. Soda wasn't a great idea because it's packed with sugar, and water was not a great solution to the "you're boring" feedback. One day in Italy, while having lunch with friends, they got talking about whether to order an extra pasta, and that led to how much they were drinking.

"We started having this conversation about what we eat versus what we drink and how this kind of health and wellness movement has really impacted how we think about food every day. But it just hasn't moved at all to drinks like alcohol. Brands don't even have to disclose what's in it. You have to say it's X percent alcohol, but you don't have to say what the ingredients are. You don't have to say what the sugar content is. There's just nothing disclosed."

This was Melanie's light bulb moment. Her first realization was about an idea for a new product, and her second was to order that second pasta because life is short.

TAKEAWAY #1: Look to the Market in Other Countries

A good business idea can be something that is successful in another country but doesn't exist in a meaningful way in your own hometown. Products in other countries can make for great research with proven figures and business models.

"The UK is where all these brands really started—I think because drinking is so ingrained in the culture. With pop culture and with drinking starting even before dinner, I would have thought that it would be the last country to maybe move to alcoholic-free beverages. But actually, they were really the leader, with something like over one hundred brands that have started over the past few years. So that was kind of our case study."

TAKEAWAY #2: Develop Your Product on Feedback

Melanie's first obstacle was to create the formula, and after speaking to many people in the industry, she found a like-minded specialist. She went through eighty-seven iterations over a year, each time getting feedback from friends and family to perfect her formula.

"It's very difficult to create a beverage that will have many notes, that will be very complex, but that will be made entirely of extracts. We were also trying to figure out how we make a drink that people can actually afford. It was also hard to create something that is concentrated but that provides value for the customers. We ended up concentrating even more so that it would be a better value per serving for them while remaining really clean. But then you have all these really potent extracts, and you don't have booze to preserve it. So how do you create a formula that's chemically stable? That was a big challenge for us."

Takeaway #3: Hire People in Your Network

Melanie realized she needed operational help and wanted to hire a COO early on. Melanie decided to turn to her network—to seek someone that she had worked with before. In many cases, a good network can be invaluable to a startup entrepreneur.

"I think for a lot of startups, you should hire people you know because you've worked with them before. I ended up hiring Henry, who was a friend that I have known for many years, who actually used to run an agency that I had worked with. He helped me really figure out the operations and the legal part of the business. We knew that there would be a lot of trademark challenges. We want to be global eventually. And so we wanted to protect our intellectual property, and there was just so much to do."

.   .   .

TakeAway #4: Get Advice from Entrepreneurs in Your Network

Melanie needed to raise capital for Ghia—or rather "her business" because the name hadn't been thought of yet. It was a tall order given that she didn't have a name or a deck or lots of market data as it wasn't an alcoholic drink or a soda—it was a new, unproven concept.

"I started tapping some people, entrepreneurs that I admire in my network, to get their advice and find out what they thought of it. They had all worked with me before and said, 'Do it, I'll invest!' And I think that was the vote of confidence that I needed. It was those first checks that were good anchors for me to be able to go out to people that I didn't know as well and say, 'We already have commitments from these admirable people.'"

With fifty to sixty back-to-back meetings, Melanie managed to raise all the funds she needed in a week.

TakeAway #5: Put in Effort to Delight Your Customers

Melanie had a challenge with launching her brand—the pandemic had hit, and it also coincided with the Black Lives Matter protests. That meant that the media had their hands full. But a successful entrepreneur has to keep pushing forward, and sometimes that means out-the-box thinking. Sometimes that means superhuman effort. I had read somewhere that Melanie handwrote hundreds (and hundreds) of notes to customers for their first orders.

"Yeah, more than 1,200 in our first week, which was a lot of notes. But it paid off!"

THREE QUICK QUESTIONS

. . .

WHAT'S YOUR "WHY"?

"I want to help people gather more mindfully. I want to create experiences that will be memorable. Someone told me once, "How you live your days is how you live your life," and for me, it's all about these really small moments and making them count."

WHERE DO you hang out to get smarter?

"A lot of learning on the internet, I have to say. I've been really thinking a lot about current events, and I've been able to find a good network of friends with whom I can have some of these debates and conversations in a really safe place."

HOW DO you win the day?

"Now that I moved to California, I have a much healthier lifestyle and go to bed much earlier and wake up much earlier. I have learned to organize my day around the times that I'm the most productive. From 7:00 a.m. to 10:00 a.m. is when I'm most productive, so I try to always be at a computer with no meetings during those times."

LISTEN to Melanie's episode to find out how she designed her labels, how tennis helps her, and what she thinks of totem poles.

36

A TRUE IKONN

MIMI IKONN: HOW AN ENTREPRENEUR CREATED THE LIFESTYLE SHE WANTED

Mimi Ikonn is a true superwoman of entrepreneurship with many successful ventures and talents. She cofounded Luxy hair, one of the world's biggest providers of premium hair extensions, which she bootstrapped through to a lucrative exit. Following that, she cofounded Love Hair, which provides natural and sustainable hair care products. But that's just part of Mimi's adventures. As a YouTube influencer with over 2.8 million subscribers and over 350 million views, she's one of the biggest names in the beauty, travel, and fashion space. It doesn't end there either. Mimi is now cofounder of Intelligent Change, which has created bestsellers like the Five Minute Journal and the Productivity Planner, with the aim to enrich your life through daily gratitude planners and productivity planners. Tim Ferris and Hailey Bieber are among their hundreds and thousands of fans around the world.

Mimi's backstory is an interesting one because we so often look at mega-successful startup entrepreneurs and think *overnight success*. It's easy to look from the outside and think they had some special opportunity that landed in their lap. But the truth is that most entrepreneurs started their journey from humble beginnings and simply a dream—often a dream that starts not with any clear direction but more of an end goal in terms of a desired lifestyle.

In her late teens and early twenties, Mimi tried her hand at many things—waitressing, working as a nanny, and later working at a bank. Although she was searching for the right fit, the one thing she did know was that she loved working with people, so she sought out customer service roles. While working at the bank, Mimi met Alex, who would become her future business partner and the love of her life. The two connected on many levels, but most importantly, they both had the same vision for the lifestyle they wanted to live. They both wanted to escape the corporate life and wanted a lifestyle of freedom and flexibility and the opportunity to travel the world.

TAKEAWAY #1: Work Is a Relationship and Should Feel Good

At the time, Mimi, like millions and millions of people around the world, was doing work that didn't make her feel good. And she trusted her intuition that it was worth taking the risk and quitting her nine-to-five.

"I think it's so important to connect to that inner intuition and calling. Just like a relationship with a partner, a relationship with your work should feel good. If it doesn't feel good, you're free to leave; you're free to go and do something else. Life is so beautiful, and there's so much variety and diversity. You don't have to be stuck in a job or relationship that you don't enjoy."

The pair found themselves unemployed for about a year

and a half, searching for what they wanted to do with their lives.

Takeaway #2: You Can Always Educate Yourself

Mimi had enrolled in college to study international business but soon dropped out.

"A lot of us grew up thinking that we need education, and I'm a big advocate for educating yourself your whole life but education is not something you necessarily need to go to school for. You can do it in many different ways, and I believe it's something that never really stops for as long as you're alive."

During an accounting class, she began to think in an entrepreneurial way.

"I decided that one day, when I start a business, I'll just hire an accountant. I think that was such an important lesson for me. I let go of the attachment that I need to have this piece of paper to be acknowledged as an educated, good-enough woman."

Takeaway #3: Self-employment and Entrepreneurship Are Not the Same

At the time, Mimi had a passion for fashion and was actively blogging, posting her outfits and spotting trends (these were early social media days before YouTube was much of a thing). She decided to grow her hobby into a business, becoming a fashion stylist and image consultant after doing a short certification program. Although she enjoyed the work and had escaped corporate life, she soon found that her career presented another trap.

It's an interesting thing to consider and a concept that

many confuse. What at first seemed like entrepreneurship was actually self-employment.

After reading the best-selling Tim Ferriss book *The 4-Hour Work Week*, Mimi quickly realized how her new career wasn't in alignment with her vision of freedom:

"If you're an image consultant or if you're a doctor or if you're anybody else who is self-employed, you are your business."

"It's very different than owning a business where you're running the show but you're not part of the equation. For example, if you were to go away on a holiday, and you have an online shop selling, the business is still going to run whether you're there or not. You need a customer service person. You need a fulfillment house shipping out the product, but essentially, you can outsource yourself out of the business."

Takeaway #4: Business Ideas Are All Around Us

For those dreaming of being a startup entrepreneur, the first obstacle is usually finding an idea for a business. As so many of our guest's stories have shown, a winning idea can often present itself through realizing that a product you use personally can be improved.

Mimi and Alex began to plan for their wedding, and being unemployed at the time, they had a very little budget. Wanting a specific hair look, Mimi purchased clip-in hair extensions. Although they were pricey, around $200, she was unhappy with them. She felt that they didn't blend naturally with her thick hair.

Having that entrepreneurial spirit, the couple realized they had spotted a gap in the market. The hair extension market was big, and if Mimi wasn't happy with the available solutions, chances are there were many others that felt the same.

Alex, Mimi, and her sister launched Luxy Hair. They had no experience in the industry and no knowledge of how to go about marketing. But they jumped in with a positive, can-do attitude, sourced top-quality natural hair extensions on Alibaba.com, tackled each element of the business themselves step-by-step, bootstrapped with a spirit of scrappiness, and built a multimillion-dollar business.

Takeaway #5: You Don't Need a Big Marketing Budget to Get Started

Sourcing product from Alibaba can of course be hit or miss. Mimi ordered ten different samples to consider, and with a stroke of luck, one out of the ten was "sensational." Bingo!

Mimi had absolutely no budget to put into marketing, but she didn't let that deter her from thinking creatively. So often, having little or no budget can be a blessing in disguise as it forces entrepreneurs to think outside the box.

"It was just me and my sister making YouTube videos, showing people how to use the products. We never even pushed the products or told people that we own the company. It was simply us sitting down and showing girls how to do all these different hairstyles."

Without a budget for social media advertising, their next organic marketing strategy was to send free product out to followers as gifts. It was an effective tactic and word of mouth spread quickly. In fact, so quickly that Luxy Hair turned over more than a million dollars in their first year.

· · ·

TAKEAWAY #6: Choose Lifestyle over Money

Even though Mimi and Alex's business was thriving, the pair didn't forget what their ultimate lifestyle goal was.

"We could have probably scaled it and grew it to be a $50 million–plus business, but for us, that wasn't the goal. The business did incredibly, and then we ended up selling it for exactly what we wanted, but for us, that lifestyle part is always incredibly important."

The couple's current venture is Intelligent Change, creating tools that make people happier and improve their lives in one way or another, be it productivity or happiness or mindfulness. Their products include best-selling books and journals, as well as an app and plans for a series of games designed to get people closer for having better, deeper relationships.

TAKEAWAY #7: Financial Success Isn't Everything

The Intelligent Change venture came out of a personal challenge that the couple faced during the heady success of Luxy Hair. Mimi and Alex learned the lesson that so many successful entrepreneurs learn—a lesson that comes as a shocking surprise to most. The lesson is that financial success is not a guarantee of happiness and fulfillment.

"I grew up with very little money, same with Alex, and we thought that when we are going to have financial abundance, all our problems will be solved, and we're going to be so happy, and everything will be perfect. But the reality is, in my case, even in the first year, making our first million and realizing that I can afford to buy anything I want or travel anywhere I want, I actually became extremely depressed, and I realized that in reality, I don't want any of these things. I just want to wake up every day knowing there's a purpose, that I'm here for a reason. So that was partly why we ended up selling our previous businesses because we just wanted to focus on what makes us the most joyful and happy and present in our lives."

THREE QUICK QUESTIONS

What's your "why"?

"For me, it's knowing that what I do every day makes the world a better place. Even with my social media content, which I never really monetized, when I put out any content, I'm always like, 'Is this going to make people feel better?' So I avoid posting on days when I'm not feeling good or if I feel like complaining or like sharing something that's not actually raising the vibrations in this world. I want to make people feel better, make their day brighter. The products have to make their life easier or improve their life in some way. It makes me feel like I'm useful in this world."

Where do you hang out to get smarter?

"I actually consume very little. I hang out with myself, and I think when I find the space to be quieter and do things like meditation, I can hear a lot of what I need to do that comes from the inside. Of course, I do listen to lots of audiobooks, and I think they can be extremely beneficial in changing your mindset, thinking bigger, believing in yourself. Also, surround yourself with great, successful people. If not in real life, then watch their YouTube channels or listen to their podcasts."

. . .

HOW DO you win the day?

"First, it's just starting the day with gratitude. I use a
Five-Minute Journal in the morning and in the evening. If I
have a really busy morning, and I don't manage to fill out
the journal, I do it in the shower, and I'm grateful for my
healthy body. I'm grateful that I present all the things that I
want to embody. I say out loud that I'm grateful for them.
Also, working out in the mornings has really helped me
have more energy and feel more like myself because I find
that when I go through periods of not doing any physical
activity, I feel more down and more lethargic. You would
think by working out, you're using energy, but it definitely
gives you more fuel and fire."

LISTEN to Mimi's episode to find out what she believes
most businesses lack, what she discovered from Tony
Robbins, and what we can learn from overpriced coffee.

37

A PERIOD OF SUCCESS

MOLLY HAYWARD: HOW AN ENTREPRENEUR BUILT A BUSINESS AND HELPED GIRLS ALL OVER THE WORLD

Molly Hayward is the cofounder of Cora—a purpose-driven fem care brand that's on a mission to build a better future for women all around the world.

Imagine not being able to go to school or go to work because you don't have the products you need during your period? Imagine having to use dirty rags instead of tampons or pads and being forced to drop out in elementary school because of your period?

For millions of girls around the world, this is a reality. Since 2016, through a buy-one-give-one scheme, Cora has donated well over fifteen million sanitary pads and has helped provide reproductive health education to roughly fifteen thousand girls in Kenya, India, Europe, and the US. Molly is one of those sparkly women I could just chat with for hours. I found her deeply inspiring.

Molly had been an entrepreneur from a young age. In her early twenties, she cofounded her second company—a sustainable fashion brand. But soon, Molly found herself impatient, wanting desperately to create a business where she could really make a meaningful social impact. She sold her shares to her partner and went in search of her next project, not knowing what that would be. But she was clear on one thing:

"The whole driving force in my interest in business was not necessarily business, per se, but being able to use that as a vehicle for doing good in the world, creating some sort of change."

You know that thing about one door closing? A friend called Molly out of the blue and (easily) convinced her to join a trip to Kenya to volunteer with women's health and girls' education. On the trip, Molly had a life-changing conversation with a local girl that had taken the day off from school because she was on her period and couldn't afford pads. Her first thought was to write a check but then:

"The entrepreneurial light bulb kicked in. I was like, hang on a minute, there are probably millions of girls all over the world like this girl, and there are probably millions of women like me who would have that same sort of visceral, empathetic reaction to hearing that."

Takeaway #1: Start with a Few Friends and Lean into Instinct

Molly's instincts were that women in the US were ready for a subscription model. It's a capital-intensive type of business, and Molly was on the search for a cofounder. She bootstrapped Cora for the first eighteen months using her personal savings. That covered basic expenses but wasn't enough to manufacture the product. However, after much searching, she found a wholesaler that didn't have minimums. But, first, she needed to validate her idea and find out if consumers would opt in for a subscription.

"I reached out to ten of my friends and was like, 'Hey, I have this idea. If I ship product to you every month, and I also give a month's supply of pads to a girl in Kenya or India, is that something you would pay me for?' They were all like 'Oh, really? Oh my God, yes!' And so I literally just started up in my bedroom, packing boxes for these ten women."

TAKEAWAY #2: Be Open to Finding Capital (and Cofounders) outside the Box

MOLLY MANAGED to raise over $30,000 through a Kickstarter campaign. She then went on a *Shark Tank*–style TV show, and it was there that she met her future cofounder (Morgen Newman). In today's world, there are so many ways to finance a brand. Crowdfunding, friends and family rounds, companies like Wayflyer and Clearco, business loans, credit card debt, grants, and so on.

"At one point, one of the investors pulled me aside and was like, 'Hey, you know, I probably shouldn't be talking to you off-camera, but I actually have a friend who is working on a really similar idea. And I feel like you two could totally team up and work together instead of potentially competing.' I ended up connecting with Morgen, and we just totally hit it off."

TAKEAWAY #3: Speak to VCs Who Understand the Problem You're Trying to Solve

Molly and Morgen went out to raise capital and successfully raised around $30 million (at the time we recorded our interview). Like so many female startup entrepreneurs, she found resistance from male investors.

"I definitely think that the category itself made those conversations a lot harder because the majority of people sitting in those rooms were men. And as a man, menstruation isn't an experience you've had. And so it's really difficult to put yourself in the shoes of the consumer who wants and needs this product. When we would go into meetings and there was at least one woman, the conversations were so much easier because I didn't have to explain why this was important."

TAKEAWAY #4: **Pitch Informally**

Molly gave some advice about pitching, explaining that she found it very effective to avoid formal "rehearsed" presentations. Take note:

"We never once went into an investors office and stood up at a projector and pitched. We would always somehow do it really informally. We would do everything we could to get an introduction to someone from someone else in our network. There was never a cold email. Then we would send our information up front and let them go through the presentation. And that way, when we got on the phone, we could walk through stuff together. But it wasn't like, 'Oh, let us have this really rehearsed kind of presentation.' And it just made it more of a conversation."

Molly continued to explain why this approach worked for her:

"I think it took a lot of the traditional pressure off, and it changed the situation psychologically such that we didn't feel like we were going in there and we were having to perform and put on a show, which I think really creates this weird power dynamic where it's this person is the one with the money and this is the person who needs the money. And even though that's true, in a sense, it sort of leveled the playing field."

TAKEAWAY #5: Being Casual Gives Credibility

The usual formal style of pitching can often create a sense of a barrier between you and the investor audience. Molly found that by being more casual, she created a sense of being "one of them." But importantly, with a casual style, it's even more important to be 100 percent on top of your numbers and pitching points.

"It lends some credibility. You look a little more seasoned when you show up and you expect to be treated as an equal than when you show up and expect to kind of be a supplicant and you come in wearing your suit and you've got a binder. Don't do that. Wear your jeans and your T-shirt and just go in as who you are and share your story authentically. Know your shit, know your numbers, know your points. But don't be afraid and certainly don't go in thinking you're going to have to grovel or convince someone that you're worthy."

THREE QUICK QUESTIONS

WHAT'S the number one marketing moment that made your business pop?

"I think it was landing on a shelf at Target. That's not like a trick on Instagram; that was really like old-school fundamentals: just get in front of people who are looking for your product in a really obvious place. It's about getting in front of eyeballs."

WHERE DO you hang out to get smarter?

"For me, that's our sister site, Blood + Milk. We have an amazing team and an amazing editor who runs that platform. The content just continues to blow my mind. Cora was providing healthier products, but there was still this education gap. Like most of us haven't had any kind of formal education or insight on these very intense experiences in a female body since ninth-grade health class, and back then it was like: don't get an STD, don't get pregnant. Even as the originator of that platform, it has grown so much that I go there, and I learn so many things."

HOW DO you win the day?

"I win the day by intentionally setting up my energy. There's this really cool method that a friend of mine shared with me, where you pick a color. Color is vibration, and the idea is that you pick a color for the day, and there is an energy about that color. And you imagine exuding that wherever you show up, with whoever you talk with. It really works. It's crazy!"

LISTEN to Molly's episode to find out how she moved from a subscription model to supplying Target, how she takes a data-oriented approach, and why she didn't put tons of millennial pink all over her packaging.

THE GREAT OUTDOORS

NICHOLE POWELL: HOW AN ENTREPRENEUR SAID GOODBYE TO BUGS, BEAUTIFULLY

Nichole Powell is the CEO and founder of Kinfield. Launched in 2019, Kinfield makes great essentials for the great outdoors, whether your great outdoors is out in the countryside or in your own backyard. Their range includes effective plant-powered skincare and body products that are safe for both people and the planet. Nichole talked to me about what makes a sustainable company. She shared insights into her company-building process and what it's like being a venture-backed female entrepreneur.

TAKEAWAY #1: Stay Away from Clip Art Packaging

I really love Nichole's packaging. It stood out as something that was crafted with love. Nichole explained the importance of not following the same rules as others in the market and thinking outside the box. It's important to distinguish yourself from what's already on the market.

"I remember when we were designing our packaging, and we were working with this amazing agency. They showed me the packaging of similar brands on the market. I just remember looking at them and saying, 'No. Clip art. Of. Mosquitoes.'"

TAKEAWAY #2: Get Experience inside an Existing Startup

After considering various career options, Nichole began work at a tech company based out of San Francisco. For many startup entrepreneurs, gaining experience inside an existing, successful startup can be a big advantage before tackling your own. They're scrappy; they allow you to learn deeply about failing fast, iterating until you get it right and, all the while, building your network.

"It was a really critical step in the journey because it introduced me to startup culture within the Bay Area. There's a really, really healthy ecosystem there around startups and entrepreneurship, and you really can create what you can imagine. It wasn't until there that my eyes were really open to this idea of 'Oh, you can have an idea and do more than just wax poetic about it with your friends.'"

TAKEAWAY #3: Identify an Industry That Is Lacking Innovation

As is the case with so many entrepreneurs I've spoken to, the seed for a business idea comes from a real-world experience—a moment where they realize that as a consumer, there is something they desire that they can't find in the market.

"I was getting ready to take a group of friends camping in Yosemite. Packing for this trip, I realized that all of my skincare and beauty even home cleaning products had become these beautiful, sustainably sourced, beautifully made brands. But the outdoor products, they were all the same brands that I remember growing up with. I thought, *Why am I still using the same products that I remember from when I was eight years old?* Surely there should have been some innovation in the space by now, and there wasn't."

TAKEAWAY #4: Make Sure Your Trajectory Is Right for You

The first product that Nichole tackled was a repellent product, which today is known as "Golden Hour" and is what Kinfield is best known for. To make this product, she needed to source a specific strain of citronella. It was no easy task and took a year and a half to formulate. To find the all-important ingredients, she decided to make it a personal mission—one that took her to Indonesia.

With each idea that Nichole came across, she would vet it with three questions:

"Is this something that I am deeply passionate about?"

"Is there a market for this?"

"Is this something you want to be thinking about, talking about for the next seven to ten years at a minimum?"

TAKEAWAY #5: Find a Mentor Who's Been There, Done That

Nichole had many questions about the industry and realized that it would be really helpful to have a mentor—someone who would be able to help with knowledge and experience. She Googled the top people in the industry, cold emailed, and attended industry events. At one of these events, one of the panel members was Gay Timmons, CEO of Oh, Oh Organic—somewhat of a legend in the industry. Nichole found that authentic enthusiasm made all the difference.

"I approached her after the event, and I was just like, 'Hi, I have so many questions.' I think she saw my enthusiasm, and she said, 'Here's my email.' And I ended up going and meeting her for coffee, and she later actually ended up joining us as an adviser."

Network and mentorship are things that come up in almost every episode of Female Startup Club. *It's why we launched our own private network for women building CPG and e-commerce brands—where you can find guests from the show readily available to help solve the problems you're currently facing in business. You can find out more at the end of the book! (Along with a cheeky discount to join.)*

Takeaway #6: Demonstrate the Real-World Need to Investors

Creating and manufacturing a product is often capital intensive, especially because of the manufacturing minimums. Nichole managed to raise funds through friends and family, which helped with developing the idea further. But soon she needed to approach angel investors.

"For my pitching, I wanted to demonstrate that there was a need for the product. I encouraged investors to go and try to find the types of products that I was looking for. That was always my favorite. They would come back, and they would say, 'Gosh, these are all really ugly, and none of them look very effective, and they don't get good reviews.' And I was like, 'Great, that's why we're here to talk about it!'"

Takeaway #7: Spend Your Dollars on PR for the Launch of Your Business

Nichole's first set of customers were people she had

directly shown her product to, and she found that word of mouth can be some of the most effective early marketing.

"If you create a product that people want, there is definitely an organic amount of word of mouth that will happen."

Her next step was to take things further and invest in the help of a PR agency. PR agencies can be an expensive investment, and there are no guarantees, but it can be a serious move at the right time.

"If there is ever going to be a time that you are going to hire a PR firm, the launch is a great moment to do that because a good PR team will help introduce you to the right editors and the right writers who are thinking about your space. You can really rely on them to help you network with the right people who are interested in brands like yours. They were definitely expensive. PR usually is. But it was a marketing investment. We had limited dollars, and rather than run ads, I elected to put that toward PR."

THREE QUICK QUESTIONS

WHAT'S the number one marketing moment that made your business pop?

"Well, it's two things. One, it's creating a memorable product in the first place. We have a repellent, which everyone kind of laughed at because "what an unsexy product." Right? But it's a *memorable* product. Second thing was that the *New York Times* wrote about the product this summer, and it was the best sales day that we've ever had."

. . .

WHERE DO you hang out to get smarter?

"My grandmother, one of my favorite people in the entire world, used to be a librarian. So I'm always asking her, 'What should I be reading next?' I read a mix of both fiction and nonfiction. I recently read the CEO of Disney (Bob Iger's) *The Ride of a Lifetime*. That was an incredible business read."

HOW DO you win the day?

"Winning the day for me starts the day before, and it starts with sleep, to be honest. And so I've done a lot of work around a good wind-down routine that works for me. That means that usually by 9:00 p.m., I try to have all my devices off, and I like to read at the end of the day. I try to, if I can, wake up without an alarm clock."

LISTEN to Nichole's episode to find out how she decided which form of company to set up, what makes a company worthy of being called sustainable, and what she thinks is the most important sentence for female entrepreneurs to say.

39

SKIN DEEP

OLAMIDE OLOWE: HOW AN ENTREPRENEUR TRANSFORMED STIGMA TO LUXURY

Olamide Olowe is the cofounder and CEO of Topicals. Founded by two young women of color, both with chronic skin conditions, Topicals is transforming the way women feel about their skin by making the treatment of stigmatized skin conditions like eczema and hyperpigmentation synonymous with the luxury and fun of self-care.

We covered so many need-to-know things, especially if you're just getting started, like the importance of marketing where other brands aren't. We spoke about how they got more than 50 percent of their launch revenue through a surprising channel, how they put the customer at the very forefront of what they do, and how they built strong relationships. Spoiler alert! We also hear about how they developed a super interesting campaign with the help of Lindsay Lohan!

Olamide grew up being fascinated by beauty but didn't really see the potential for creating a career out of it. Following in her family's medical career footsteps, she enrolled to study dermatology and attended UCLA on a full scholarship. At UCLA, she was also a competitive runner.

She quickly realized that juggling her late-night studies and early-morning gym routines was super hard. So she thought about doing something entrepreneurial—also a family tradition that she grew up around. She set out to try something that mixes med school and the skincare dermatology side of things.

TAKEAWAY #1: Apply a Playbook You Know

Olamide had previously worked at Moisture, and she was able to apply insider knowledge that she had learned from her time there. Working with a big brand before going out on your own can often give a head start through having real-world industry experience.

"The big thing about Moisture is that they saw that there was this discrepancy between the beauty hair care aisle and then the ethnic hair care out there. It was like this segregation. As I was doing my own research, I started to realize that dermatological skin conditions, like eczema, psoriasis, and rosacea, were relegated to the equipment aisle. And then the other skin conditions that had kind of become mainstream, like acne, were in the beauty skin care aisle. And I realized that there were no brands that people had an emotional affinity to in the aisle and realized that I could pretty much take the same playbook that I learned at Moisture and apply it to the skincare market. And that's how Topicals came about."

TAKEAWAY #3: Ignore Those around You—You Got This!

I was interested to learn about the reactions Olamide got from those around her when she decided to switch from med school to startup entrepreneurship—first, as a twenty-one-year-old and, second, as a female. Unfortunately, the combination of those two often means a lack of support and belief from others, and that's an obstacle many young females have to face, even in 2021. (Eyeroll.)

"My mother was absolutely horrified. She was like, 'You've worked so hard to get to UCLA; this is what you wanted to do.' And my dad, who is just as wacky as I am, was like, 'Who cares? You'll never be twenty-one ever again. Do wild things at twenty-one!' My boyfriend was super support- ive. He actually gave me my first $2,500 to incorporate the company. He was like, 'You have a dream to do this thing. I have seen how meticulous you are about other things.'"

Olamide's friends were generally incredulous and gave her lots of "what on earth are you doing?" advice. And, as is so often the case with young girls, the business world didn't take her seriously.

"I think, at the time, people in the business sphere were like, oh, she's so cute. Like, you know, she doesn't realize how hard this is. I don't think they discouraged me, but they were also just like, this twenty-one-year-old girl has no idea what she's getting herself into. And to be very frank, I didn't fully know. But I think I adapted well."

TAKEAWAY #4: Entrepreneurship Should Be for Everybody

As a startup entrepreneur, people around you may call you naive, but in many cases, that can be a big advantage. Many startup entrepreneurs look back on their journey and say that if they knew how hard it would be, they may have been too scared to take the leap. Naivety can help people get started, and that's the most important step to success.

"I think you're absolutely right. There's such a risk in starting a business, and if you know too much, or you have too many responsibilities, then it's very difficult to make the jump if you know you have to pay X, Y, and Z bills. If you know you have to support X, Y, and Z people. I hope to see more programs get started for people at that stage who have student debt or have children or some other financial oblig- ation where starting a company isn't exactly in their cards. I think entrepreneurship is a beautiful thing, and I think it helps our ecosystem. It changes people's lives. And so I don't think the opportunity to be an entrepreneur should only be gifted to those who are privileged enough to have access to networks that have access to capital."

Takeaway #5: Listen to Your Future Customers (Hi, Twitter)

Olamide had always been super obsessed with consumer behavior and spent a lot of her time under- standing why people buy what they buy. She knew that she wanted her products to be accessible to people online and potentially in stores, but she hadn't yet decided what kind of products she would create, how she would approach marketing, branding, tone of voice, and so on. So the first thing she did was to get close to the customer by doing lots of interviews and asking as many questions as possible. Olamide also extended her research to the online space.

Research is critical to launching a business. Talk to people. Talk to more people. Trawl the internet. Find new data points to prove your theories.

"I think another way to do that outside of just talking to people is social listening. I love to listen on Twitter. I will search for certain words and just read people's tweets to see what people are talking about."

As a third method of research, Olamide read different industry journals.

"There are a lot of reports that came out saying this is going to be a big industry in 2021 or these are the top interesting ingredients or top interesting categories. So I took a compilation of all of that, and that's when I started to plot out what this brand could be."

TAKEAWAY #6: Know How to Surprise and Delight Your Customer

I wanted to talk about something that I saw in one of Olamide's ads that she posted; it's a video of Lindsay Lohan using a platform called Cameo. If you haven't heard about it, Cameo is a platform where you can hire celebrities to do shout-outs for you or your brand, and it's an exciting approach if you can find the right folks aligned to you and your marketing.

"That was so much fun and such an honor to work with Lindsay Lohan through Cameo. She's so sweet. And it was a very seamless process. Cameo has a business platform, which is more like an ad-based platform where you can connect with people who you think really align with your brand. And so we worked with Lindsay as part of our Facebook campaign. If anyone has watched Mean Girls, we put a spin on people talking about other people, where we talk about beauty status instead. It was a really fun activation to just again poke fun. That's our whole brand—we're super nihilistic. We poke fun, and we always say we know the world's ending and we want to go out with a bang. Our community loved it; they went wild for it. And I was so happy because it's this whole thing about consumer behavior and understanding who your customer is, how to support them, how to delight and surprise them."

THREE QUICK QUESTIONS

WHAT'S **the number one marketing moment that made your business pop?**

"The number one marketing moment has been our threads on Twitter. That was the key to creating a community. Fifty percent of our revenue at launch came from Twitter."

WHERE DO **you hang out to get smarter?**

"Oh, I have a list! I absolutely adore Web Smith, who is the founder of 2PM. That is the playbook of my life. Additionally, I love *How I Built This* by Guy Raz. I love the *Side Hustle Pro* podcast by Nicaila Matthews Okome. That's a great one with a lot of women of color creating businesses out of nothing, no investment, nothing. Additionally, some books that changed my life over the last two years are *The Tipping Point* by Malcolm Gladwell and *The Lean Startup* by Eric Ries."

IF YOU ONLY HAD **$1,000 left in your business bank account, where would you spend it?**

"There's a lot of different ways I can answer this question. In a business way, I'd say paid marketing through Instagram or TikTok or Twitter ads. But I think, honestly, where I'd leave that last $1,000 is with our community.

Donating it to a mental health organization because if we say our mission is to transform the way people feel about skin, that doesn't always have to do with sales."

LISTEN to Olamide's episode to find out how she went about developing her product, what charities her company supports, and what her mother wouldn't allow.

40

HIGH SOCIETY

OLIVIA ALEXANDER: HOW AN
ENTREPRENEUR BECAME QUEEN OF THE
CANNABIS MARKET

Olivia Alexander is the founder of Kush Queen. In fact, she *is* the Kush Queen. The former beauty queen launched her premier luxury lifestyle cannabis brand in 2015. With over seventy SKUs, Kush Queen's CBD- and THC-infused products include edibles, wellness supplements, skincare, and bath bombs, and Olivia quickly rose to fame as a true leader in the industry. As one of the most influential figures in the world of cannabis, she had over 2.5 million followers and an average of 100 million monthly impressions on social media. Dope magazine crowned her Social Media Influencer of the Year in 2017, and Elle Magazine named her "The Mariah Carey of Weed."

Olivia's multimillion-dollar operation, which distributes to more than a thousand accounts, began humbly in her garage. Looking at where she is today, just several years later, it's as hard to believe as it is inspiring.

At first glance, many would call Olivia's venture an overnight success. However, just as with every successful entrepreneur, it took years of hard work and experience to get to her "overnight success." Olivia explained her leg up was that she started working in the industry before it was an industry. She started right at the bottom with the entry-level job of "bud tender." When a friend opened a dispensary, she followed and built up more and more experience in the industry. It was a perfect fit for her.

"It was from that moment that I fell in love with the plant and the people that use it. And I knew that there was going to be a whole world that was going to be built around people who were not stoners. Because I wasn't a stoner. I just used cannabis, and I had no idea what I was going to do. I just knew this is it for me forever. I love it. I love connecting with people."

TAKEAWAY #1: Experience Is a Form of Capital

By the time Olivia embarked on her own journey, she had many years of on-the-ground knowledge, genuine passion, and experience with the ins and outs of the industry from the humblest beginnings. This kind of in-depth experience can itself be a greatly valuable asset in building a startup.

"When I started Kush Queen, I had been working in the industry as well for many, many years, and I was able to use my experience as a form of capital when it came to starting my business and chasing my dream."

TAKEAWAY #2: Train Yourself to Listen to Your Intuition

Olivia had always had an entrepreneurial spirit, and she started her first company, Sky High Treats, at just eighteen. The venture failed but didn't deter her.

"I'm an entrepreneur who really believes in training

yourself to learn how to listen to intuition. Believe it or not, you can train yourself in meditation. And so I've always been listening."

Takeaway #3: Listen When Opportunity Knocks

The journey to ascending the Kush Queen throne started in an unusual way before the opportunity presented itself. Her story illustrates how important it is for an entrepreneur to always be aware and on the lookout for opportunities. Even when you think you've had your "aha" moment, it may be the first of many.

During a period of heavy focus on yoga and meditation, trying to open her mind and energy to opportunity, Olivia had what she described as "the most important week of my life" in the summer of 2013. Having always been involved in the entertainment industry, she attended a small premiere party with an actor friend. She had casually done some creative nail art, and to her complete surprise, a photo of her nails appeared on the Glamour.com beauty blog, and it credited "Celebrity Olivia Alexander's Nail Art." This got her thinking, and she began experimenting in the space. A few days later, she was at a store where she had purchased a pen battery, and the owner saw that she had embellished it with Swarovski Crystals. The store owner immediately wanted to buy some, and this is when Olivia felt that her first "aha" moment happened. She felt that this was the kind of opportunity that she was trying to manifest.

Olivia borrowed $700 dollars from her father to start her business of crystal vape pens, nail art, and embellished sunglasses. Her venture exploded on social media, and she soon had a large and loyal community of followers.

However, this was in a time unlike today, when there was still very much a stigma around the industry.

"I was posting images of the products, posting images of myself, really showing people a luxury cannabis lifestyle long before this was even socially acceptable. I had so many people tell me, you're ruining your life. Why would you post yourself smoking on the internet? You're never going to have a job. And I was like, well, I was not making money like this before. So the money kind of had people settle down with the stigma very quickly, and then a lot of organic natural support developed."

Calling in favors from her Hollywood friends, before long, Miley Cyrus tweeted a photo of herself with Olivia's glasses.

Her vision was to make a cannabis brand for "everybody else." As she explained: "I wanted to make beautiful, amazing products that speak to people in a way that is wellness and that isn't just about getting high."

TAKEAWAY #4: Sometimes a Disaster Can Be a Blessing in Disguise

Startup entrepreneurial journeys almost always have their disaster moments. At the time, they can seem truly earth-shattering and disheartening, but sometimes, in hindsight, they turn out to be blessings in disguise.

Under her Crystal Cult brand, Olivia had amassed a community of over three million followers on Instagram. However, CBD violates the terms and conditions of most social media platforms, and this led to a true nightmare of a day in 2015.

"I lost a million and a half followers in one day. My

biggest pages were deleted and taken away from me by Instagram and never given back. And in that moment, I had my real dream right in front of me, which was Kush Queen, and I took it as a great 'aha' moment to focus on what I truly wanted and not be distracted by all of these cannabis clients and all of this social media advertising."

I get to hear a lot of entrepreneurs talk about their experiences with failure. And what I keep picking up on is that things that seem like disasters can, in hindsight, be important steps in the journey to success. Olivia explained the Instagram nightmare:

"I was beyond upset; I was depressed. Like I built my home on somebody else's land, and they evicted me."

However, two positive things came from the experience. The first is that it helped her toughen up.

"The truth is it set me up for having a lot more roadblocks because I hadn't even seen the start of the roadblocks. I hadn't even seen the beginning of what I would face as a CBD and cannabis business. I had so many challenges ahead of me, and it really helped me get some good battle armor."

Second, it turned out to be a case of one door opening after another closed.

"I look back on it, and I thank the universe that happened to me. I know when people hear the story, they're like, wow, that sounds awful. But I've never, ever been the kind of person who stops. I never stop with forward motion. And for me, like I just said, this is leading me to my real dream—Kush Queen. I actually sold the remaining pages that I had and really used that capital to put into building Kush Queen."

. . .

THREE QUICK QUESTIONS

How do you win the day?

"I try to wake up between 5:00 a.m. and 6:00 a.m. I immediately go outside, and I walk my dog. I stay off my phone for at least a good hour. I also avoid caffeine for at least an hour and normally drink tea or water. And then of course I take CBD in the mornings. I exercise. I have a treadmill that I have to get on around like 8:00 a.m., and I also do a lot of like burning of sage incense. I really find the smell resets my body. I'm known as kind of a nonpartier for being in cannabis. I'm kind of an old lady, and I like to go to bed around nine, ten o'clock."

Where do you hang out to get smarter?

"I am a huge fan of coaching in general and personal development. I think a huge part of being an entrepreneur is staying committed to your own personal growth. I've always been a huge fan of Malcolm Gladwell and all of his books. I also really, truly just enjoy sitting in on a lot of Clubhouse rooms. Clubhouse is really giving me a way to connect with a lot of people outside my space."

How do you deal with failure?

"Just keep going, and don't ever frame it like a failure. I see it as that wasn't meant for me. The mind is powerful, and you can reframe. I reframed losing everything as the best thing that ever happened to me because I got to start Kush Queen. I did the same with my mom's brain tumor, the same with my personal struggles—reframe and just never give up because they can't stop you if you don't stop."

LISTEN to Olivia's episode to find out how she got creative with her spending, how she harnessed the energy of unicorns, and what she knows about the power of giving your customers crowns.

41

GOOD VIBRATIONS

POLLY RODRIGUEZ: HOW AN ENTREPRENEUR ELEVATED FEMALE SEXUAL WELLNESS

Polly Rodriguez is the CEO and cofounder behind the sexual wellness company Unbound. Since its start, Unbound has gone from a labor of love operating out of a tiny New York City apartment to a leader in changing how people explore and enjoy their sex lives. Their mission is to make sexual wellness products that are body safe, affordable, and elevated in design.

Polly discussed the harsh realities of building this business for the first few years and the kind of sacrifice and commitment that comes with launching a startup. She also shared her advice on marketing regulated products, standing out, and dealing with the bias that exists between men's and women's sexual health companies. And also why it's important to be weird.

The origins of Polly's career path began when she was just twenty-one years old and was diagnosed with stage-three colorectal cancer.

"Before radiation, my doctor sat me down and said, 'This is going to beam through all your reproductive organs, and as a result, you'll never be able to have children.' And it wasn't till I was about a month into treatment that I started having hot flashes and all the symptoms. So I Googled it, and that was how I felt—I was going through menopause. No one told me that was going to happen. I found that there would be a dip in libido. I would have vaginal dryness, like all these very unsexy things, but things that I thought my doctors probably should talk to me about."

"So, in an effort to try to reclaim my sense of sexuality, I went and bought a vibrator and lubricant, and the only place that sold them was a Hustler Hollywood at a strip mall next to the airport. And it was just a really embarrassing shopping experience."

Polly ended up working for Senator Claire McCaskill from Missouri, focusing on the Affordable Care Act. Feeling disillusioned about the slowness of making change in DC, Polly moved to Deloitte as a management consultant and then worked for a dating startup. While there, she developed a passion for starting her own business.

"I started working on Unbound with my cofounder Sarah-Jane Adams in 2014, with the goal of trying to change the shopping experience that was really bad for both of us growing up in the Midwest. We wanted to create a destination online that felt like the place that we both would have wanted to find when we were trying to answer questions about our sexuality."

Takeaway #1: It Takes Years to Reach "Overnight Success" (and Profitability)

It took a long time before Polly's company became profitable, and I think it's an important thing for entrepreneurs to hear about, as we often get bombarded with out-of-the-gate success stories that aren't necessarily the more real-world cases.

"I felt like a failure every day because you see all these PR stories of how these startups just took off. How they launched the product, and they had a waiting list of two thousand people. And I'm sitting here, you know, going to every event I can, doing pop-ups at random flea markets, trying to write witty marketing emails. And I just felt like no matter what I did, it didn't move the needle. But, eventually, things started to grow slowly. The thing I've finally realized, being six years into this, is that so many of these startups that have those Cinderella stories usually have millions of dollars in funding, and they are putting that into a PR agency that they're paying $10,000 a month to get them in a lot of big press."

Takeaway #2: Be Bold with Early Marketing

As businesses grow, branding often becomes more controlled and conservative as it settles into a cohesive brand identity and marketing department decisions. Polly found that there is freedom in the spontaneity and risk-taking of early-day marketing that's worth taking advantage of.

"You just have to keep doing it. The thing that is actually really liberating in the beginning is that you can take as many risks as you want. You don't have to tone the brand down. As your audience gets bigger, you have to be much more thoughtful about everything, and you have to kind of scale it down and tone it down a bit."

Takeaway #3: Make Your Email Marketing Entertaining

There's a concept in the advertising industry, which is that if you're taking up someone's time, you have a responsibility to at least be entertaining. Polly applied this idea to her marketing, and she found she had a natural knack for copywriting.

"I think email marketing is like knocking on someone's door. And if you're going to knock on someone's door, you better have something worth opening the door for. And so I started to write weirder and funnier copy that was really relatable, and I think things started to turn a corner where people would be like, 'Oh my God, I read your emails. They're so funny. I shared them with my friends.' I highly encourage brands, whether it's social media or email marketing, to just take a risk and be weird because there are so many generic emails out there. You want yours to stand out, and it doesn't cost anything."

Takeaway #4: Do Customer Service Yourself

By taking care of customer service herself, Polly was able to gain insight into her customers' needs. Startup entrepreneurs know the secret to a successful blueprint is that getting close to your customers gives you invaluable insights.

"As I was the person that was doing all our customer service, I noticed that people were paying like $150 for these brand-name vibrators that were breaking and that also had no return policies. Customers were getting really frustrated with that. So we had a very good sense of what was missing in the market and what we wanted to create, which was a much more affordable product by cutting out distributors but also making sure it was medical grade because most of the products in this industry aren't regulated by the FDA."

. . .

TAKEAWAY #5: **The More Rejections, the More Persistence**

Understanding what the market wanted, Polly set out to develop her range and then raise capital. And as so many startup entrepreneurs find out, raising capital can be a truly grueling process. Every startup entrepreneur's story includes many rejections, and it's persistence that leads to success.

"A lot of the things that people were buying, they were using on one of the most absorbent parts of their body, and it had carcinogens in it. So we did two things. We proved that we could build something that had significant traction. And then I was just relentless about fundraising. And it took two and a half years before I raised our seed round of capital. I got over three hundred rejections from investors before I got my first yes."

THREE QUICK QUESTIONS

WHAT'S **the number one marketing moment that made your business pop?**

"The one that probably put us on the map the most was when we did "Vibes for Congress" in 2017. This was when Trump was attacking Planned Parenthood. We launched a campaign that allowed you to put in your address, and it would look up your local politicians and federal politicians, and you can send a vibrator to any politician for fifteen dollars. And all the proceeds would go to Planned Parenthood. Thousands and thousands of people did it. We got a lot of PR coverage as the company that was sending four hundred vibrators to Mitch McConnell!"

WHERE DO you hang out to get smarter?

"I'm an avid *New York Times* reader, and I also read a lot of biographies. I try to read as many of the business books as I can. I think one of the better ones is *The Hard Thing about Hard Things* by Ben Horowitz. It's a brutally honest book about how tough it is to be a leader at times and having to do the hard thing."

IF YOU ONLY HAD $1,000 left in your bank account, how would you spend it?

"Assuming I had inventory on the shelves, I would probably commission the weirdest Instagram, like, micro people. I would pick four that would do it for $250."

LISTEN to Polly's episode to find out about her experience with fundraising, the way she turned handcuffs into jewelry, and the problem with people's hands going numb.

42

INCOMING FEMALES

REBECCA MINKOFF AND ALISON KOPLAR WYATT: HOW TWO FEMALE ENTREPRENEURS HELPED THOUSANDS OF OTHERS

Rebecca Minkoff and Alison Koplar Wyatt are the cofounders of Female Founder Collective—a network of businesses led by women, supporting women, with a mission to enable and empower female-led businesses to positively impact communities both socially and economically. Rebecca and Ali spoke about the challenges that women face in the corporate world and in entrepreneurship and what we need to do to tackle these big issues. I've long admired both of these women and was especially excited to speak with them, given we have so many synergies in our mission to empower the female entrepreneurs who are solving global issues right now.

Rebecca founded "Rebecca Minkoff"—a global fashion company built with the idea of outfitting the modern woman. She soon developed a collective.

"Our collective was really started with the idea of being frustrated at the wage gap conversation, being frustrated at seeing the same familiar faces as the only women leaders showcased as examples, whether it was on magazine covers or panels or a part of certain lists, and knowing that in the United States alone, there are over thirteen million female-founded businesses. And so I thought, *What if we could provide, as an organization, a community, a recognizable CEO, that way one could get the education to really bridge the gap from their passion to their business?* Ali found me and has really ushered in a new era of what it means to educate a woman and to give her power in her knowledge."

TAKEAWAY #1: **Women Look before They Leap**

Ali came from a long line of startups, including helping Gwyneth Paltrow bring Goop from London to Los Angeles. After moving with her husband from Los Angeles to New York, she started consulting for a lot of female-founded businesses.

"It got me really excited about what women can do and how impressive women are as founders. They really plot out what their existence is going to look like years ahead. They're incredibly thoughtful about planning. It feels like more men leap and then look, whereas women make sure that they look before they leap, but they also really have a game plan in place for how they're going to succeed as a business."

Ali started to get really excited about female founders, not only as a consultant but as an angel investor too. She came across Sophia Amoruso, the author of the hugely popular *#GIRLBOSS*, and partnered with her to launch that as a business. When she left that in 2018, she reached out to Rebecca.

TAKEAWAY #2: **Modern Moms and Businesswomen Rock**

I asked what their first meeting was like, and each gave a rather different answer. But what it proved was that we don't need to hide the struggle of being a multitasking mom— sometimes it can really impress (as it should!).

Rebecca: "I saw her email, and I was like, 'Oh my God, it's the woman I talk about all the time!' I was really nervous. I was pacing in the hotel room as we spoke on the phone, like how do I get this woman to want to work with me?"

Ali: "I saw Rebecca on the floor of a bathroom in the most unsexy, unglamorous area just sitting there pumping. And I knew that she had her baby with her there. And I was so impressed. She had literally just come from doing this big panel. And I was like, this is a woman that I want to work with. She is who I want to be. She has three kids. She is overseas. She brought her kid with her. Nothing is stopping her. And I was just so impressed that she was living the modern mom/businesswoman life that I think so many of us feel like can't be for us but actually can be."

TAKEAWAY #3: Be as Confident as a Man

Ali discovered that there was a common difference in how women and men pitch. It's a similar dynamic to our personal lives—men tend to be overconfident, while women tend to underplay themselves. A stereotype perhaps, but coming from truths nonetheless.

"This might sound a little controversial, but I see an element where women's own confidence is getting in the way of their funding opportunity. I witnessed it myself when we were going out and fundraising for the last company I was part of. We got pulled aside by one of the female part-ners on the investment committee, and she said, 'You have to be more bold and bullish when you're presenting.' And she's like, 'You guys don't sound confident enough. It doesn't seem like this is going to be a big enough business. You seem to be defending your numbers as opposed to having it be more affirmative.' Investors typically give men's estimates a 30 percent haircut, as far as what they think growth will be, whereas with women, investors have to increase it 30 percent because they always do much better than they say they're going to do. So women have a tendency to underestimate what they're capable of, whereas men overestimate what they're capable of. There's this confidence gap."

Takeaway #4: If She Can Do It, You Can Do It

Rebecca and Ali had recently held a super successful three-day virtual summit with founders and women in business from all over the world. One of the things they realized from the summit was just how important it is for startup entrepreneurs to have role models—but not just any role models. So often we look to the most famous businesswomen for inspiration, but sometimes it's more powerful to look toward entrepreneurs that look like you, entrepreneurs that are more relatable.

"I think that there are so many unsung heroes. We read and know tons of famous business leaders, but the general public doesn't get access to these women, and they are so smart and so motivating and so inspirational that I was really happy that we could provide such a vast and diverse group of women that you can now follow and know and learn from. And it just goes to show you—if you can see it, you can be it. It's just more inspiring than having a famous person, famous for being famous. You know, that seems very unachievable. But you could look at any of these women and say, 'OK, if she can do it, I can do it.'"

. . .

TAKEAWAY #5: It's All about Having a Clear Game Plan

It's vital for startup entrepreneurs, as well as for anyone with a big project or goal, to have a plan. Running on instinct and passion can only get you so far without an actionable plan in place. However, that doesn't mean your plan can't change many times along the way.

"Put together a plan. I see a lot of people that launch businesses, and then they're like, 'I don't know what my goals are; I don't know where this is going.' If you don't, you're going to pivot a million times. So you definitely don't need to know where it's going. But what you do need is 'what does execution look like for me in the next twelve months, next thirty-six months?' Because that way, you're at least tracking it, and you know what success looks like so that you don't end up one day looking at your bank account and seeing it at almost zero and being surprised."

TAKEAWAY #6: Build Your Business the Old-Fashioned Way

Many startup entrepreneurs see early investment as a quick-fix boost to power up their plans. But there is wisdom in building a business "the old-fashioned way"—step-by-step progress, one building block at a time. Focusing on building your business this way can lead to a solid foundation and ultimately create a business with proven sustainability that is attractive to investors. This was the route the pair took, and Rebecca explained their thinking:

"Everyone thinks they have to go into a business, raise a ton of money, and then end up working for your investors. That wasn't trendy when we started Rebecca Minkoff. So we had to do it the old-fashioned way. You had to find a product that people wanted. Then you sold it, and then you took that money from the profit, and you put it into the business. When you're bigger and more successful, and you have traction, and you have customers, and you have awareness, and you do want to do a raise, you're just coming off of that from a much stronger position. So I just think, *Stop looking at all that noise, make your business successful, have something to show for it, and then raise money if you even need to.*"

THREE QUICK QUESTIONS

WHERE DO you hang out to get smarter?

[Alison] "Newsletters, I believe, are the key for me in the sense that I love getting stuff served up to my inbox. Otherwise, I won't remember to go to it."

How DO you win your day?

[Alison] "I think happiness is the key to working productively. And the number one thing for me from a happiness perspective is contrary to what I read from a lot of founders saying like, 'I get no sleep.' I have to get sleep, or I don't work. I'm like a car that has no fuel. I need at least seven hours. Seven and a half is like my sweet spot."

IF YOU ONLY HAD $1,000 in your business bank account, how would you spend it?

[Alison] "People. I had a boss that said everybody is replaceable, and this was in the beginning of my career, and that couldn't be further from the truth. Amazing talent is what makes an organization. I don't care if you're a product organization or a service organization; if you have amazing people and an amazing team, then you're going to be able to accomplish whatever you put your mind to. So I think investing in somebody on your team who needs it, that also is a great performer, is where I'd put it."

LISTEN to Rebecca and Ali's episode to find out what they think the future holds for female-led businesses, how they go about their marketing, and how pumping schedules should be integrated into video meetings.

43

INDIA-PENDENCE

ROOSHY ROY: HOW AN ENTREPRENEUR INTRODUCED INDIAN BEAUTY RITUALS TO AMERICA

Rooshy Roy is the cofounder of an amazing Indian-inspired skincare brand called AAVRANI. First-generation Indian American Rooshy grew up watching family members making traditional Indian skincare treatments, using ingredients like turmeric and almond oil. Through a chance encounter at business school (on just her second day), she started her exciting entrepreneurial journey with fellow student and cofounder Justin Silver. In 2020, Rooshy secured around $2 million in funding. She has developed a brand rooted in Indian culture that aims to empower and inspire women worldwide through ancient rituals.

I started out by asking Rooshy about her background. How did she transition from a successful finance career in private equity to starting her own business? In most of my interviews, this kind of question prompts a short answer. In Rooshy's case, I found it so interesting that I wanted to share her full story with you.

. . .

TAKEAWAY #1: Let Go of Validating Your Worth

Rooshy was born and raised in Detroit, Michigan. Raised by Indian-immigrant parents, she had opposite feet planted in two very different cultures. In school, differences between Rooshy and her peers left her feeling lonely at times. After several years of working in New York's corporate world, she studied at a prestigious Ivy League business school. She shared what enrolling at the Wharton School of the University of Pennsylvania meant to her.

"Going to Wharton was an opportunity for me to really step back and figure out, like, 'Wait. OK. I did the thing where I worked as hard as possible in an environment that was competitive. I am comfortable with that. I don't need to continue trying to validate who I am or my competence anymore.' And that inflection point gave me the freedom to explore what I do care about."

TAKEAWAY #2: It's OK to Not Have a Clear Path

Rooshy's early days at Wharton brought back childhood memories of feeling different and alone, but this time, she found a new way of thinking.

"When I got to Wharton, interestingly, I was already a little discouraged by my peers in the sense that I didn't really realize a lot of people come to business school in order to get a very specific job afterward. It's one of those things where you come in, you start recruiting right away, and then you're off into a new career track. I had no idea what I wanted to do, and that lonely feeling started coming back. But instead of letting that bog me down the way it had my whole life, it was kind of a freedom. Like, 'Wow. This is a good thing! I'm not thinking in this way because I've done that. I've left that, and now this is a real opportunity for me.'"

Takeaway #3: Make Room for Serendipity

On her second day at Wharton, Rooshy met fellow student Justin Silver. They would later found a business together, but she couldn't have known. At first, Rooshy thought she had Justin pegged as "another finance guy," and she expected the same old boring conversation. Justin soon surprised her with his energy and passion. He excitedly told her about a skincare brand he'd helped build through a private equity firm he worked at previously. Justin's infectious enthusiasm coaxed Rooshy out of her usual introversion and challenged her reservations. The two soon found themselves in animated conversation.

"I was like, 'Let me tell you all about this skincare from my culture.' I grew up making turmeric masks. My grandma would put coconut oil hair masks in my hair, almond oil on my knees and elbows for hyperpigmentation. All these sorts of knowledge and beauty secrets that I was privy to growing up . . . I didn't even realize it was special or unique in the context of the world."

I wanted to know how Justin reacted to Rooshy's stories about homemade Indian skincare products.

"He's like, 'What do you mean you can't get a ready-made turmeric mask? Why would you make them?' The idea of creating your own skincare (even from a cultural perspective) is very different when you want to indulge or self-care these days. It's a really expensive spa day, right? With the high-end technician, aesthetician, masseuse, whatnot. In India, it's a very personal and community-driven effort where you're creating these treatments with the women around you: cutting the turmeric, really distilling the oils to a point where you're appreciating the treatment for what it is and not just trying to consume it."

I found that fascinating! It's such a different way of looking at, essentially, the same thing (skincare). The whole approach, however, the ritual and ceremony around preparing and applying the products is completely distinct.

TAKEAWAY #4: Not Knowing Enough Is a Façade

Rooshy and Justin took a bold and decisive step. They took all the cash they were going to spend on business school tuition, put it in a joint account to get an LLC, and took out student loans so that they could get started with the business right away. I asked Rooshy what was the first step that they took to get going?

"The very first thing we did was Google skincare manufacturers. And so, just to reiterate, this idea of not knowing enough or not being enough to start anything is a complete façade. Anyone can do anything. Information is so democratized these days, and I'm realizing more and more—especially for women—we are the only things in our own way. You know the idea of, 'Oh, I don't have the experience.' Like, what if you just started doing it? You suddenly have experience."

TAKEAWAY #4: Your Pitch Should Be about Heart and Vision

Rooshy and Justin raised funds for their startup as soon as they launched. They chose to be bold and have confidence in their forecast of great success. For that, they needed investment. But Rooshy experienced an all-too-common challenge faced by female entrepreneurs.

"I was like, 'I know what this is. I come from finance. This is my thing.' Meanwhile, Justin and I are walking into rooms, and people think I'm the person that's going to get them water and start asking Justin about how his experience in skincare is going to make this a billion-dollar company. And when people are asking me, 'Why do you think this is going to be great? Why should we invest in you?' I didn't realize how much of my own heart and my own vision was critical to that decision."

TAKEAWAY #5: Be Proud of What You Stand For

So often for female startup entrepreneurs, it takes a lot of personal conviction to weather the storm of negative (even hurtful) comments from family and friends. This was a challenge for Rooshy. She explained such a relatable family dynamic I could identify with too.

"I don't get the headline of business school to fall back on when I'm too shy to say, 'I'm a CEO; I'm starting a company,' when I would go back home, for example. In between business school, there are those certain aunties and uncles who are like, 'Oh, what are you up to?' They're so proud I'm at Wharton. I'm not about to tell them I just dumped all my savings in a beauty brand, right? They're just going to be like, 'What?!'"

Rooshy experienced imposter syndrome at first, and it took time to own her entrepreneur identity, to claim it with conviction.

"On my LinkedIn, having *entrepreneur* written . . . I mean, my heart was just racing. What are people going to think of me? 'Who does she think she is to go out and do this?' Like, how could it possibly be that she thinks you can start a beauty brand and be herself? Now, I finally feel like I can stand in front of you and say, 'I am the founder and CEO of AAVRANI, an Indian-inspired skincare brand. We are pioneering Indian-inspired beauty, and by the way, this is awesome. Because this is the thing that I needed to feel beautiful and confident growing up. And I don't really care if it resonates with you. Because I know it resonates with me.'"

TAKEAWAY #6: Even Successful Entrepreneurs Are Still Working on Their Mindset

After our long chat, I was touched by what being part of the *Female Startup Club* meant for Rooshy.

"This is amazing. Just sitting in front of you and having you tell me about all these amazing entrepreneurs that you've interviewed. And to decide that I belong in that bucket, that's a mindset that I have to work on every day."

THREE QUICK QUESTIONS

How DO you win the day?

"In the morning, I do a seven-minute meditation. I am the type of person who wakes up and reads her emails in bed. I already start getting anxious by the time I'm in the shower. *I have to respond to this person. I need to make that call.* You can't win in that kind of day because you're in a cycle, so taking a moment to breathe and remember where you're at, center yourself, and set your intention for the day—that's really important. It's really as simple as it sounds."

. . .

WHERE DO you hang out to get smarter?

"I would encourage others to follow or read up on things that they don't naturally gravitate to. I don't think we realize how much of an echo chamber we can get into by going toward things that are comfortable and things that we like. It's only when we talk to people from different experiences and actually hear them out that we can open our own minds to getting stronger as people."

HOW DO you deal with failure?

"I deal with it in the now by preemptively addressing it. So, when I sense a big thing coming, like a decision being made, or I find out about something and am anticipating it, those are my worst nights or lead-ups where I just inundate myself with self-doubt and the what-ifs. I think isolating who you are in the moment from who you know you can be is critical to dealing with that failure, because that failure is no longer a "failure." It's a lesson. It's a pivot to where you're supposed to go. It's what makes you an even better, truer version of yourself."

LISTEN to Rooshy's episode to find out how she raised $2 million in funding, why she thinks being vulnerable is so important, and what she has to say about the beauty of asymmetrical ears.

44

MILKING IT

ROXANA SAIDI: HOW AN ENTREPRENEUR FOUND INSPIRATION AT A FAMILY LUNCH AND INTRODUCED A NEW

product to the US

Roxana Saidi is the cofounder and CEO of Táche—a family-run business that produces the first true pistachio milk available in the US. The benefits of their pistachio milk are plentiful: it's healthier than oat milk and tastier than almond milk as it can be regularly consumed alone with no added oils. It's low in carbs and sugar, and it steams and foams extremely well. Oh, and it has a smaller water footprint too. So it's a product that makes a lot of sense for today's health-savvy and environmentally conscious consumers. And being first to market is a great coup! Táche was launched only four weeks prior to our interview, so it's a great opportunity to hear from an entrepreneur that is in the thick of it, making it all happen.

Before our usual takeaways, you may be wondering what pistachio milk tastes like.

"It's a little nutty, and it's got a little natural hint of sweetness. It has a beautiful, creamy consistency, very velvety. And it works really well with coffee without overpowering it. It's great in smoothies and protein shakes, as well as an ingredient for baking. The brilliant thing is that it is also great tasting on its own."

(So now you can explain pistachio milk to your friends and family.)

I'd say that in most cases, or at least in many of them, I find that entrepreneurs have their light bulb moment that makes them look for a solution out of personal necessity. If you have a necessity in your life for a solution, chances are there is a market full of people just like you.

Roxana recalled a time in 2015 when she was having a lazy lunch with family in Paris. Having recently cut dairy milk from her diet, she was craving an almond milk latte, but it wasn't available on the menu.

"I thought, *Wait a minute, I'm Iranian. Pistachios have been in my household my whole life.* If you ask any Middle Eastern immigrant, they will tell you that they grew up with pistachios in their house. And so, I just thought, *Hold on a second. I don't have to wait to get back to the US. I could literally go back to my uncle's house, and I could blend up pistachios and make pistachio milk!*"

TAKEAWAY #1: Bring Good People on Board (Even Your Dad)

Many successful startup entrepreneurs understand the value of creating a strong team around them. Entrepreneurship is a skill in itself—the visionary driving force of a startup. But it can take many different skills to achieve success, and bringing the right people on board is very much a job description for an entrepreneur.

Roxana's father was an engineer in Silicon Valley, and she recalls that tech startup funding was a constant subject in her household while growing up.

"I first went to my dad and pitched him on it in the hope of getting him on board and out of retirement as a cofounder. Having founded and exited three startups, his expertise lends so well to building this business. He knew exactly the trajectory, how to go about this, what kind of outcomes you should be building toward."

Spoiler alert: He said yes.

TAKEAWAY #2: Find Expert Help from Industry Veterans

Roxana's first obstacle was that the ingredients were at a premium, and she needed to find a way to make it an accessible price point. So again, she found expert help.

"The very first thing we did is we found a consultant who was a thirty-year veteran in the industry. She's the buyer of North America for 7-Eleven. She had this very incredible career of understanding the cost of goods and margins."

TAKEAWAY #3: Go Legal but Do It for Free!

Roxana gave me the most amazing tip that I had never thought of before. While she was reading about the food business industry, one book recommended that if you don't have the capital to bring on a patent trademark attorney, you should go to a law school and see if the law clinic at the university will take on your case pro bono.

"The UCLA Law Clinic took us on, and they did all of my legal work for free. It took three semesters of work to get to a name as a lot of the names that are derivatives of the word *pistachio* were already taken. I always suggest to founders who don't have their bootstrapping and they don't have a ton of capital to put toward attorney fees, around trademarks to go that path."

Takeaway #4: Be Creative in Raising Funds

Roxana needed a manufacturer that specialized in shelf-stable products and found they were quite rare in the US. All the ones she met with had super high minimum order quantities—typically around the 250,000 unit mark for a first order. She needed capital of around $2 million, and this made Roxana realize that she couldn't simply bootstrap the business—she would need to raise funds. Her first port of call was friends and family, which proved to be a good early success. However, the COVID-19 pandemic ground things to a halt. Roxana needed to approach institutional investors, and she got her lucky break when the owner of the food distributor she had signed up called her and proposed an investment deal. Then she had another trick up her sleeve:

"I did a digital *Shark Tank*–style pitch competition. And it led to investment from Gary Hirshberg. He's a legend in the industry. He was the cofounder and CEO of Stonyfield Farm—Stonyfield Yogurt is the largest organic yogurt company in the US."

Takeaway #5: Do Research but Take Some Goddamn Action

Roxana noticed that many female entrepreneurs take too long between the phase of research and the phase of taking action, so she gave some advice on the matter:

"What I saw in myself, and I see in other women is we're excellent researchers, like really digging into podcasts just like this one. Learning so much, absorbing so much. We're fantastic at synthesizing information. But you also have to remind yourself, actioning it is just as important. And sometimes I think, as women, we wait a little bit longer than we need to. Be assertive and push the thing over the line or just start the thing."

THREE QUICK QUESTIONS

WHAT'S YOUR "WHY"?

"My "why" is to help young women and girls champion their dreams and become entrepreneurs and successful women out in the world."

WHERE DO you hang out to get smarter?

"I've always loved the podcast *Unfinished Biz*, and I start every single morning with *The Daily*. I love everybody's favorite, Guy Raz. One of our investors and a mentor of mine has an episode on *How I Built This*. I couldn't recommend it more."

HOW DO you deal with failure?

"I try to meditate at least three times a week. It helps me to not fixate on how I could do better and all that kind of stuff that we get stuck on from time to time. Also, I think that therapy is an enormous gift to add to your toolbox."

.   .   .

LISTEN to Roxana's episode to find out about Three Ring Circuses, how Roxana educated her market, how she got the coolest domain name, and why she likes bad TV shows that annoy her husband.

45

LASH IS KING

SAHARA LOTTI: HOW AN ENTREPRENEUR DISRUPTED THE EYELASH INDUSTRY

Sahara Lotti is the inventor and founder of Lashify—a DIY eyelash extensions company that garnered a serious cult following. And when I say serious, I mean it. Our conversation was full of raw, candid, pure-gold advice, as we spoke about the absolute importance of patents, the ins and outs of how people can screw you over in any industry, and how she found her manufacturer, and spoiler alert, it involves karaoke! These are the learnings of a woman who has a clear mission and isn't afraid to chase her dreams.

Before founding Lashify, Sahara was in the movie business. For much of her career, she was, as she described, "a jack of all trades." But with a mind that needed constant stimulation, she found herself working as a movie screenwriter. It's the first time I've heard this comparison, but here's how Sahara connected screenwriting to being a startup entrepreneur and the lessons learned along the way.

TAKEAWAY #1: Everything about a Product Needs to Make Sense

With entrepreneurship, no prior skill or experience is wasted. Often, our previous experiences in a completely different industry can pop up as an invaluable source of wisdom in unexpected places.

"In movie screenwriting, you're creating a new world, and everything has to make sense. Every word that the character is saying has to match their personality, and it all has to be fluid and in line and very logical. And so what I found was that that way of thinking is the way that products are invented as well."

TAKEAWAY #2: Problem Solve Your Own Problem

In essence, entrepreneurship is all about problem-solving. One day, Sahara was battling to apply her lashes, and with her problem-solving mind, she became obsessed about finding a solution.

"I wanted to get the logic; I'm an obsessive personality. Like if a word doesn't come to your tongue, and you're like, what was that word? And then you just can't think straight until you find that word. I'm that person. So when it came to lashes, it's like I take it and I stick it underneath. And then I have this tweezer, and it peels it down. And I was looking for it, Googling the alternative, and it didn't exist. And so when you so vividly can see something, but it doesn't exist, it's your job to bring it to fruition. Does that make sense? You kind of have to."

TAKEAWAY #3: Think Big and Then Think Even Bigger

For much of her career, Sahara never focused on "I need to make tons of money." But after getting involved with natural medicine for animals, she had an epiphany on how important money can be. Not all entrepreneurs are driven exclusively by the money side of things. But through money, one can make an impact on causes close to the heart.

"I found that the number one way to heal these animals was to use natural medicine. But I also found that there was no money for research, and it bothered me. I was thinking, wow, I just saved my dog's life because I used this natural thing. But the doctors refused to give other dogs the natural thing because there's no research. So I thought, *Well, where do we get the research from?* Their response was, 'Oh, research needs millions and millions of dollars.' I pushed and asked, 'Why aren't you doing research on turmeric?' And they're like, 'Well, there's no King of Turmeric who's going to fund it.' So in my mind, I started thinking differently—I need more money. Not in the sense of having a cool apartment or a Chanel bag. I need *real* money. How do you get that? So I thought, *I'm going to have to create a business that is very lucrative.* I thought about it, and then I decided I should go forward with this idea because I'm obsessed with it. So I began to strategize how I would basically create this market, create this product, and basically own a space that would have a revenue model that would allow me to do what I wanted. So my intention to blow it up was very clear."

TAKEAWAY #4: Patents Are Important, but They Also Need to Be Defended

For many entrepreneurs, one of the first steps of setting up a venture is to apply for patents. It's sometimes the most costly element of getting started, but in many cases, it's a smart move. I had read that Sahara had obtained something like seventy patents all around the world. She explained both the complexity and the importance of patents.

"I knew what was going to happen if I didn't protect myself because I watched it happen to other female entrepreneurs in space. What happens is for every patent that you get in the United States, let's say there's the manufacturing patent, then there's a method patent, then there's the system patent. Then there's the patent for the law and the patent for the cartridge, the patent for all of them that work together. So you really have to go in. Otherwise, competitors will try to get around your patent."

However, simply having a patent isn't always enough to protect you from the competition out there, who have never-ending tricks to get around things.

"It's terrible because patents inspire manipulation and getting around it. So a lot of these companies, all they know is getting around your patent. They don't know how to market. They don't know how to connect with their people, but they know how to get around your patent. So, you know, a patent doesn't mean anything unless you're willing to defend that part."

TAKEAWAY #5: Use CAD to Build Your Prototype Design

Initially, raising capital wasn't on Sahara's mind. Her focus was on how to make her first product, and she began to experiment with what she had. Startup entrepreneurs often start this way—in fact, it's very much part of the fun! But sometimes it's worth bringing in the help of a professional, which can ultimately save time and money and result in a better product.

"So I had an idea that if I had this tweezer that wrapped around my eye like this, I could get the extensions on. So I was melting jewelry because I told you, I'm the chick that becomes obsessed with things. So I was like, I can build my own one!"

Her first step was to get the form right with a twisted wire. Then she had to find out how to actually get the prototype made. This led to her discovery of CAD (computer-aided design).

"After mad research, I realized that you need something called a CAD designer. Once I figured out what a CAD designer was, my life changed. What's in your head, they put it on the computer."

Takeaway #5: Don't Bring In Friends

To develop her ideas further, Sahara brought in friends to help. This is always an interesting topic, and I've heard different experiences from different entrepreneurs about working with friends. Some advise that friends are ideal colleagues as they're trustworthy and often inexpensive as they're happy to help. But some find that working with friends is a wrong move for a variety of reasons—in Sahara's case, it was that her friends had the right heart but lacked the necessary skills.

"I was like, 'OK, you guys, I'm going to create a factory like Andy Warhol, and then I'm going to have five beauty ideas, and this is going to be one of them.' So I brought in friends and realized that they really didn't know what they were doing either. So it's a really bad idea to ever bring your friends. Do not get in business with your friends."

Takeaway #6: Sing Your Heart Out

Sahara's next step was to find a manufacturer—not an easy task with such a new, innovative product. She turned to

Google and got in touch with a manufacturer that owned glass factories—of course, an altogether different industry but they seemed to have experience with adhesives, which was an important and challenging element of her product. She contacted their agent and presented her idea.

"The guy was startled and said, 'Wait, say that again?' And I said, 'It's like this ... and then it's like this that you put on your eye. And all he could say was 'Oh, OK.' He later told me that when I came in, he looked at me and thought, *This is either insane or completely genius.*"

The agent put her in touch with a Korean manufacturer who he thought could be a good fit.

"I met with them, and it was like, boom, he got it. With Koreans, a lot of the friendship forming has to do with getting really drunk and karaoke. I don't drink, but I got wasted in the name of laughter. I sang Celine Dion. I sang Guns and Roses; you name it."

Takeaway #7: Commit to Loyalty and Building Strong Relationships with Your Partners

Convincing a manufacturer to take on your business can sometimes be quite a challenge. Sometimes it takes money, sometimes an offering of equity. In Sahara's case, it came down to something that is both invaluable and costs nothing.

"I had to actually go to Korea and meet with the owner. Now you have to remember something—we're dealing with a very, very, very different culture. Men absolutely dominate, and especially in Korea. So I actually met with the owner; he was in his sixties and very serious. And I was basically like, 'I am going to create a new market. It's my market.' I said, 'What I can tell you is that I will be loyal. I don't fuck

around. If you do this for me, I will own this marketplace.'
We had Korean sushi, which was the best thing I ever had.
Again, everybody drinks beer like they are the party animals
of Asia. You have to keep up. And then we had a celebration,
and then he agreed to give me more of their capacity."

TAKEAWAY #8: Keep Your Process a Trade Secret

Working with manufacturers is rarely as simple as it
looks. Factories have high pressure to keep their machines
running twenty-four seven. When working with manufacturers, Sahara found that because she had developed a
unique process, it became her trade secret, and that
prevented early-stage copycats.

"When you're dealing with factories, you're dealing with
capacity. It's in their interest that every single day, they have
production. Right. So let's say, for five days this week, they're
filling Chanel lip liner [for example]. They have to come in
and give you that room. I invented a new process of making
this, so in order to make it, we had to train people. That's
why it took so long for the copycats to copy me because they
didn't know how to make it. It's a trade secret."

THREE QUICK QUESTIONS

WHERE DO you hang out to get smarter?

"I'm a Twitter fan. I'm an information junkie, I'm literally an encyclopedia of information. I like to absorb, absorb,
absorb, absorb."

. . .

IF YOU ONLY HAD **$1,000 left in your bank account, where
would you spend it?**

"Products. If you don't have the products, you don't have
anything to sell. If you have shitloads of products, then
you're going to put it in marketing. But first and foremost,
product, and this is really important, you want to always
leave yourself a very healthy margin. When you work with
really low margins, it's just not fun."

How DO **you deal with failure?**

"OK, so here's the thing with failure. If you're failing, the
universe is telling you something—you're not on the right
track. I was a very good actress. I had a natural ability to
read lines, but it was uphill, man. So then I started writing,
and all of a sudden, there was this smooth ride. And I was
like, OK, I'm on the right track. So it's like when you're in a
bumper car and you're trying to go forward, that's failure. So
you have to turn. It's never failure. It's a lesson. It's teaching
you something."

LISTEN **to Sahara's episode to find out how she protected
her IP, how she went about her digital marketing, and
how she was the first to wear clogs.**

46

GLOW YOUR BUSINESS

CHRISTINE CHANG AND SARAH LEE: HOW TWO FEMALE ENTREPRENEURS INTRODUCED KOREAN SKINCARE TO THE WORLD

Christine Chang and Sarah Lee are the cofounders of Glow Recipe Skincare. The brand is more than just another successful product—it's achieved the enviable status of a cult brand, and it has a long line of loyal (and obsessed) customers. Initially, with the intention to educate, Glow Recipe started out as a curated e-commerce site with the coolest of Korea's indie skincare brands. In 2017, Glow Recipe launched its in-house skincare brand with the industry- and life-changing Watermelon Glow Sleeping Mask. The mask, which went through 1,024 iterations before being perfected, was an instant hit and quickly went viral, leading to an over five-thousand-person waiting list at the time of its launch! The popularity of the Watermelon Sleeping Mask (now just one of its products) has continued to grow with no signs of slowing down. At the time of this interview, a Watermelon Glow Sleeping Mask is purchased every fifty-one seconds, and to keep up with the demand, fifty watermelons are cut by hand daily (at the time of our interview). The brand's following is evident on social media with over

940,000 followers on Instagram, and their online video "How Our Watermelon Mask is Made" has close to three million views.

Sarah and Christine were both in marketing and product development at L'Oréal. They originally met while working for L'Oréal Korea and quickly became friends, both sharing a passion for beauty. Coincidentally, the two ended up in New York around the same time, and they began to have discussions about how their jobs evolved into really focusing on product development and the fact that they were looking at Korean beauty as the next big thing.

TAKEAWAY #1: There's Opportunity in Being a Middle(wo)man

With entrepreneurship, where you start isn't always where you finish. A business can pivot many times, but it's getting started that's key. Before considering launching their own line, the two saw an opportunity in the market to represent existing brands that were unknown in the US market.

"We were kind of that middle person taking the Korean beauty technologies but launching them under the L'Oréal brands. And then we had this "aha" moment where we felt that we could actually do this at a faster speed but also help the brands in Korea that don't necessarily have the expertise or experience to go overseas, especially the US market. And we thought that this was a unique opportunity for us because we were the only two Koreans in the company at that time of ten thousand employees in the office. We just had this moment and thought, *Hey, we could do this ourselves!*"

Sarah and Christine decided to take the brave step and quit their jobs to focus on their new business venture. They created Glow Recipe—the name alluding to the skin ideal in Korea, which is to "glow." The pair got started with a very simple low-overhead operation.

"I think the first time we flew out to Korea, we came back with nine new contracts with exclusive brands that we were able to partner with. And that's how it all started. But it was very nimble, bootstrapped. It was just the two of us. We had maybe an intern or two in the beginning to help pack our boxes from our office, but that's how it all started."

TAKEAWAY #2: Listen to Your Gut Intuition

Christine and Sarah started by each putting $25,000 of their own personal savings into the startup. For a while, they remained bootstrapped and independent. However, they kept an open mind to exploring their options, and at the end of 2018, they appeared on *Shark Tank*.

Their pitch on the popular TV show was a success, and the pair got three investment offers, ultimately shaking hands with Robert Herjavec. But the reality of investment from a shark didn't turn out to be the right fit for Sarah and Christine. It's an important lesson that if something doesn't feel right, it's OK to listen to your gut intuition, say no, and walk away.

"Months after the show and going back and forth with his team, we realized that the goals that we were looking for in an investment partner were a little bit different. So we amicably parted ways. So that was the closest we've ever come to getting investment. From day one, we've been very careful about our cash flow, our spend, how we approach certain investments in resources. And because of that, we've been cash-flow positive. And that's given us the luxury to really take a step back and make sure that if we do potentially consider any partners down the road, it would have to be a strategic partnership where we're looking for other aspects in partnership outside of just funds."

Takeaway #3: Be Resilient and Patient

Building a brand takes resilience and patience. There's no such thing as overnight success; every successful business is the result of hard work. From the outside, the path to success can look glamorous and easy—Sarah and Christine's business is an example of one that looks ultra glossy and glamorous, but the pair were quick to shed light on the behind-the-scenes truth.

"I think for any new entrepreneurs, it's important to know that it's not what you see. There's a lot of behind-the-scenes. It's a one-step-at-a-time approach; you need to be resilient and patient and stay focused on what matters for your business. And there's a lot of hardship along the way too. And ups and downs. But everything kind of builds up together and creates one beautiful story at the end of the day."

Takeaway #4: Friends Can Make Great Partners

It's a hotly debated subject—whether friends make good business partners. In Sarah and Christine's case, they found that there were great advantages—from a special level of trust to the power of having a shared background.

"We've been friends for fifteen years or even more, and I think that's also why the cofounder relationship has been smooth from the very beginning. I think we already had trust and understanding of each other, and we also had similar backgrounds working at L'Oréal. So even though we had a crazy busy schedule from the very early days of our business, I think what really helped was efficient communication because we didn't have to add a lot of context to what we were trying to convey. Everything was very quick and easy. We still sit together today; our desks are pretty much attached to one another."

TAKEAWAY #5: Transparency Is Key

In every business, and in much of life, good communication is fundamental for success. Above all else, transparency is vital within a team. It creates trust, a shared understanding, and a basis to work as a unified team.

"Being transparent is the key to creating a partnership because I think that as a company grows, your team will grow, and you do have to divide up your projects. Of course, all the decisions are made together, and anything that involves a lot of budget, for example, we always make sure to discuss before decisions are made. So that's kind of our promise to one another. But I think when it's so busy, there is this underlying understanding that we're going to be flexible with allowing the other person to make some quick decisions."

ONE BIG QUESTION

What's your key piece of advice for women starting out on their entrepreneurial path?

[Christine] "For me, I think one of the key pieces of advice would be to just really find your network and your tribe. And what I mean by that is personality-wise. I'm actually quite introverted. So finding my own network over the years has been a personal challenge for me. And I think that what I've come to realize is that really you can't do it alone. Whether that's finding an amazing cofounder like Sarah to help you grow and help you get there faster or to find people that are in a similar position. So, for example, other founders, other female founders, other entrepreneurs, whether it's through networking events or other kinds of avenues and really connecting and trying to find these people who will be there for you to support, to give you ideas, to give you inspiration. It's a key thing as an entrepreneur because it can get quite lonely. The highs are high, and the lows can be low. So having that sense of emotional support is invaluable."

Entrepreneurship doesn't need to be lonely. Learn more about Female Startup Club's *private network for women building CPG brands at the end of the book.*

LISTEN **to Sarah and Christine's episode to find out how they did DIY PR, what their grandmothers taught them, and how skincare routines can be like a movie.**

47

CLEANING UP THE MARKET

SARAH PAIJI YOO: HOW AN ENTREPRENEUR TAMED A SHARK AND HELPED SAVE THE PLANET

Sarah Paiji Yoo is the cofounder and CEO of Blueland, a forward-thinking company that's reimagined cleaning products and is on a mission to eliminate single-use plastics. The name may be familiar to you—if you're a *Shark Tank* fan, you may have seen her pitch that clinched an investment from Kevin O'Leary. If you follow Kim Kardashian's Twitter account, you may have seen her there too. And I guess if you're a *Female Startup Club* fan, you'll now have read about her here! Sarah shared her journey and what it was like in the early days, trying to create something that literally didn't exist in the world, and how she made $200,000 worth of sales in her first month alone!

Before Blueland, Sarah had spent many years as a serial entrepreneur, as had her cofounder John Mascari. Both were very interested in having a positive impact on the world, beyond simply building a new company. As a new mom, Sarah became a lot more conscious about what was in her son's food and water. In her research about bottled water vs. tap water, she was shocked that both options contained hundreds of pieces of microplastics. She committed to cutting back on her plastic consumption; however, Sarah didn't find much choice in the stores to aid her intentions— which of course rings alarm bells for any serial entrepreneur. The pair set out to look at different ways they could disrupt the market and offer a product that bucked the omnipresent trend of single-use plastic.

TAKEAWAY #1: Don't Fall in Love with Your Ideas

Sarah and John played around with many ideas, trying to find the right product fit for their vision. She gave some interesting advice, which is to not fall in love with your ideas. Sometimes in the early stages, entrepreneurs can become too fixated on a specific idea to be genuinely open to feedback. A good skill set to have in entrepreneurship is the ability to allow your ideas to evolve, pivot, and constantly be iterated on.

"Cleaning products was the last category that we arrived at. Initially, we threw ideas around, everything from bulk refills, things like shampoo and body wash and conditioner. We would go out to friends and survey them on the ideas. We would try to be really honest with ourselves, try not to fall in love with ideas, try to be open to the honest feedback that people were giving us."

TAKEAWAY #2: Find Help on LinkedIn and Don't Stop until You Find Someone Who Can Help You

Sarah and John settled on an idea to create a tablet that would dissolve in water and be an effective cleaning solution. The concept of adding a tablet to water was intuitive to customers, and the barrier to switch wasn't as high as with other products such as deodorants and hair products. However, the pair didn't know if it was actually possible to create their vision. Reaching out to manufacturers, they were consistently told that it can't be done. And if they were to have a chance, they would need a chemist to create a formula. Sarah found that LinkedIn was a useful platform for the task. The thing to keep in mind here is that it's a numbers game. Keep chugging along until you find someone who can see the vision and help you bring it to life.

"We had no chemists in our network, and there's no place you can just go to find them. So we turned to LinkedIn and reached out with direct messaging until we found the right one out of a list of hundreds."

Takeaway #3: Raise Capital with Momentum

Sarah realized that the R&D needed was going to cost more than she and John were able to personally put into the business. So they approached investors, starting with those they had worked with in the past, as each had successfully founded and sold startups. But it's no walk in the park to get investors on board with a product that doesn't exist in the market and has no proven track record. This can call for a change in strategy, and Sarah found that she was able to attract investors with the fast-paced energy of momentum.

"With fundraising, I'm a big believer in momentum. I think it's really important, especially when there isn't a product to be shown and there isn't traction that you can show. So it was kind of a speed game for us. And we made it pretty efficient."

. . .

TAKEAWAY #4: Gain Mass Exposure

Although not always easy, it can be a great strategy to find a way to gain mass exposure for your brand and get the message out to a large audience.

Sarah appeared on *Shark Tank* in an effort to raise capital and get a successful investor behind her brand. With or without investment, the public exposure of being on a popular TV show can itself be a turning point for a business —you never know who's watching.

"It's always been a dream of mine to go on *Shark Tank* if I were working on the right type of business. Kim Kardashian caught the episode and tweeted about it. In fact, she was so excited about the product she tweeted three times!"

Sarah had wondered (just like I had) about how things would pan out post-investment. With the sharks investing in so many companies over so many years, did they have the time to really be involved and hands on?

"Kevin [O'Leary] has been incredibly accessible. We text or talk probably once every week or two. He's very engaged. He's always thinking about us when he's out talking to the press; he's really down to do it, do anything. I mean, we even ended up shooting a TV commercial with him that's been running for the past few months."

TAKEAWAY #5: Be in Control of Your Own Content

Sarah focused her marketing attention on social media —a world where sustainability is very much a topic of our times. She found that there was great value in personally taking control of all the content the brand put out. Sometimes entrepreneurs get outside help to produce content, but doing it yourself can really get across your vision like no one else can.

"That's been an area we've invested a ton of time into from the very beginning. I continue to be very (very very) hands-on with every post and every story that goes up. It is quite time consuming, but then I just realized it was so valuable in so many respects. I think, as a marketing channel now, I continue to believe it's the most important channel for us."

Sarah, Queen of 305,000 followers on Instagram, continued:

"It's the only channel where our audience is coming on multiple times a day and actually wants to be there. The opportunity to show up as a brand every day and speak to your audience in a very organic way is very powerful. From a customer feedback perspective, I think Instagram is invaluable."

THREE QUICK QUESTIONS

WHAT'S YOUR "WHY"?

"With climate change, if we don't act fast and truly solve this problem in the next twelve years, the world my son's going to live in is going to be vastly different from the world that we've enjoyed. And I think that's made it all very concrete and real for me."

WHERE DO **you hang out to get smarter?**

"It feels lame, but I learn a lot on Instagram. I'm so grateful for that platform."

. . .

How do you win the day?

"A big one for me, in the mornings, is making sure that I have quiet time. I try to reflect on a few things that I'm very thankful for. I think it's just a good way to ground myself each day and give me perspective."

Listen to Sarah's episode to find out how she educated a market, why she dropped out of Harvard, and what her relationship is with Justin Timberlake. Ah, bet that last one will grab your attention.

48

TO A TEA

SASHEE CHANDRAN: HOW AN ENTREPRENEUR REIMAGINED THE TRADITION OF TEA

Sashee Chandran is the founder and CEO of Tea Drops. Founded in 2015, Tea Drops is a super innovative planet-conscious tea company with a simple philosophy: to make drinking tea more fun and also environmentally friendly. By making an assortment of bagless organic leaf teas, their products shed 20 percent less waste than traditional tea bags, and they've become a favorite among new and experienced tea drinkers alike—including Michelle Obama and Tory Burch. Sashee told me about what her startup story was like, what it took to get it off the ground, and how you can go from having no network when it comes to angel or institutional investors to having a thriving community of people ready to invest their money in you. We also chatted about what it means to have controlled luck and what you can do to bring it to life in your own business today.

Also, it's worth mentioning the tea bag shapes—little love hearts, little flowers—love that for us tea drinkers!

Sashee came from an entrepreneurial family and was inspired by her parents, who both always had side hustles in addition to their nine-to-fives. In terms of tea drinking, Sashee has the ultimate heritage—her mother is Chinese and her father is Sri Lankan.

Following her parents' example, Sashee started working from a young age with her own side hustles. At thirteen, she had babysitting jobs and worked at the gym, and throughout her teens, she had various side gigs at school, selling jewelry and other things.

TAKEAWAY #1: Take Note of What Frustrates You

Like so many ideas for startups, the initial inspiration came from personal frustration. As a consumer yourself, if you're frustrated with something, then there's a good chance there are others out there just like you.

"I grew up in Southern California and ended up working at eBay and Silicon Valley. At home, there was always tea at the table, and I love the ritual of tea. Working in a fast-paced corporate environment and trying to make tea wasn't really working out great. I would have an arsenal of equipment; I would have my kettle, my strainer, my loose-leaf tea. I would boil the water, strain the tea for five to seven minutes, and by the time I made it, I had to run to my next meeting. I didn't really have the time to enjoy it. And tea bags for me were just not as flavorful or aromatic. They are often made with what's called tea dust. That's the last part of tea harvesting and production.

So that was my own personal frustration. That's really the point at which I set out to investigate why there is no convenient way to make tea. And I saw that even though the tea market itself, which is a $65 billion global market, and [tea] is the most consumed beverage in the world, there were no simple or convenient options on the market. And so that really was that first 'Hmm, maybe I should investigate this moment."

TAKEAWAY #2: Failed Concepts Can Lead to Bigger Things

Sashee's entrepreneurial spirit continued after high school, and she tried her hand at several businesses before coming across her tea concept. Many startup entrepreneurs (myself included) will agree that on the journey to finding the business that's "the one," it's so important to try out many other ideas. Statistically, most business ideas will fail quickly, and this is where invaluable lessons are learned. In addition to that, one business can open a door of opportunity for another, sometimes in the most unlikely way.

"I always had this hope that I would be an entrepreneur in a way, and I don't think I recognized it at that time. But I always knew starting a business would be fun. And actually, prior to Tea Drops, I had a lot of other failed concepts. Like I had this cookie concept, which I actually still think is a great idea if someone wants to take it. But I would go to artisan shows, and the whole concept was baking a custom cookie on the spot. So basically, you would have your cookie dough; you would come up and choose your mixes, whether it's walnuts, chocolate chips, M&M's . . . I had a basic convection travel oven. I tested out that concept, and it went well. Except, one day, I was invited to this fair at the height of summer, and it was going to be over one hundred degrees. And I was like, there's no way people want freshly baked hot cookies on a summer day. And in the meantime, I was already working on these prototypes for tea drops—probably forty to fifty! I brought those prototypes to the show to sell in case I couldn't sell the cookies. And what ended up selling out were the Tea Drops and very few cookies. So I think that was really the point of validation to say, OK, like maybe I should give up this cookie thing."

Takeaway #3: Find Inspiration from Other Products You Love

Sashee experimented with finding a solution, and she found inspiration from another altogether different product. When experimenting with a formula, sometimes it can be a good idea to look around and see what other industries have come up with creative solutions.

"In those initial early days, what I was thinking about Tea Drops was not necessarily as a business but just my own fascination with how do you make tea in a more convenient format. I was just literally buying tea and spices and then going into my apartment kitchen after work and on weekends. I would just start experimenting with different tea leaves and really learn the properties of the tea leaf itself. A year and a half later is when I really developed this concept. I was inspired by a bath bomb and seeing how it works; like, you just drop it in your bath, and it magically makes this amazing bath experience. Why can't we do that with tea? That really was that point of inspiration to start putting the tea into these fun shapes. And that took me a while to figure out how to do it."

Takeaway #4: Test the Market with Trade Shows

While working at eBay, Sashee was faced with the dilemma of most startup entrepreneurs: do I quit my job and do this full time? She asked herself many questions in an attempt to make a decision, and it left her with self-doubt. Sashee decided that in order to make a decision, she would attend trade shows, learn more about the industry, and have a go at selling product.

"I took every opportunity at these gift shows to create a small booth and sell my product directly and see how people responded to the tea drops. Like, did they like them? What was the feedback? And I must have done thirty or forty shows that first year. It gave me a good sense that after that period of time when I really thought tea drops like this could be a path for me. It was around six or seven months in, and I still was working in my corporate job. And at that point, I kind of made the decision that I had enough feedback. I have done enough trade shows. I was actually working on making this product in my home kitchen, and it was selling like crazy. But I love that process. And so at that point is when I decided I want this to be my full-time work. I didn't really have a plan, per se, but I was also debating at the time whether I was going to pursue my MBA."

Takeaway #5: Take a Risk in Raising Your Own Capital

So now Sashee had a second decision to make—startup or MBA? Both would be a costly move for her, and she decided on where to place her bets.

"Instead of paying what would have been maybe $75,000–$100,000, I just decided to take a step back and use what I would have used for education and put it into the business."

Startup entrepreneurs usually share a common challenge in needing capital to get going. Using personal savings to start a business is a high-risk game, but it's a decision many successful entrepreneurs have taken, Sashee included.

"At that time, I had just purchased a home, and I went and did something that probably people would consider risky. I took a home equity line of credit on the house, and I used some of that to start the business. So in total, I had around $125,000 really, but I didn't think of it that way because it wasn't necessarily savings I had in my bank account. They were reserves that I knew I was going to spend eventually on either education or my property."

However, as many startup founders quickly find out, money goes fast. As part of Sashee's bootstrapping strategy, she took on a lot of the work herself.

"I was naive to think how much would be involved in actually growing and starting a business. So once you start purchasing, packaging, and also buying ingredients and attending trade shows, which are expensive, you soon real- ize, wow, there's a lot of costs that go into building this! So those early days, I was literally making the product in my kitchen and packing and fulfilling orders. And then on my weekends, I would be doing these artisan trade shows."

TAKEAWAY #6: The Harder You Work, the Luckier You Get

Sashee continued to build the business step-by-step, including an aggressive strategy of attending pitch competi- tions. This eventually paid off, as she gained a $100,000 investment from the Tory Burch Foundation. A big turning point for Sashee was a public endorsement by celebrity Chrissy Teigen. How she got there shows two valuable lessons—the first is that you should start with thinking about exactly what you want, whether you know how to get there or not yet. The second is that with hard work, you can make amazing things happen without having to spend a fortune on marketing and PR.

"On a team retreat, we were thinking about who would be our dream celebrity influencer that we would want to connect with our brand. And we just felt that Chrissy Teigen really aligned with the values and our brand ethos. And so I investigated what it would take to work with her. I soon learned from her team that it's like hundreds of thousands of dollars for a post—we definitely didn't have that kind of budget. So I was like, OK, I went to my team and said, 'Let's send product to every address that we can find that's affiliated with her in some way.' I found some addresses from other sources, and we just sent product everywhere.

She repeated the same strategy for other dream influencers.

"That's also what we did with Oprah magazine too. And then five or six months later, we see this tweet. Isabella, who runs our social media, is running down the hall and screaming. And I'm like, what's going on? I thought someone died. And then I saw this amazing, amazing organic endorsement of Tea Drops. And it was so genuine. It was better than anything you could ever really pay for. There is something that I think is really encouraging for any entrepreneurial journey. It's that there is this notion of luck, but there is 'controlled luck' that you have agency over, and these magical things happen. It's like that notion that the harder you work, the luckier you get."

THREE QUICK QUESTIONS

WHAT'S the number one marketing moment that made your business pop?

"That shout-out tweet from Chrissy Teigen was a huge turning point for us, and it's not marketing that we really had much say or control over, but our direct consumer website went crazy. Amazon went crazy. It's hard to quantify because it's been the gift that keeps on giving. We had all this additional PR that came from the tweet."

WHERE DO you hang out to get smarter?

"There's a Facebook group called LMG. If you're just starting out, it's a really great ecosystem. People ask questions, and people answer them. And then just generally, I have a network of founders that I love turning to for different questions. I find them to be most valuable in terms of what I listen to. I obviously love podcasts like yours. And I think that just learning earlier in the journey of what the experience is like is just invaluable."

Find out more about Hype Club, our own private network for female startup entrepreneurs, which we launched after hearing so many people credit their network as invaluable support. Details at the end of the book.

IF YOU ONLY HAD $1,000 left in your business bank account, where would you spend it?

"I have to say, I think it's going to be digital paid ads. We have this machine of an operation, and I know our head of digital growth would love to hear that!"

LISTEN to Sashee's episode to find out how she patented her formulas, what advice she has on pitching for investment, and why she thanks God for moms.

49

A WELL-OILED BUSINESS

SUSAN GRIFFIN-BLACK: HOW AN ENTREPRENEUR DISCOVERED THE ESSENTIAL VALUE IN ESSENTIAL OILS

Susan Griffin-Black is the founder of EO (which stands for Essential Oils). EO produces body, skin, and hair products made from active botanicals that are accented with essential oils. They also have a sister company called Everyone, which is the more accessible line that's affordable for, well, everyone. Susan is an OG. She's been an entrepreneur for over twenty-five years.

In 1995, she launched as a four-piece collection to Bloomingdale's, making the products in her garage, all while being a single mom and hustling every single day to pay the bills and keep the lights on. Fast forward to today. The business remains independently owned by her, alongside her cofounder Brad, and pulls in around $50 million in revenue each year. I loved my conversation with Susan. She gave key pearls of wisdom, like the importance of pursuing the journey and the actual day-to-day of building a business rather than the pot of money at the end. She also explained why it's critical, as we move forward in this world, to have

women in complete control of their lives and at the forefront
of leadership.

Susan started her career as a clothing designer. She was
greatly inspired, interacting with many leading fashion
industry names and working with the top creatives around.
On a research trip to London, she stumbled across a small
quaint courtyard in Covent Garden called Neal's Yard. I go
often and can vouch for it if you're ever in London! She was
attracted to a small apothecary and went in to poke around.

"There were dried herbs and tinctures and essential oils.
I picked up this bottle of *lavender angustifolia* (English lavender), and I inhaled, and my life was changed! I looked
around just to see if anyone was watching me because I felt
like I was totally transported. And I thought, *This is really
what I want to do. I want to learn everything about this, I want
to work with this.*"

Takeaway #1: Don't Ignore What Makes Your Heart Sing

When considering a startup, sometimes the best advice
is to do something that you genuinely and naturally
resonate with. After all, your business will become your day-
to-day life, so if it's around something that you're passionate
about, it makes the ride that much easier, enjoyable, and
authentic.

"I would just urge everyone to always think about those
moments when you receive information and it's not really a
thought process. It just goes right to your heart and soul. It's
very easy to dismiss afterward because it's like, 'Oh, that's
crazy.' But those are the moments that are the essence of
what gives us courage and vision."

.   .   .

TAKEAWAY #2: There's Plenty of Opportunity to Learn

The world of essential oils was new to Susan. There's an important lesson that I've learned from so many of my interviews. It's that not knowing an industry you want to go into isn't a barrier to entry. It's totally achievable to learn, and there are many ways to do it, whether enrolling in a course, getting first-hand experience, or teaching yourself. Perseverance, curiosity, and a dose of humbleness go a long way.

"I worked in a friend's store for a bit to learn everything, and I studied aromatherapy. I took a crash course in cosmetic chemistry at UCLA. I was tinkering with essential oils and blending and learning. So I'm pretty much self-taught through trial and error."

TAKEAWAY #3: Happiness Is a Positive Cash Flow

In the early days, Susan's business was barely breaking even, and it forced her to be practical about money and, in particular, her cash flow. For a startup, it's often cash flow that is the most important element for survival.

"I would do anything to get people to pay up front; it was worth a couple of points of a discount because I really became the 'cash flow queen.' And to this day, I would recommend that for everyone because it really is the lifeblood of the business. Even if you're very profitable, without cash flow it's a no-go. You don't have enough money for payroll. It doesn't matter how good the margin is."

TAKEAWAY #4: Marketing Is Getting Product into People's Hands

EO launched in the days before the internet. Well, at

least in the days before the internet as we know it today. Remember that *eeee-e-e-eee-eee-ee* dial-up noise? (If you were born in the 2000s, ask your parents about what patience looked like in the 1990s.) We're so used to the internet as being the focal point of marketing, but in the days of Susan's startup phase, her focus was on her product and innovative ways to get it out there.

"For us, it was a matter of, can you make a beautiful product inside? Make it stand out. We like type; we like simplicity. And everyone else had packaging with leaves and all sorts of botanicals. So we made ours quieter. We moved hand sanitizing wipe stands outside of every office. People tried it, and they were like, 'Oh my God, it smells so good; where do I buy this?'"

TAKEAWAY #5: **Women Rock**

Susan has been in the game for a long time, and she's witnessed so much evolution in the workplace, specifically around attitudes to females. At *Female Startup Club*, we're of the opinion that being a woman is a huge advantage in many ways, and it's just a matter of time before the business world will universally realize this. Susan gave her thoughts on the subject.

"I think that women-owned businesses and female leadership is the way. There's just no question about it. I can see from my experience of having children and being a mom that the way for women to be in the workplace is to have a flexible work schedule that meets the demands of their lives and is reasonable. I think women are more intuitive, compassionate, and emotionally intelligent, and they bring so much to the party. So I just encourage every female that wants to have a business to just do it and to think about the next steps without getting too carried away about the cash-out moment, thinking that that's the moment of celebration —because it really is about the day-in-and-day-out journey."

THREE QUICK QUESTIONS

WHAT'S the number one marketing moment that made your business pop?

"This COVID-19 situation and our partnership with Lyft was incredible. We donated hand sanitizers and hand wipes to Lyft to keep their drivers and passengers safe. And that had a really incredible ripple effect."

WHERE DO you hang out to get smarter?

"I'm a Zen Buddhist student, and so I find that going to a Zen Center or just paying attention to that community allows the information that I do get from all of these other sources to sort of integrate and settle."

HOW DO you win the day?

"I like to get up particularly early, like seven, and then I read for a good hour and a half. I read everything from the *Times* to *Fast Company* to *Harvard Business Review*. So just really having a good look at everything that's happening and how things connect."

. . .

LISTEN to Susan's episode to find out how she expanded her business, how she adapted to the new world of e-commerce, and what she learned from picking up her son's towels in the bathroom.

50

THE GOLD(E) STANDARD

TRINITY MOUZON WOFFORD: HOW AN
ENTREPRENEUR ADDED WELLNESS TO
SKINCARE

Trinity Mouzon Wofford is the founder of wellness-meets-skincare brand Golde. She founded Golde with her partner Issey when they were both only twenty-three.

Golde has partnered with big-time retailers such as Urban Outfitters and Nordstrom, as well as Revolve and goop. In 2020, Trinity was named to the Forbes 30 under 30 list. She told me about her journey and building the brand as a Black female founder, her lessons learned along the way with her cofounder/fiancée, and some great insights into the world of wholesale.

From a young age, Trinity had always been interested in health and wellness. Her mom had an autoimmune illness, and her holistic approach inspired a young Trinity to want to be a doctor. She attended NYU, but when her mom was denied health coverage and could no longer afford medical treatment, Trinity decided that she no longer wanted to be a doctor if it wasn't something available to everyone.

Still considering what she wanted to do with her life, she began a fast-paced career in marketing. Although she still kept the dream in the back of her mind about working within the wellness space.

Takeaway #1: Take Advantage of Your Sweet Youth

Starting her business at just twenty-three years old, Trinity had the advantage of youth on her side. For many entrepreneurs that start young, there's a big plus in the youthful attitude toward the success and failure of the business world. Young startup entrepreneurs often have a certain naiveté that proves to be a major asset. Often, the older and mature among us face the obstacle of knowing and experiencing too much and having anxiety about risking it all.

"My high school sweetheart [Issey Kobori], who's now my cofounder, grew up in a family business. So he had that window into entrepreneurship, and that gave both of us the context that one day we could do something like that. I definitely think that was a big chunk of the secret ingredient—being young enough to be so fearless. I think that that naiveté that it'll all work out is very powerful. I think that's the beauty of starting something when you're young. It's like, OK, well, worst-case scenario, I'll just move back home, and my parents will be a little annoyed with me. But I can see the path out of failure."

Takeaway #2: Working with Your Significant Other Takes Maturity and Empathy

Trinity took the brave step to partner in business with her significant other. Everyone has their thoughts about this —I've spoken to entrepreneurs who've found the experience enriching and others who shout, "run a mile!" Trinity found it a positive experience but warned that it's not for everyone.

"My answer to that question is always if you have to ask, you already know. I don't think it's for everyone. And I don't think that's a sign that you don't have a strong relationship. But I think it's a lot to put on your relationship to be in it twenty-four seven. Ultimately for us, I think it has really strengthened our personal relationship because it forces a certain level of maturity and empathy that I feel you can kind of skirt around when it's just your significant other."

TAKEAWAY #3: Ask Yourself What You Want as a Consumer

Golde was launched in 2017 with a single product—an original turmeric blend. From her own experience of feeling left out of the prestige brand space as a consumer, her vision was to make her products more accessible to the mass market. While it's important to listen to the market and identify their needs, if you are yourself part of the target market, your own insights are of great value too.

"We found that people were coming to Golde because they loved our ethos around wellness. I was looking at my own experiences as a consumer in the wellness space, and I was feeling very caught between this crunchy granola stuff that I grew up with (I come from 'Birkenstock land') and then the other side of it, which was luxe and prestige and like seventy-five-dollar powders. Even if it did appeal to me, I definitely couldn't afford it. So I wanted to do something in the middle. The fascination with the brand seemed to really be this new perspective. And we found that over time, we wanted to be able to apply that perspective more broadly because there was so much value in saying that wellness should actually feel good. It shouldn't be a punishment."

.   .   .

TAKEAWAY #4: Be the Only Cook in the Kitchen*

*except maybe with a cofounder sous chef.

Trinity was faced with the decision of whether or not to seek investment capital to get her business going. While many entrepreneurs seek the investment route without much thought, it's not always a good fit. Investors can mean less freedom when it comes to making business moves and decisions, and that can be frustrating to the entrepreneurial spirit.

"I had a little bit of savings because I had been working at a fancy tech startup, and I was one of those people that's obsessively frugal. Like tuna noodles frugal. We put a couple thousand dollars into it between the two of us and just went with it. To be honest, we didn't really know anything about investors. I think my experience at a startup also turned me off of venture capital. It just always felt like the founder didn't have the ownership that they wanted to have. There are always other cooks in the kitchen."

TAKEAWAY #5: Explore Different Options for Raising Capital

Trinity and Issey kept the bootstrapping ethos alive, but the cash-flow strains of supplying big retail clients led them to a stage where they needed the help of extra cash. Most startup entrepreneurs will be faced with this challenge and will have to make a decision on how to do that. Sometimes the traditional VC route is the right one; however, there are other options for entrepreneurs to consider first—options that allow for more freedom and more control. In Trinity's case, she opted for borrowing small amounts of money from friends and family, which she paid back in a short time with a little interest.

"With our growth, we're now exploring different options because there are so many different places that you can get working capital or inventory funding. So I am open to raising more money from investors, but I want to be very thoughtful about doing what's truly right for the business and not just whatever is the trending solution at the moment. We've seen this crazy fallout of a lot of these over-funded, venture-backed brands that were the industry darlings two years ago when I first started talking to investors. So I'm very hesitant to just do whatever people are telling me to do. Two years ago, they were telling me to raise $10 million, and now they would never tell me to do that at this stage."

Takeaway #6: As a Founder of Color, There's More to Prove

Sadly, even with all the changes and advances going on in the world, business remains a male-dominated space, and female startup entrepreneurs often find raising invest-ment is tough as a woman. There's also a challenge in being a woman of color too, so Trinity had a double challenge on her hands.

"People would say that my business, which was prof-itable and had revenues doubling every year, was 'too early.' But then I would see that they had invested in a pre-revenue business from a white female-founded brand. It took me a while to really sit with the fact that part of that was because I'm a Black founder, and there's just more for me to prove compared to the average white founder. I am very interested to see what is going to shift now in the landscape now that there is such an over response to trying to bring more diversity, specifically Black voices into entrepreneurship."

I had read an article that Trinity wrote for the *Huffington Post* about this being a strange time for Black-owned businesses. A line stood out in my mind: "It can be challenging to separate the profound from the performative." Trinity expanded on the concept:

"I can't remember who said this, but someone, a Black woman, was talking about this, and the question that she was asked was 'Do you think that these people are actually being sincere, or are they just making these pledges because they have to?' And she said, 'I don't care if they're being sincere or not as long as they're doing it. If we're getting Black people where they need to be, where they've always deserved to be, I don't care if a white person is doing it because they feel like it's just going to look good or like they have to do it.' So I think that the first step is inherently a little bit superficial, but maybe this will create momentum toward positive change."

THREE QUICK QUESTIONS

WHAT'S the number one marketing moment that made your business pop?

"The past two weeks of this [Black Lives Matter] movement to support Black-owned businesses has been ridiculous. The level of visibility and attention and enthusiasm and new customers that we've acquired has been incredible. Kourtney Kardashian was posting about us, and I'm like DMing with her, saying thanks so much. One of my favorite tennis players was giving us a shout-out. I was like, "What?""

. . .

How do you win the day?

"I love a good routine. I am very much a morning person, so I wake up very early, like five or six usually. I always try to start the day with two big glasses of water. I also make a smoothie every day that keeps me hydrated. It's got celery, lettuce, and fruit."

Where do you hang out to get smarter?

"I talk with other female founder friends. I find it really valuable to talk to someone who's twenty years in, and it's like, "Oh yeah, don't worry about it. Here's how you handle it. Onto the next.""

If you're looking for Modern Mentorship and Network from the people who have been there and done that, tune into the end of this book where we tell you more about our private network Hype Club and how to join.

Listen to Trinity's episode to find out how she started an ambassador program, what the difference is between indie stores and mass retailers, and how she was inspired by candles.

51

ACQUIRING HEALTH

VALENTINA MILANOVA: HOW AN ENTREPRENEUR EDUCATED WOMEN AND THE INDUSTRY ABOUT FEMALE HEALTH

Valentina Milanova is the founder of Daye, a company that's reimagining women's health. Daye aims to bridge the gap in health care through medical research and innovation—and they're raising the standards of health by creating effective products and services that fit conveniently into women's lives. Right now, they have two groundbreaking products: the Naked tampon and a CBD-coated tampon to help with period cramps (and, yes, I've tried them; and yes, my period was much better than usual; and, yes, I'll be using them from now on!). Valentina explained how she was inspired to educate herself on women's health, where the inspiration for her idea came from, and how she pushed past the critics and naysayers to bring her vision into a reality.

Valentina was born and raised in Bulgaria, but she moved to London to study business, economics, and law at the University of Buckingham. After considering various careers, including journalism and event planning, Valentina found herself drawn to the startup world. This led to working at Techstars and as a venture associate for Founders Factory.

Valentina described her first two innovative products, which she took from conception to launch in three and a half years. The first is the Naked hyper-absorbent tampon, which is free from any nasty chemicals and is sustainably sanitized to prevent the risk of toxic shock syndrome. The second is a pain-relieving tampon, which has a cannabinoid coating.

Valentina explained that she wanted to bridge the gender gap in medical research and innovation (something that I—and I imagine many others—weren't even aware of as an issue). She explained:

"One of the biggest pain points that exists in front of us as people with vaginas is that there hasn't been enough research into products that work for us. As a female health research and development company, we aim to change things."

One of the ways Valentina has already made an impact on the industry is that she recently drove a change in prescription guidelines for ibuprofen. You know when you're on your period and go through ibuprofen like Tic Tacs? Well, it turns out the recommended dose of 250 milligrams works for the male physiology, but the female of the species actually needs 800 milligrams. As a woman, you may have worked that out already, right?

I read on Valentina's website and social media that it wasn't until 1993 that women could even be part of medical trials, which seems so recent! That really highlights the need for what Valentina is doing and how important a voice like hers is for women's rights.

.   .   .

TAKEAWAY #1: **It's up to You to Educate Yourself**

Valentina's journey and passion for educating herself and other women about female health dates back to her years of puberty. Puberty was a traumatic experience for Valentina because she had no female guidance about all the physical changes she was experiencing. She felt ashamed about her period, seeing it as a "disease," and when she saw a TV show describing how to examine yourself for breast cancer, she mistook her small developing breasts for the cancerous lumps they were describing.

In addition to those traumatic experiences, when she was fifteen, she found out that she had a number of cysts on her ovaries. They were only discovered after an incorrect diagnosis and a surgery for what doctors thought was appendicitis. Valentina explained:

"This was the part of my personal story that formed the seed inside of my core that made me constantly think, *OK, how can I educate myself about female health? How can I become the person who has every single research paper, so that I can have an educated conversation with my doctor?* I formed the habit of reading lots of research papers. I subscribed to PubMed and started getting newsletters to my inbox with various research papers that were coming up on topics that I found interesting. So that's my personal experience that inspired me to found the company."

In 2017, as part of her part-time MBA studies, Valentina was given an assignment to develop an idea for a business that would be socially impactful. Valentina focused on an impoverished area of northern Bulgaria and began researching its history.

"I started reading into the history of Bulgaria and what that area had traditionally been good at. As it turns out, it's growing industrial hemp! Before the communist takeover in the 1940s, northern Bulgaria was the largest European producer and exporter of industrial hemp—and it was a Bulgarian scientist that initially synthesized cannabinoids."

This piece of forgotten history intrigued Valentina and inspired her to research further:

"Reading about the properties of industrial hemp, there were two things that really stuck with me. The first one being that hemp is one of the most absorbent natural fibers. And the second is that the extract from the flower CBD has potentially pain-relieving effects. And this idea was born in my mind around combining the two of them and forming one product, which would be more absorbent and relieve pain."

But her MBA presentation didn't quite go as planned.

"It was dead silence in the room. People had their eyes wide open. 'Why are you talking about tampons? This is so bizarre. No one wants to hear about tampons. Like, it's taboo. This is a "proper" MBA. Why is she doing that? She should have just presented some kind of an IP business. This is ridiculous. Who is this weird woman?'"

It's always interesting to me that outright resistance to an entrepreneur's idea seems to be an unavoidable step on the journey to success!

TAKEAWAY #2: Ignore the Critics and Do Things Quietly

Valentina decided to ignore the critics and soldier on: "I decided, 'OK, well, you can still work on a company or on a product without letting people know.' So I just quietly started developing this product idea so that I could see whether I could make anything of it."

Moving back to London, Valentina took a job in early-stage venture capital. This allowed her to fund her evening product development. She focused on the clinical validation of the IP and securing the supply chain but hadn't developed the branding as her hope was to partner with one of the big players in the industry, like Kimberly-Clark or Procter & Gamble.

TAKEAWAY #3: Don't Be Scared to Cold Message Investors

So many entrepreneurs try to get in touch with big industry leaders, but it's a challenging task. Traditional advice is often to not cold call. But traditional advice isn't always the only option, and Valentina did things her way, proving that cold calling can indeed work.

"Because I worked in a really early-stage venture capital firm, people often think that that's how I had contacts. But that's not really the case because I was a lowly associate, and my job was to look for companies to invest in. So the way that I fundraised was really unconventional. You know, everyone says, 'Don't message investors on LinkedIn. Try and find a warm introduction.' I didn't have any warm introductions, so I went on LinkedIn, searching for investor venture capitalists and seeing what kind of people came up, and then just started sending them messages."

TAKEAWAY #4: Many Presentations Help You Perfect Your Pitch

I've heard from other entrepreneurs—who happen to be women—that pitching female-centered products to a largely male-dominated investor space can be difficult. This is especially true when it comes to understanding the product and need. Whenever I hear about the journey of startup pitching, I'm always amazed at just how many rounds it takes to achieve success. While the schedule can be grueling, entrepreneurs often find that the repetition of pitching is actually an opportunity to keep refining and perfecting the presentation.

"Initially, I pitched angel technology accelerators. Really, anyone that would listen, and this experience was very humbling because people did not understand the business. And the most common question that I got was people saying, 'Is this some kind of a charity because you keep talking about sustainability. You keep talking about social purpose. Is there a business in what you're trying to sell us here?' But this whole process did allow me to perfect my pitch and also perfect certain elements of the business model and the way that everything was presented."

THREE QUICK QUESTIONS

WHAT'S YOUR "WHY"?

"I want to create a world where every woman can have complete understanding and complete control over hormonal, menstrual, and vaginal health. I want to create this beautiful culture where everyone can show up as their effortless self to work every day."

WHERE DO you hang out to get smarter?

"I like to read biographies or documentary-style books that show human stories and how people overcome challenges. Or how they develop emotionally as human beings. I do coaching twice a month, and I do therapy twice a week—and that really helps me become smarter in the way that I manage my time, in the way that I manage myself, in the way that I manage my emotions."

How do you deal with failure?

"I wish I could feel better with failure. My therapist recommended that when I go into an internal self-bashing role, that I try and analyze the way that I speak to myself and see whether I would speak like this to a person who wasn't me. And that helps me put things into perspective."

Listen to Valentina's episode to find out how she developed her brand, how she got a twenty-thousand-person waiting list before launch, and what watching *Mad Men* inspired her to do.

INVEST IN SHARES

HOW YOU CAN MAKE OUR DAY!

Thank you for reading my book. I'm so grateful for you – you're a shining star (or five)!

DID you know that people who help others experience higher levels of fulfilment, live longer and make more money? Well, it's true in my case at least :)

I HOPE you've enjoyed the read and taken away some useful insights and inspiration. If you have, I'd love for you to be a Hype Girl (or guy) and leave an honest review online via Amazon. Reviews are one the best things you can do to help support an author. By leaving an insightful review online it helps other people understand why they might like the book too (and it pleases The Algorithm Gods!)

AND WHILE I'M HERE… Since we're all social media superstars, if you'd like to post a shout-out, remember to tag

us so we can reshare and give you some love back.
#femalestartupclub #yourhypegirl or if you have the time
#yourhypegirlisthebestbookeverandyoushoulddefinite-
lyreadit. (I kid! Kind of.)

FINALLY, I'd love to meet you and get to know you too; what
you're up to in business, and where you are in the journey so
far. So please get in touch through one of the accounts
below:

INSTAGRAM: @dooneroisin / @femalestartupclub
    Twitter: @dooneroisin
    LinkedIn: @dooneroisin
    TikTok: @dooneroison / @femalestartupclub

OUR HYPE CLUB

YOU IN?

Are you a female startup entrepreneur looking for a network of like-minded women and the support of a 24/7 community? As an extension of Female Startup Club, we've launched "Hype Club" – an online space for e-commerce and CPG entrepreneurs, and we'd love you to join us!

Launched in 2021, Hype Club was created out of a response to hearing from so many of our listeners who found value in the podcast and were seeking further connection, particularly in answering their specific questions. We've also found that many of our listeners are finding their entrepreneurial paths lonely and are looking for the support of a positive and caring network. The invaluable power of having support has been mentioned by successful female entrepreneurs in almost all of our episodes.

In addition to Hype Club we've created an industry vetted e-commerce blueprint by experts as well as the insights learned from 280+ founders. It's the every-step-you-should-be-doing when launching and scaling an e-commerce brand type guide packed with recommended tech, resources and how-to's. There are over 350 steps and it's made for YOU.

If you'd like to learn more about our Hype Club sisterhood, check us out via the link below. We have some cheeky discounts and offers for anyone who reads this book:

www.femalestartupclub.com/yourhypegirl.

BIG LOVE

Female Startup Club wouldn't be possible without you. My army of supporters. A special mention to Marc Hoberman and Ben Guest for the endless advice and guidance in creating my first book. Big love to everyone who's been involved so far and in the future... Especially our Hype Girls.

ALISON LEDDY, Amber Boutiette; Founder of Marin Skincare, Ami Bateman; Founder of Pleasant State, Candice Shelley; Founder of Good and Clean, Carron Mitchell, Casey Dworkin, Catarina, Catherine, Christel Mena, Cristina Iraheta, Danielle Kar, Dotun Abeshinbioke, Emily Pyke; Founder of Bare Thrills, Fatima Ahmed; Founder of Shimmer Me Gorgeous, Gina Farran, Haeley Gjesvold; Founder of Nightwork Candle, Heidi Happonen; Co-Founder of Heideq, Jacqui Hayes, Jade Head, Jenelle Manzi, Jenna Rodrigues; Founder of The Cure•ist, Julie Klukas; Founder of Shy Wolf Candles, Kat Joyce, Kelsey Reidl; Founder of The Visionary Method, Kianna Magelaki;

Founder of Kianna Magelaki, Kiera Egger, Kimberly Rubio, Kourtney Brooks; Founder of Tinge Beauty, Larissa Hildebrandt; Founder of Henrie, Laura Rubin; Founder of Nurture, Olivia Koennecke; Founder of Maison Essentiele, Marika Adamopoulos, Marlene Jungen, Megan Broderick; Co-Founder of a|dash, Melissa Epifano; Founder of Winnoh, Nergiz De Baere; Founder of Magi, Fiona Simmonds; Founder of Pinkie, Prajvali Gupta, RaeDawn Brooks; Founder of Balaeyon, Rayna Larson; Founder of Bota, Regina Osei-Bonsu, Ruby Wallen, Sarah Brown, Sharon Russell, Shenae Rae; Founder of SwearBy Skin, Silvia Avramut, Siobhan McDonagh, Stephanie McGuigan; Founder of Elwyn Bridal, Supraja Yenigandla, Yasmin Zeinab, Yolanda Joy, Zepha Jackson; Founder of Standard Procedure.

(And to everyone who's joined us since I wrote this section!)

Printed in Great Britain
by Amazon